SAWBILL

History and Tales

*For Ann and Dick
Wishing you great memories
of Sawbill always*

Mary Alice Hansen

Mary Alice Hansen

**Tofte, Minnesota
2005**

Illustrations by Lida Storch

Cover photos
Paddlers — Dave Freeman
Cow Moose — Bill Ivy
Island Pine, Sunrise — Tom Kaffine

Copyright © 2005 Mary Alice Hansen

All rights reserved. No part of this book may be used or reproduced in any manner whatsoever without written permission, except in the case of brief quotations embodied in critical articles and reviews.

Published by Sawbill Press
4620 Sawbill Trail
Tofte, Minnesota 55615
www.sawbill.com
mah@boreal.org

Printed and bound in Canada
Friesens Corporation, Altona, Manitoba

First edition

ISBN 0-9761627-0-9

Dedication
To Wilson "Nibs" Arbogust,
the very first Sawbillian

Acknowledgments

Very little is ever accomplished single-handedly. This book has been written with the help of innumerable friends.

Information from personal interviews came from Olga Erickson, Ron and Jerry Gervais, Earl Hansen, Robley Hunt, "Casey" Tofte, and Florence Wehseler.

Phil and Fran Higley provided many pictures, as well as stories, about Sawbill Lodge. David Freeman, resident photographer at Sawbill Canoe Outfitters, has generously shared a number of his pictures. Jay Brooker and Robley Hunt also contributed pictures as well as shared memories.

Photos beyond my own and those mentioned above were graciously provided by Bill Lane, Tim Norman, and Bob Olson. Keith Morris shared pictures as well as information written by his father, Emerson Morris. Color photos by Bill Ivy and by Tom Kaffine appear on the cover.

Advice, support and encouragement came from my writing friends: Beryl Singleton Bissell, Virginia Reiner, Kirsten Stasney, and Stephen Wilbers. Gratitude also goes to Barbara Soderberg for her great help with U.S. Forest Service information.

My most dedicated and helpful writing friend is Wilson Arbogust, who read and edited the entire manuscript. He provided the early history of Sawbill Lodge, of which he was a major part. His efforts and encouragement over the past several years are deeply appreciated.

Thanks also go to Wilson's sister and brothers, Jane Arbogust Howell, Harold "Hedge" Arbogust, and Bob Arbogust, who read the chapter on Sawbill Lodge and added memories of their own.

Writer and publisher Pat Bell has been a valued adviser and friend over many years and deserves great credit for guiding me through the process of publishing a book.

Many thanks are due Rosemary Wallner of Minnetonka, final developmental editor of the manuscript.

Lida Storch, University of Minnesota art student and Sawbill's resident artist, generously produced the line drawings that introduce each chapter.

Final production credits and kudos go to Maryl Skinner and Denny FitzPatrick, of M Graphic Design, who were the fine stewards of the layout and appearance of this book and its cover. M Graphic Design provides far more than technical support to a book. In this case, they organized, proofread, and attended to the endless details involved in a publication. Most appreciated was their enthusiastic support and encouragement at every step of the way.

Family support is always important but, in this case, very special gratitude is due my husband, Frank; my daughter, Ranna; my sons, Karl and Bill, and their spouses, Lee and Cindy. They were not only helpful and supportive, but they lived many of the events that make up this book of history and tales.

Karl and Bill have each harbored the intention to write this book. Perhaps there will be a sequel some day!

Contents

Introduction	viii
1. Our Story Begins	1
2. 1958 – Our Own Building	20
3. Forest Service – Then and Now	27
4. Saga of the Telephone	42
5. Sawbill Lodge	56
6. Becoming Full-Timers in 1976	83
7. Sawbillians – The Crew	94
8. Corps Values – The CCC	108
9. The Sawbill Trail	117
10. Neighbors at Sawbill	130
11. Wild Animal Tales	139
12. Animals, Not So Wild	160
13. Feathered Friends	172

14. Emergencies	183
15. Fire in the Woods	205
16. Customers Remembered	220
17. Operating a Small Business	227
18. Work Credit	235
19. BWCAW – Federal Role	247
20. What Is Wilderness?	274
Notes	282
Bibliography	284

Introduction

Sawbill! It's a place and a destination but it is also a feeling that delights you when you are there and tugs at your heart when you are away. It is a peaceful, quiet, natural place in sharp contrast to busy cities and crowded, noisy highways.

This book is written especially for the people who have come to Sawbill over the past 48 years. While filling out fishing licenses, ringing up sales, and writing rental agreements over the years, we have so often been asked questions about Sawbill and about us. Time constraints required a short and incomplete answer. Now, in retirement, I have the opportunity to provide detailed answers to the many questions.

"How did you ever happen to get involved with this place?"
"What happened to Sawbill Lodge? When did it close?"
"I was in the CCC here. Do you know about that?"
"Why don't they blacktop the Sawbill Trail?"
"Where can I see a moose?"
"Why do I need a permit to go out on Sawbill Lake?"
"What is an outfitter anyway?"

I hope you will read this book to find answers to these and many other questions.

Let me introduce the cast of characters at Sawbill Canoe Outfitters. The business was started in 1957 by Frank and Mary Alice Hansen. Our children, who played a large role at first, are Karl, Ranna, and Bill. They were all under 10 years old when we started out. In the 1970s, Karl and Ranna moved on to other pursuits. Bill stayed with the business. His family grew to include his children — Adam, Ruthie, Clare, Carl — and his wife, Cindy. Bill and Cindy have been in full charge of the business since 1994, and the children all participate as valued crew members.

Being a canoe outfitter means renting canoes and camping equipment. Business starts when the ice goes out of the lakes each year — about May 1 — and continues until lakes freeze in early November.

The outfitting business in the Superior National Forest began just after World War II as people became interested in canoeing and camping for recreation and vacations. Businesses doing canoe outfitting usually include a retail store that serves campers' needs. In recent years, gifts and souvenirs of the trip have become of major importance in the store. Many of the Gunflint Trail outfitters are associated with lodges or resorts. Sawbill Canoe Outfitters started with a great deal of help from Sawbill Lodge but became totally independent after four years. Sawbill Canoe Outfitters is also the concessionnaire for the Sawbill, Crescent, and Temperance River campgrounds. These are typical National Forest campgrounds.

This book contains memories about Sawbill Canoe Outfitters. All memories are personal and subject to personal interpretation. These memories are mine and not necessarily absolute fact. Others in my family or acquaintance will certainly remember the same events differently and they may be more accurate. I only claim that this is the story as I saw it and remember it. Some chapters are not about Sawbill Canoe Outfitters. The information in these chapters comes from other sources as noted.

· Chapter 1 ·

—— Our Story Begins ——

The story begins in western Maryland in the Appalachian Mountains where Frank's parents had summer camps for children: Camp Whitethorn for boys and Camp Minnetoska for girls. Camp lasted for eight weeks and all campers came for the entire eight weeks. From the time he was a youngster of seven, Frank went to camp every summer. Over the years, he became first a camper, then a riding instructor and a counselor, and eventually a manager. After we married in 1946, we both went to camp every summer. We could do that because Frank was teaching at the University of Minnesota on a nine-month appointment. The school year was September through May.

I was an enthusiastic camper, too. I grew up in Hutchinson, Kansas, where there was not a single lake and consequently not a single boat and not much camping either. There were hardly any trees until the "Great Dust Storms" came in the 1920s, and it was suggested that a "shelterbelt" of trees would give some protection from the wind as it swept across the cultivated fields carrying the topsoil in its clutches. When, as a child, I read stories involving a forest such as Little Red Riding Hood or The Three Bears, I could not envision "a forest." (Now Kansas has trees and human-made lakes and boating is very popular.) As a youth, I went to Pilgrim Fellowship Camp where we hiked, learned crafts, and swam in swimming pools. I loved being a camper.

Frank grew up in Baltimore, Maryland, where his father was a physical education instructor and wrestling coach for Polytechnic Institute, a Baltimore public high school. Pop (as he was known to everyone at camp) had spent some time working as a camp director during the summer and then had bought his own property about 1926.

Inspired by his camping experience as he grew up, Frank became an expert horseman and a competitive swimmer. After he graduated from Loyola College in Baltimore, he decided to study child psychology. This interest, too, related to his experience working with children at camp. He did graduate work at Fordham University and then the University of Minnesota where the two of us met. We were both teaching assistants at the Institute of Child Development during the 1944-45 school year. We spent the next long year apart. Frank was called into military service and stationed at Camp Lee in Virginia, and I had a job as a research associate with the University of Chicago. It seemed an eternity to me until August 1946 when we were married.

During our first years of marriage, Frank and I made an annual trek from Minnesota to Maryland to go to camp. As the babies came along, they accompanied us. By the time we had spent eight summers at camp as a family, Frank's parents were ready to retire. We spent a lot of time during our summers at camp dreaming about how we would run the place if we had free reign. During these summers, Frank's father often threatened to sell the camps. At first, it wasn't a serious threat but as time went by, we sensed that the elder Hansens were thinking seriously of retirement. We knew they weren't going to give us anything so we did a lot of figuring about how we would finance a purchase. We had talked to our bank about a loan based on the equity in our Duluth home. We felt that we were quite ready to make an offer when the camps went up for sale. Early in 1956, Frank's mother wrote that the camps had been sold to a teacher who had worked at the camps with us the previous summer. We both wept. What were we to do?

Our routine of camp in the summer was disrupted and our summer was free. That summer of 1956 was the only one we had free for the next 40 years and we enjoyed it. Frank took 9-year-old Karl camping on Island Lake outside Duluth. We explored the immediate area with such activities as a picnic on Park Point. It was a delightful summer but not very comfortable financially since we had no income. Looking back, I am amazed to realize that we never considered giving up "going to camp." That simply wasn't an option. Frank's parents told us they hadn't considered selling us the camps because we lived too far away. This led us to the conclusion that we should start our own camps in Minnesota.

We had never visited the Superior National Forest or explored the area beyond Duluth, but Frank knew that canoeing was a popular activity. He thought that our camps should feature canoeing rather than the horseback riding that was the popular recreational activity in Maryland. He also knew that the headquarters of the Superior National Forest was in Duluth and one day he went to talk to them about our dream of starting camps in the area.

It was that day that the first of many very lucky events occurred. Frank met with J. Wesley White, Assistant Supervisor of the Superior National Forest, who turned out to be our patron saint. Wes said, "You know, in this part of the country, private camps are not so popular as they are in the East. Organizational camps such as the Y camps and the Scout camps are well established and provide the camping opportunities in the area." Sommers' Canoe Base, the Boy Scout facility, was one of those already well established in 1956 as were Camp Menogyn, the Minneapolis YMCA camp, and Camp Widgiwagan, the St. Paul YMCA camp.

But Wes White was not totally discouraging. He had another suggestion. He said canoe camping was gaining in popularity and that the Forest Service was concerned that the Ely and Gunflint areas were becoming overcrowded. He pulled out a map of the Superior

National Forest and showed Frank the myriad bodies of water in the area. Ely is on the western side of the area and the Gunflint Trail is toward the eastern edge, he pointed out. Halfway between is an area with a great many lakes that are relatively small but close enough together so that it is feasible to portage from one to another. Wes said there was a business located in this area at Sawbill Lake. It was Sawbill Lodge, an American plan resort owned by Jean Raiken. (American plan means one fee covers lodging, food, boat rental and all related services.) Guests would come to this resort for a week and settle into a cabin. Then at some point during the week, they often liked to have camping gear and food packed for them so that they could travel even farther away from civilization and stay out in the woods for a night or two. This was usually inspired by the hope of spectacular fishing. Jean Raiken was doing some canoe outfitting in the sense that she packed food and equipment for these trips, but she tended to view this as a nuisance that took time away from her mission of running a first-class eating and lodging establishment. When the Forest Service approached her about going into the business of outfitting canoe trips, she wasn't at all interested. So Wes suggested that we might want to visit with her about this type of business.

Fortunately, we were willing to listen to Wes's advice and we promptly began to arrange a canoe trip for ourselves in conjunction with a visit to Sawbill Lodge. My parents were coming from Kansas for a visit and agreed to stay a few extra days to look after our three young children while we made this expedition into the woods. The date was set for the day after Labor Day, shortly before school was to resume at the university. Then we had to round up equipment. We borrowed a square stern Grumman canoe along with car racks plus a motor from our friend, Ellis Livingston, who also taught at the University of Minnesota, Duluth (UMD). We rented a heavy canvas tent from Duluth Tent and Awning. We had sleeping bags of our own and we gathered up some old cooking and eating utensils to round out our gear. Our menu was planned around canned goods. I remember that we took Dinty Moore beef stew for one dinner and canned shrimp along with Minute Rice for the other. Each dinner was planned as a special treat — something we would never eat at home.

We drove up the North Shore to Tofte and then up the Sawbill Trail to The Grade and over that to Peterson Lake where we met the local ranger, Rudy Peterson. We met there because he wanted to show us the place where the Forest Service envisioned an outfitting service. It was on Baker Lake. The old Grade Road went by the south end of Peterson Lake and Baker Lake was nearby, with no road access at that time. The Forest Service was seriously promoting the idea of having an outfitter in this mid-forest area. After visiting with him for a while, we launched our canoe and fired up the three-horse motor.

The day was growing short by this time so, after motoring up Peterson, we chose to stop and make camp on the portage between Peterson and Kelly lakes. There was a fire ring already built showing that others had camped there before us. We set up our tent and built our campfire and all was well. Then we cleverly decided to rig up our can of Dinty Moore beef stew on a makeshift tripod over the fire so that the stew would heat in the can thus saving dishwashing. By this time, we were very hungry, even ravenous. Just as the stew appeared to be hot, our tripod collapsed and our can of stew tipped into the fire. Once again, we had options to consider. If we abandoned the stew and started another dinner, what would we eat the next night? I had carefully planned and rationed our food so there wouldn't be any extra weight or any leftovers to deal with. "Well," we said to each other, "there's no reason to believe that wood ashes will hurt you," so we scooped the stew out of the fire and gobbled it down. Shortly after that, we crawled into the tent to sleep. Frank slept well but I lay awake most of the night, imagining that I heard a bear prowling around our camp.

There was no evidence of bear or any other animal the next morning, but we did awaken to overcast skies and much cooler temperatures. We hadn't thought of bringing warm clothes because the weather in the first few days of September had been very warm and summery. It didn't occur to us that it could change quite suddenly. We hadn't been around Northeastern Minnesota long enough to appreciate the weather's capricious behavior. We weren't even well prepared for rain and it rained all that day as we motored up the Temperance River chain of lakes. Dinner was much more successful that night and sleeping went well, too.

However, the new day was again cold and rainy and we were decidedly uncomfortable. If it had occurred to us to paddle, the activity would have helped to keep us warm but we continued to use the motor. The breeze that the motor created added to the wind that was blowing and chilled us through and through. Jean Raiken later told us that the temperature had never gone over 40 degrees.

Frank carried the awkward 90-pound canoe over what seemed long portages while I carried the motor over one shoulder and a heavy gas can in the other hand. We had packs as well and made a second trip with those. One thing we did on the trip was to visit the cabin on Kelly Lake that belonged to Bill Plouff. It was a log cabin with handcrafted log furniture. I remember an enormous throne-like chair made of logs. We knew that Bill was gone by this time but the cabin looked as if he had planned to return the next day. We found out later that Bill had been found dead in his cabin one spring a few years earlier and his body carried out.

Bill Plouff's story was that he was the younger son of the Plouff family who lived at the intersection of what is now Plouff Creek and the railroad grade, west of the Sawbill Trail. Bill acted as a guide for fishermen in the 1920s and 1930s and the family had a rustic cabin or two that they rented to anglers. In the early 1900s, many people were attracted to the area by the promise of valuable minerals. Bill was a prospector for silver. John "Casey" Tofte told us years later about Bill Plouff. He had built his cabin on Kelly Lake and sunk a mine shaft there. About that time, silver was found in western states and the price dropped drastically, so he never made his fortune from silver. Silver was never found in the area anyway.[1]

On the third day of our trip, we made our way back to our car and changed into dry clothes. The miracle of the trip was that we thought we had had a great time and were thrilled with this camping experience. We drove back to Sawbill Lodge where we had an appointment with Jean Raiken. She was such a warm and cheerful person, the perfect host for a vacation resort. We felt accepted immediately. She promptly began to plan for us to take over the outfitting business at Sawbill.

In 1956, we meet with Jean Raiken (center) to discuss the outfitting business at Sawbill.

Her proposal was that we live at Sawbill Lodge the following summer while we were arranging our own accommodations. She had a log cabin named Pulpwood that she wasn't renting any more because it had no plumbing. It was a fairly large one-room cabin with beds enough for the five of us plus our dachshund. Frank was assigned to be the dock worker which involved getting the guests out on the water for fishing in the morning and then welcoming them back in the afternoon, admiring and cleaning their catch of fish. She had a tiny cabin named Cedar that I could use to handle the outfitting business which she proposed to turn over to us. These cabins were just up the

Pulpwood Cabin, our home in 1957

hill from the dock. No cash was involved in this arrangement, which was beneficial to both parties.

Another problem Jean was having involved the seven-site Forest Service campground just up the lake from the Lodge. The campers kept appearing at the Lodge asking if they could buy milk, bread, or eggs. After all, it was 24 miles to the nearest store and Jean was Mrs. Hospitality, unable to resist giving any nurturance she could. Still, she felt that it was more than she could handle while maintaining the Lodge as a top-notch facility. So she wanted me to keep a small stock of goods that would supply the needs of people on the campground. In return, we could eat at the Lodge and use other facilities there, such as her washing machine and the Lodge sauna, which included shower facilities.

Another cooperative arrangement that Jean had just engineered was with the Osmans. Vi and Ken Osman lived in a family-owned cabin on Brule Lake in the summer. They had recently retired from their work with the MacMillan Oil Company in Milwaukee and wanted to live in the Sawbill area year round. It was not practical to live on Brule Lake in the winter, so they had made the deal that they would build a cabin at Sawbill for winter use. It was later named Viken Cabin. In the summer while the Osmans were at Brule, Jean would rent the cabin to Sawbill Lodge guests. She was ahead of her time, envisioning and developing the condominium concept!

We were invited to come back in October to the Osman's housewarming party for Viken Cabin and to bring our children as well. It was our introduction to many local people — local meaning residents of Tofte, Schroeder, and Lutsen. Among these were Bob and Shirley Bierbaum who had just bought the hardware store in Schroeder from the Pecores and were getting started in their business. Later they gave us two handmade wooden display counters that they were discarding from their store. These became primary fixtures in our new store and after some 25 years were retired to our bunkhouse where they served as storage units for our crew.

During that winter, the YMCA sponsored an overnight workshop on canoe camping and we seized the opportunity to attend. We learned how to roll our sleeping bags and how to pack a Duluth pack most efficiently. Bill Trygg, an Ely realtor and renowned forester, instructed us in the safe use of a single bit axe. In the evening we sang camp songs and did some

Vi and Ken Osman built Viken Cabin.

square dancing. It was like being at our camps and we had a most enjoyable time. We were reassured about our camping skills and picked up some valuable tips. The most valuable experience, though, was meeting people who were in the camping business in the area.

One of the people we met was Janet Hanson, who ran Gunflint Outfitters in partnership with Gunflint Lodge. There were not many outfitters in business in the 1950s and Janet's operation was a strong thriving concern. It was also a close parallel to our plan of working in conjunction with Sawbill Lodge.

Janet had been a teacher before she got into the outfitting business 10 years before, so we had a lot in common. She had a friendly word of advice for us though. She said, "Lots of people are trying to go into the outfitting business these days and they generally don't make it. Let me warn you, you kids won't last three years."

When school was out in May 1957, we headed up the North Shore and then up the Sawbill Trail to Sawbill Lake. Frank had bought 40 sleeping bags and a paper bag full of fishing tackle. Cedar Cabin was transformed into a store by putting shelves around the walls. On these, we stacked the new sleeping bags and the other camping gear from the Lodge's stock plus some essential canned goods. We had coffee and oatmeal, Spam and Dinty Moore beef stew. I remember the oatmeal particularly because I used an empty oatmeal box to hide my cash every night. A gray metal tackle box was the cash receipts box during the day.

Hiding the cash was a good precaution because we were robbed before the summer was over. One morning I found that the cabin had been broken into and the gray tackle box was gone, along with a few candy bars. The hidden money was probably less than a hundred dollars but it was very gratifying to find that it was still there in its oatmeal box. The sheriff investigated the crime and soon caught the perpetrators, two teenage boys who had stayed briefly at the Lodge. The good news was that the gray cash box was recovered. It had been thrown into the woods and had a dented corner but was still usable and was returned to service with great satisfaction. It is still in use today as the storage place for cash before it is taken to the bank. Now it is locked in a sturdy safe at night.

The other furnishings in our new store consisted of a decrepit display case with a glass front and our discarded electric refrigerator, which we had bought through a co-op in Minneapolis. The refrigerator was for the milk and eggs that campers might want to buy. That refrigerator is still in our store, now used for bait. Candy, gum, and tackle went in the display case. The tackle arrived at Cedar Cabin all jumbled together in a paper bag. It wasn't packaged in neat little boxes or plastic bags as it is today. I had never paid any attention to tackle before. Suddenly I was faced with the task of disentangling and identifying it. My first course of study that summer was entitled "Lures, Leaders, and Line 101."

One of our cooperative agreements with Sawbill Lodge was that we would hire college students to work nominally for us but also for the Lodge as fishing guides. This benefitted the Lodge because Frank, by virtue of teaching at UMD, had a large pool of potential employees. It benefited us because we had help at very little cost to us. The arrangement was that we would guarantee our employees a salary of $200 a month and Jean would provide them with room and board. Their primary duty was to guide Lodge guests on day or overnight fishing expeditions. Jean paid us a set amount, $10 a day, for each day that any one of them worked as a guide for her, and that amounted to enough to cover a sizable share of their monthly salaries. When they weren't guiding, they were our employees and we would find things for them to do. In those years, we didn't worry about such things as health insurance or being sued for some negligence.

Our best instructors, in addition to our sponsor and mentor, Jean Raiken, were our customers. First and foremost was Art Towner. Art was also the patron saint of Sawbill Lodge. He had built his own cabin on the lake. He and his wife, Ruth, spent most of the summer there each year. His business was the American Hospital Supply Corporation and he persuaded many of his salespeople to vacation at Sawbill Lodge, a tribute to his sales ability. Art had a beautiful Thompson cedar and canvas fishing boat that got a new coat of green paint each year before Art arrived. Each day, he and Ruth zoomed up to the north end of Sawbill with their 35-horsepower motor. Arriving at the prime fishing spot, they switched to a three-horse trolling motor.

The fish they caught were cleaned by the Lodge's dock worker and usually prepared for Ruth's breakfast the following morning. If they caught a lot of fish, the guests at the Lodge shared the largesse at dinner. Early in the summer, Art took Frank and me out separately and shared his knowledge of fishing. I was lucky enough to catch a 3-pound walleye on my first trip, which amazed and delighted everyone, especially me. He selected a tackle box for Frank and filled it with suitable tackle. We have it still.

We outfitted 35 parties that first summer of 1957. That didn't count canoe rentals. When people rented canoes for a day or more, that was the Lodge's business because they owned the canoes. I developed a menu for my customers and packed the food, which included canned goods plus fresh food for the first day. I also packed the equipment. When the party returned, I cleaned up the equipment. I hung the tent and sleeping bags out on a clothesline, washed the dishes, and polished the cook kit. I remember that it was hard work.

While Frank and I were working, our three children were playing around the area. At the beginning of the summer, Karl was nine, Ranna was seven, and Bill had just turned

Art and Ruth Towner were two of our best instructors.

Bill, age 4, naps on the dock.

four. Karl and Ranna often played with children on the campground. The games very often centered around "The Big Rock," which was on the path between the Lodge dock and the campground dock. Bill was more likely to hang around the dock with Frank. At least once every day, he fell into the lake. There was undoubtedly a message there that he needed to get more attention. We were preoccupied with other things. Frank would fish him out and send him up the hill to Mom for dry clothes. It was a chore to get his wet clothes off and get him dressed again. Clothes manufacturers had not at that date thought of making clothes easy to get on and off.

Then there was laundry to do. I packed all my dirty clothes in a Duluth pack and hiked over to the Lodge. The washing machine was in the basement of Pine Ridge, Jean and Dick's

14 SAWBILL

Mary Alice hangs out the laundry, unaware of the attacking blackflies.

winter home. They had a wringer-type washing machine. The clothes were agitated in the machine and then hand-fed one by one through the wringer into a tub of rinse water. They were rinsed by hand typically in warm water first and then put through the wringer again to a tub of cold rinse water and through a final wringing before being hung out on the clotheslines to dry. Under the clotheslines was tall grass. After all, this was not a city backyard. My first experience with hanging out the clothes was almost fatal. I had never heard of blackflies. They bite silently and painlessly. Soon after I hung that first load of clothes, I felt sick and my feet and ankles were swollen to twice their normal size. I had to stay in bed for several days with my feet elevated until the swelling subsided. After that I always did laundry wearing high leather boots with my jeans tucked securely inside and there were no more blackfly bites.

In that first July, another of our important customer/instructors arrived. It was Dale Koopman, Boy Scout leader extraordinaire. He brought a Boy Scout troop from Chicago for a week-long trip. He had a wealth of experience in canoe camping. A few years later, he announced that it was his 40th trip. He invited Karl, who was turning 10 in July, to go along on the trip around the Little Saganaga loop even though the Scouts on the trip were all teenagers. This gave Karl wonderful first-hand experience in canoe camping, which benefited us and all our customers from then on.

One suggestion that Dale had for us was that we get an embroidered patch that would say "Sawbill Canoe Trip." He said that Boy Scouts always needed to buy patches to sew on their uniforms or badge sashes. He provided us with the name of a company in Chicago that made embroidered patches and he designed the patch, using our logo. The next year, we had them for sale in our store. Forty-five years later, we still have the identical patch, the only change being that now the patches are "iron on" instead of "sew on." We still order from the same company and probably sell 200 a year, mostly to Boy Scouts. Now we have another patch that says "Paddle the BWCA," which is more popular with people other than the Scouts.

We hadn't been at the Lodge many weeks when an exciting event occurred. It was mid-morning and all the guests had headed out on their day's fishing expeditions when the big dinner bell suddenly clanged and we realized that there was a fire. Frank thoughtfully picked up the fire extinguisher that he had provided for the boathouse and we all sprinted for the Lodge. Black smoke was pouring out of Pine Ridge, the newest cabin. While everyone else milled around in panic, Frank pulled off his shirt, wrapped it around his nose and mouth, dropped to his knees and crawled into the building. He found the source of the fire very quickly. The guests had left their wet boots from the day before on top of the grating of the floor furnace. Once they dried, they caught on fire. Frank extinguished the fire and carried the grating and smoldering boots out. He was hailed as a hero while his family breathed deep sighs of relief!

When the smoke cleared, the damage was assessed. The wood

paneling near the furnace and the floor around it were burned and had to be replaced. The painted walls in the two bedrooms were not burned but hopelessly smoke damaged. They had to be repainted and all the curtains and bedding had to be washed. Jean could think only of the fact that she had promised the cabin to guests the following week and it had to be made ready. An innkeeper never reneges on a reservation. My help was enlisted to paint the bedrooms while the available guides pitched in on the carpentry. The Lodge did have other employees — the cook, kitchen helpers, the receptionist — but they were very busy with their regular duties. We had the cabin ready when the guests arrived.

Jean and Dick were close to 60 years old by this time and beginning to think of retirement. Dick took care of the electricity-producing diesels, did some maintenance, and kept the grounds manicured. Jean did the ordering and book work. She was a county commissioner, which meant that she went to Grand Marais at least one day a week and had extra work for that. Sunday was smorgasbord day at the Lodge. This was an unbelievable feast for its day, served on handmade platters made out of natural materials such as spruce burls and polished moose horns. It attracted diners from all over Cook County and also numerous North Shore tourists. Many people in Cook County still picture this event when they think of Sawbill.

In the midst of all the excitement and flurry of this first summer at Sawbill, we also had to think of providing our own building for our new business. In the fall of 1956 when we first agreed to start an outfitting business, Frank had immediately taken the first step, which was to apply for a special use permit from the Forest Service. Since the land was all part of the Superior National Forest, there was no possibility of buying it. As agreed, he applied for the special use permit for land near Baker Lake. As the summer of 1957 was flying by, we looked in vain for approval of our permit. Our relationship with the Lodge was going well, so Jean suggested that we build our building on her special use permit at Sawbill. We obtained interim approval from the Forest Service to do this. They chose a site up the hill from the lake, just above the public boat landing. The

The 1958 crew: (left to right) Dick Flint, Jerry Plumb, Sam Overland, Don Hempel, Tom Kubiak.

Forest Service did not want any buildings to be seen from the lake and they decreed that we could not keep any boats or canoes on the lake shore. So the building site was chosen just east of the Sawbill Trail and our guides began using their spare time to clear the land.

One of our neighbors in Duluth was a young architect just starting in business. He drew up plans for us, envisioning a Swiss chalet type building with living quarters on the second floor above the business. We thought that would be wonderful until the Forest Service informed us that only one-story buildings were allowed. Plans were redrawn for an L-shaped building with living quarters at the east end and the outfitting warehouse at the south end and a small store area at the northwest corner. It was also decreed that the building would be made of logs — stained brown. At Jean's suggestion, we ordered 600 8-foot logs, known as pulp sticks, and stockpiled them for curing.

The first of many family canoe trips

On Labor Day, the canoeing business was essentially over. We closed up shop and our family set out on a greatly anticipated canoe trip. The University did not start classes for several weeks and we chose to keep our school-age children, Karl and Ranna, out of school the first week.

We started out on a dreary, windy, overcast day. Sawbill Lake was choppy and we entertained ourselves by riding up the waves and bouncing off while singing cowboy songs.

Karl and I paddled one canoe while Frank and Ranna handled the other one. Frank had to carry both canoes over the portages while the rest of us managed the packs. We easily reached our destination of Phoebe Lake. We were all alone at that time of the year. We lured minnows by throwing bread crumbs on the water. Then we used them to bait our hooks. One stringer of fish left in the lake over night was gone in the morning. We consoled ourselves with the thought that the turtles were surely grateful to us for providing easy food and we vowed not to make that mistake again. We stayed there for three more days, then packed up and headed back. Our four-year-old Bill was not quite as enthusiastic as the rest of us. In an effort to include him, we had him carry the coffee pot, which contained a few remaining minnows. At the end of the portage, we discovered that he had discreetly set the pail down before starting his trek. We didn't go back.

The "after Labor Day canoe trip" became a family tradition for many years. Our goal was to explore the many lakes and portages so we took a different trip each year and tried to cover as much territory as possible. It was very valuable not only in becoming familiar with the area but also in experiencing the challenges that our customers met when they were on the trail. That week in September was inevitably rainy and cold so one of the first things we learned was that the tents we were using were not waterproof and they were soon replaced. Thus, we learned to value good equipment.

That first year, 1957, was the year that we became dedicated canoe campers and canoe outfitters for life.

· Chapter 2 ·

——— 1958 – Our Own Building ———

During the winter of 1957-58, a contractor from Grand Marais put up our building for canoe outfitting. He must have been greatly challenged to find carpenters to work in this remote location. Driving 50 to 100 miles as part of a day's work was not done at that time. Lumberjacks always lived in the woods where they were working, unlike the present loggers who drive to work every day. Neither did we drive from Duluth to see what was going on. Although Frank made a few weekend trips, I didn't see the building until the following Easter vacation when it was nearly complete.

The crew that built our building were Ray Bystrom and his son, Dick, and Claude Anderson. Ray was especially nice to our little children, among other things making them a little stool out of scrap lumber. Ray's home was in Tofte and the others lived in Grand Marais. They moved a travel trailer to our site and lived there during the week. Ray was the cook.

Building proceeded from crisis to crisis. The first crisis was that the 600 pulp sticks that were supposed to make the outside walls

1958 – Our Own Building

were all used by the time the walls were four feet high. It turned out to be a good thing because they were really quite inadequate building materials. Still, the dilemma remained. Now what? We settled on board and batten siding and construction continued.

It goes without saying that money was a major problem. We had almost no resources. We naively assumed that banks were a source for loans to start a business but we soon discovered otherwise. It makes sense from the bank's standpoint but it makes it very difficult for young people who are not already well supplied with resources to start a new enterprise. We tried the Grand Marais Bank and the bank we used in Duluth and were turned down. Finally, we went to Northern City Bank in Duluth. We knew the loan officer through attending the same church. He in turn knew what a canoe outfitter was because he knew Jim Pascoe who ran Wilderness Outfitters in Ely. He agreed to a small loan provided that we transfer our personal accounts and home loan to Northern City. We had to put up all the canoes and outfitting equipment, a meager lot, as collateral. So began a long and friendly relationship. Northern City became First Bank and eventually part of a huge impersonal corporation, now called Wells Fargo.

Still, as the building progressed, the money was all spent. As a last resort, we decided to cash in on our years of work for Frank's parents and reluctantly asked them for a loan. They agreed and we managed to complete the shell of the building. It took ingenuity, luck, and a lot of help from our friends to finish that building. The SAGE building had just been completed in Duluth. Frank and friends salvaged the concrete forms used when they poured the massive concrete walls. This rough marine plywood became the paneling for the inside of our building. It was cut into chunks and the edges were beveled in an effort to make it look like paneling. It was full of holes that we stuffed with corks and some spackling before we stained the wood. It remained as the ceiling paneling of our store until 2002. It served well as the subflooring. We covered the house and store floors with the cheapest possible asphalt tile that we installed ourselves, not very skillfully. The outfitting warehouse floor was left unfinished.

Our new building goes up during the winter of 1957-58.

Next we needed furnishings. Jean and Dick Raiken provided us with all the discarded furniture, cooking utensils, and dishes that they could round up from Sawbill Lodge. They also gave us a lovely new wood-paneled bar and four bar stools that Dick had made a few winters earlier at the request of a lodge guest from Kansas City who never took delivery. That became the primary store fixture along with our old glass-front display case and some shelves nailed to the wall. It led to our applying for an on-sale beer license — a move we came to regret. For several years, our store became a bar in the evening and bar customers did not accept our closing time of 10 p.m. Bars don't open again at 7 a.m. as we did. After a few years, the wood-paneled bar had to go, although we still use it as furniture.

Jean located an institutional-size gas range that a restaurant in Grand Marais was discarding. I remember spending a beautiful Easter weekend in 1958 in the parking lot in front of our building scraping layers and layers of encrusted grease off this stove. It was never beautiful but it worked. We had the old refrigerator we had used in Cedar Cabin and we built in a counter between the kitchen and living room to serve as our eating table. I shopped at garage sales in Duluth for odds and ends. My best buy was a very functional electric toaster, which I got for 25 cents.

The fellows who worked for us that summer had plenty to fill their spare time as they helped us add the finishing touches to the building. The personnel was the same as the first year, with the addition of Jerry Plumb, a high school student who lived with us and helped out. He and Frank spent many hours making a small round coffee table for the living room. The base was made of a section of a spruce tree with three branches splitting off. Turned upside down, this formed the legs. They used heavy planking for the top and spent much time sanding and shaping. Dick Raiken made artistic, rustic lamps out of spruce burls. We received a floor lamp and a small table lamp. With much help from friends, we settled into our new home and business.

The Forest Service permit continued to be an issue. After our first summer in business, we still had heard nothing from our application to build an outfitters on Baker Lake. It was evident that we were firmly settled at Sawbill so we applied for our own permit and received it without too great delay. Four years later, we were notified that we had been granted the permit at Baker Lake. We said, "No, thank you." In retrospect, Sawbill Lake certainly was a far better location.

On the way home from meeting with Jean Raiken in the fall of 1956, Frank and I brainstormed a name for the new business. Our first choice was Caribou Canoe Outfitters, but we had concerns because it might imply a connection with Caribou Lake in Lutsen. When it became apparent the following year that we were going to build on Sawbill Lake, we asked Jean if we could call our business Sawbill Canoe Outfitters and she agreed enthusiastically. (Sawbill is the nickname of the ubiquitous merganser duck.)

The building begins to take shape in the deep snow.

We started the business as a partnership with Sawbill Lodge, patterned somewhat after the relationship of Gunflint Lodge and Gunflint Outfitters. Jean Raiken and Justine Kerfoot of Gunflint Lodge were both county commissioners at the time and certainly compared notes on their respective businesses. Our arrangement was that the Lodge would contribute the canoes and outfitting equipment that they had and we would give them 10 percent of the profits at the end of each year. We would continue to store and rent all the canoes at the Sawbill Lodge dock.

There were endless other things that Jean and Dick did for us. All our fresh and frozen food was stored in the Lodge walk-in cooler and freezer. When Jean drove 50 miles to Grand Marais each week, she took orders from everyone at Sawbill and did the shopping. She looked after all of us in a motherly fashion, even choosing clothes for us and

Our building is completed in 1958.

bringing them home for approval. Before we had given a thought to the upcoming winter, she brought Frank a Woolrich red and black plaid mackinaw jacket. Earlier she had picked out a Forest Service green cruiser jacket for him. Both of these gave him the proper North Woods appearance. All the guides also wore the olive drab cruiser jackets.

We never went to Grand Marais in the early years or to Tofte for that matter. Jean did all the errands. We caught glimpses of Lake Superior and the North Shore on our annual moves from Duluth to Sawbill in the spring and back to Duluth in the fall. However, we did establish a relationship with Anita and Cliff Johnson who had a grocery store, bar, and gas pump in Tofte, with their residence in the same building. They had a covered porch in the back of their building and that became our freight depot. There was no UPS in those days. North Shore Freight trucks delivered our merchandise. Then, as now, there were specialized trucks for such things as milk, bread, and pop. This was all delivered to Cliff and Nita's porch and picked up by anyone bound for Sawbill.

Early on, all our employees and friends were trained to stop in Tofte to pick up anything that was there and to call on the telephone to see if we had any last-minute needs. This rule became so embedded in Sawbill procedure that Eric Hoekstra, former crew member, called one day from New York City to ask if anyone needed anything! Now crew members perpetuate the joke by calling from all over the country when they are away.

We stopped to visit with Cliff and Nita on the rare occasions when we were on the shore. Nita and I made a few trips to Duluth together. One of the bonds she and I had was that we both pumped gasoline at a time when this was strictly a man's job. We had good laughs about the male customers' reactions.

In 1962, it was discovered that Nita had cancer. Cliff took her to the University of Minnesota Hospitals but nothing could be done and she was gone within a few days. Cliff was distraught and was not able to cope with his loss. He tried to carry on the business by himself but he was heartbroken at losing Nita and it was all too much for him. In a short time, he was dead too. Their building was torn down.

A new grocery store was soon built on the north side of the highway by Florence and Henry Wehseler. Soon, the North Shore Market was the hub of the community. They were kind enough to let us establish our freight depot there and they have continued to be faithful friends over all our years at Sawbill. The ownership of the North Shore Market has since passed to Cliff and Nancy Iverson, another pair of wonderful neighbors.

· Chapter 3 ·

—— Forest Service – Then and Now ——

Sawbill Lake is in the Superior National Forest, which is administered by the U. S. Forest Service, a division of the Department of Agriculture. The jurisdictional distinctions of the area baffle many people. The Superior National Forest is the land part of the area and it is managed by the federal government. The water, which constitutes a large part of the area, is controlled by the Department of Natural Resources (DNR) of Minnesota. Fishing regulations are the province of the state, which leads to the misconception that the whole area is overseen by the DNR. National forests must also be distinguished from national parks, which are managed by the Department of Interior of the federal government and operated under different rules.

The Forest Service provides campgrounds in almost all national forests throughout the country. They are predominantly primitive campgrounds, with no electricity or water hookups. They have campsites with a tent pad, wells with hand-operated pumps for water, and outhouses. They are often on lakes, with docks or boat launching facilities provided. In recent years, in the Superior National Forest, running water from a faucet is available at some campgrounds, made possible by solar operated pumps.

The Forest Service charges a daily fee for camping at many of the larger campgrounds. Most of the 28 campgrounds in the Superior National Forest are free, but a fee is charged at a few of the larger ones. A rule is that no campsite may be occupied for more than 14 consecutive days. This prevents people from setting up a permanent or seasonal home as often happens in private campgrounds. The Forest Service has the responsibility for building and maintaining the roads into and through campgrounds, keeping campsites and privies clean, removing fallen trees or "hazard trees," which are ones that seem likely to fall on campsites in case of a high wind, and collecting the fees where these are charged.

When we first came to Sawbill, there were seven campsites on the Sawbill Lake campground. Four or five were on the left as one walks down the road to the lake. Two or three were on the lake shore on the right-hand side of the boat landing. These were popular with those who wanted to keep their boat at their campsite. The dock included a boat launching ramp. There was one water pump and one set of privies — his and hers.

As we were establishing our business at Sawbill, the Forest Service was actively working on improvements. There was increasing demand for camping facilities at Sawbill so they built additional campsites. They soon closed the campsites on the south side of the road to the boat landing and made two of them into "picnic sites." They also closed the sites that were on the immediate lakeshore and put the new ones up the hill a little way from the water. This was to prevent lake pollution. People who were accustomed to camping at Sawbill were extremely unhappy about these changes. They yearned to continue camping on exactly the same campsite they had come to cherish. The Forest Service blocked the driveways to the old campsites with huge rocks and put up signs advising people that no camping was allowed. At first, people sometimes moved the rocks and continued to use the old campsites. Change is difficult to accept.

Forest Service — Then and Now

The Sawbill Lake boat landing, 1960

We had cleared out a small space for our customers to park their cars while they were out on canoe trips. We could probably have accommodated six cars if we had ever had that many customers at one time.

After a few years, the Forest Service decided there should be a real parking lot and they cleared out a huge space just opposite our store. We thought it was ridiculously large but the Forest Service looked into the future with great foresight and built it to fit the demands of the next 50 years. Seventy-five cars could park comfortably.

At present, the parking area rarely has many empty spaces. Earl Hansen, who was the Tofte ranger at the time, remembers that he, too, thought the planned space was outlandish. The decision went all the way to the regional office in Milwaukee where they approved the large size.

I protested that they were cutting down my beloved trees. My kitchen windows overlooked that portion of woods and we enjoyed watching birds there. The ranger consoled me with the promise of a new planting of red pines in a strip between the parking lot and the road in front of our place. Forty years later, these trees are about 40 feet tall and are known to many folks in the Forest Service as Mary Alice's red pines.

The funniest incident occurred one winter as we looked out the window at the nearby woods before it was cut down. We had a stale loaf of bread that we decided to put out for the birds. We straightened a wire coat hanger and strung the slices on it, expecting that it would provide food for many birds for several days. Almost immediately, a Canada jay arrived and grabbed the middle of the coat hanger in his beak and flew off with the whole thing. Our dismay turned to amusement as it flew into the woods. The jay's "wide load" would not fit between the trees and he dropped it right there at the edge of the woods. We thought it served him right!

As our business was getting started, the Forest Service made Sawbill into a fee campground. They hired a retired insurance salesperson, Les Coyer, to be in charge. He drove a green Forest Service pickup from Tofte each morning, 24 miles up and then 24 miles back to the ranger station. It was his duty to check the privies, keeping them supplied with toilet paper, and then to visit each campsite and collect the fee. He joined our crew for coffee break each morning. Then he drove on to service other campgrounds at Crescent Lake and at Temperance River.

One year, the Forest Service looked at the books and realized that campgrounds were losing money, due to the cost of the employee and the vehicle involved. They decided to open the job for bids from private individuals or businesses. The system is that the Forest Service continues to take care of road maintenance and major improvements while the concessionaire is responsible for the daily upkeep. The concessionaire pays the Forest Service a percentage of the receipts. Sawbill Outfitters has regularly been the successful bidder for the concession at Sawbill and Crescent campgrounds. It is a profitable operation for us since it doesn't require a lot of extra driving or hiring an extra crew member. During much of the summer, a campground host camps on each campground. In exchange for free camping and a small stipend, the host interacts with the campers and does the daily chores.

When we were still hosting morning coffee breaks, I felt an obligation to supply homemade cookies each day, adding to my already overwhelming list of duties. Still it was a great opportunity to socialize. The gathering always included any guides who were not out, some lodge guests, and anyone else who happened to be around. Two interesting guests were game wardens from Louisiana who came to pick up black bears that the DNR had trapped. They hoped to establish a black bear population in Louisiana. The DNRs of the two states had arranged a trade in which the state of Minnesota would receive wild turkeys to be released in southern Minnesota. Minnesota enjoys its wild turkey population to this day. I wonder if Louisiana is equally happy with the deal.

Sawbill Lodge attracted some very interesting guests who often ended up at our morning coffee. One was young Sandy Keith from Rochester, who in later years became Chief Judge of the Minnesota Supreme Court. Another was Chick Hanscomb, who was chief of security for the University of Minnesota. He had a reputation as a successful sleuth and was one of a team consulted by Erle Stanley Gardner when he was trying to solve big crimes. Erle called the lodge one night looking for Chick, throwing all of us mystery fans into a frenzy of excitement. He was working on the Sam Shepherd murder case in Cleveland, Ohio.

Before any businesses had been established in the area, the Forest Service had started its work. Hugo L. Sundling remembers working for the Forest Service in 1922.[1] He was a sophomore at the Michigan Agricultural College and needed summer employment. He was hired as a forest guard by Supervisor Calvin Dahlgren of the North Shore unit of the Forest Service headquartered in Ely.

The first challenge of the job was getting there. The North Shore was still a primitive frontier, similar to the East Coast a century earlier. Hugo traveled to Duluth by train, spent the night there, and then took another train to Two Harbors. From there, he boarded a steamship (probably the *America*), which was the only means of transport to Grand Marais. In Grand Marais, he checked into the North Shore Hotel (later named East Bay Hotel), operated by a Mrs. Giddings. There was no running water but the hotel room was equipped with a washbowl and a pitcher of water on the commode, and a night chair within the commode.

The North Shore unit of the Forest Service was comprised of the northern portions of the Gunflint, Tofte, and Isabella districts. Ranger Charles Taylor was senior ranger in charge of the entire unit. Ranger Jack Valentine, headquartered at Four Mile Lake, was in charge of the western area along the Alger Smith Railroad as far as Brule Lake. Ranger Ed Mulligan handled the area along the southern boundary of the unit, and Ranger Taylor had the eastern portion and the area along the Gunflint Trail. The southern boundary of the unit did not go all the way to Lake Superior as is the case today.

The Forest Service facilities were quite different then. The Grand Marais ranger's office was on the second floor of a frame building with meager furnishings. Correspondence consisted of handwritten memos. When typing was necessary, the rangers had to do it as well as doing filing and all other office chores. There was a grounded telephone line connecting Grand Marais with Ely, but it was not always dependable.

Hugo's first assignment was tower lookout at the Pine Mountain Fire Tower. It was 25 feet tall but still provided good vision over the tops of the trees because the area had been burned off in 1910. It was not an exciting job as there were very few smokes and there was very little traffic on the Gunflint Trail. He did see Native Americans from Grand Portage passing by, heading up to the Gunflint Lake area to fish and pick berries. Men came first with rifles, in case they scared up deer or moose, followed at some distance by children and the women with papooses on their backs. Most traffic for the Gunflint at that time went by way of the wagon road to the South Brule River where they hit the Gunflint Trail.

His next assignment was to Rangers Mulligan and Valentine. They went by boat to Lutsen where the trail to the back country started on the west side of the Poplar River. George Nelson Sr. was operating a small resort with very good food, Hugo recalled. The trail had been developed for moose hunter guests of Lutsen Resort by

George's father, C.A.A. Nelson. The Forest Service people would hike eight miles to Honeymoon Cabin, work there several days, and then walk to Four Mile Cabin, 10 miles to the west.

Hugo remembers assisting Rangers Mulligan and Valentine with the telephone lines and trail maintenance going as far north as Sawbill Cabin. The Sawbill Trail was not yet in existence so access to the cabin was by way of foot trail going north from Honeymoon Cabin past Peterson Lake, Burnt Lake, and then to Sawbill Cabin.

He went on to Silver Island Lake to the cabin there for patrol work. Patrol work consisted of being alert to any smell of smoke as well as climbing hills at intervals to see if any smoke could be sighted, meanwhile doing maintenance on the trail. "Mosquitoes and blackflies were pretty bad that summer," he

Sawbill Cabin Ranger Station was originally accessed only by foot trail.

said. "We had to use bandannas to cover the backs of our necks while working. In the evenings, we would put coals in a can and cover them with grass. This made enough smoke to discourage the mosquitoes. In the daytime, we used a lot of citronella mixed with pine tar."

Hugo started work on April 15 and continued through September 14. He earned $90 a month, less an allowance for lodging and food.

John "Casey" Tofte remembers the early days when the Forest Service was developing canoe routes. Local boys worked for the Forest Service during the summer vacations from school.[2] Casey remembers doing this in 1933 and 1934. He was in his early 20s at that time and on vacation from college. Three different crews worked in the Sawbill area. Each crew consisted of about 15 men, and they established a tent camp where they lived all summer, occasionally canoeing out on weekends.

The portage crew built portages and established canoe routes. They put in the railroad tracks from Sawbill to Alton and from Alton to Kelso. They built box-like docks with heavy 12-foot-long timbers, held together with big spikes. Then they filled the docks with rocks to hold them in place. They built dams on rivers to decrease the amount of portaging. They put up big signs with the name of the next lake and the distance to it. To locate portages, they followed established trails made by Native Americans, trappers, and prospectors, but they straightened the trails to make them as short as possible. The trappers had strong objections to this trail-building activity. They didn't welcome other people coming into their established territory.

The original trails tended to follow the contours of the land. The portage crew chose the shortest possible distance between lakes. They cleared a width of about nine feet, three feet on each side of the walkway. They sometimes laid timbers along the edges of the walkway. They grubbed out the trail to level it and then, using wheelbarrows, hauled dirt to fill the low spots. They built simple bridges where necessary to keep the trail dry. They built canoe rests — two posts with a log across the top — about every 50 rods or wherever a canoe carrier might be tired, as at the top of a hill.

The portage crews carried all their supplies and equipment into the woods. They took food in cans and 100-pound sacks of staples such as flour and sugar. They hauled in tools and big bags of the heavy steel spikes for dock building and big wooden boxes, each containing 50 pounds of dynamite. Each camp had a full-time cook. The camp on Sawbill Lake probably had more than 15 people. Another camp was at Hazel Lake and there was another somewhere east of Sawbill Lake. The boss on this job was Quentin Meussen. The Forest Service Ranger was Ed Mulligan.[3]

Around this time, there were still many small unnamed lakes. As maps were being developed, the crews out in the woods were encouraged to give names to all the lakes. With thousands of lakes to be named, this became quite a chore. One can easily imagine the feelings of some of these early workers who chose such names as Disappointment Lake, No Sleep Lake, and Louse Lake! Many lakes were named for their shape such as Horseshoe Lake, Pencil Lake, and Round Lake.

With this system, there was a great deal of duplication. There are still 200 lakes named Mud Lake. The DNR has renamed some major lakes to correct the confusing repetition. Not surprisingly, many lakes were named Pine Lake. This was the original name of Crescent Lake, which got its present name in the early 1960s. Lichen Lake, next to Crescent, was also renamed at the time. It had been one of many lakes named Beaver.

Many of the larger lakes were, of course, named by the Native Americans who first traveled the area. These are the names that are hard for many visitors to pronounce — Kawishiwi, Saganaga, Gabimichigami. (I'll share a secret. Ojibwe names always have the accent on one of the last two syllables.) Moose Lake was also named by the Ojibwe. The Ojibwe name for the animal became the English name as well.

Given the opportunity, many of the workers immortalized themselves by giving their own names to lakes: George, Karl, Frederick, Jack, or last names Davis, Winchell, Nelson, Baker. Most names are men's names, not surprisingly, since it was men who worked in the woods. A notable exception is the Lady Chain, one of Sawbill's most popular canoe routes. Names are Beth, Ella, Grace, Phoebe, Hazel, and Polly. Ed Mulligan, the ranger on the district, named these lakes for his sisters and other relatives.

A family of mergansers, nicknamed "sawbills" for their sawtooth bills.

Sawbill is a fairly unique name, although there is a large lake in the Quetico named Sawbill. "Sawbill" is the nickname for the merganser duck with its sawtooth bill. It is a common denizen of the area.[4]

It may be well-known that the Temperance River was named by Father Baraga, a Jesuit priest who traveled Lake Superior in the 1800s, because it is the only river flowing into the lake that does not have a sand bar across its mouth. Two of our early customers and friends, Dr. Bernard Zimmerman and his wife, Elizabeth, wrote a wonderful song called "The Temperance River Ballad" sung to the tune of "There's a Tavern in the Town." Their fellow paddlers were encouraged to keep stroking to the rhythm of this song.

Verse 1:
Oh, Father Baraga was pious and brave.
He crossed the water 'midst the wind and the wave.
But, he said, "Dear Lord, I've gone a bit too far
'Cause the Temperance River has no bar."

Chorus:
Now it's northward we are heading
And we've got our tents and bedding
And we've packed a little bottle
Just in case of need.
Adieu, adieu kind friends, adieu, yes adieu,
Now we'll be taking our canoe, our canoe
'Cause there ain't no trains
And there ain't no trolley car
And the Temperance River has no bar, has no bar.

Verse 2:
The loons will laugh at us and the wolves will cry,
And the rain will soak us when it pours from the sky
But we'll steer our course as true as yonder star
'Cause the Temperance River has no bar. (Chorus)

Verse 3:
You climb a mountain and you tramp through a ditch
'Cause the Sitka portage is a son of a bitch,
And when you reach the top, how sorry then you are
That the Temperance River has no bar. (Chorus)

Verse 4:
The tent is cozy and it's buttoned up tight,
But who's that grow-el-ing out there in the night?
It must be the wind or the thunder from afar
'Cause the Temperance River has no b'ar! (Chorus)

By the time we arrived in 1957, the Forest Service was still hiring college students who worked under the direction of regular Forest Service personnel to take care of the portages over which canoeists traveled from lake to lake and the campsites where they camped. Each portage was marked with a sign that named the next lake and gave its distance in rods. Rods were used to measure portages because it was a measure that surveyors used and that practice has never changed. A rod is 16½ feet — an average canoe length. Portages consisted of a wide path through the woods with canoe rests approximately every 50 rods.

A campsite in the woods consisted of a picnic table, a fire grate, a tent pad, and a box latrine. The rules were in place even then: camp only at established campsites, build fires only in the fire grates, burn all your trash, and leave your campsite clean. Forest Service seasonal employees made the rounds cleaning campsites, replacing latrines and tables and canoe rests as needed, and cutting fallen trees off portages. When they needed to replace a picnic table, the Forest Service airplane would drop it off. If necessary on a smaller lake, it would be towed upside down across the lake behind a canoe. Latrines came disassembled in a cube-like package and were assembled on the site. Both the tables and the latrines were made of thick lumber and were very heavy. Some of the first picnic tables on the sites had been built by the CCC men in the 1930s. These tables were constructed on site and were made of rough hewn lumber, often halves of large cedar logs.

Campsites in the 1950s often had amenities that were not provided by the Forest Service. Benches and chairs were built around the fire grates by campers. Clotheslines were hung from tree to tree and nails and pegs were arranged on tree trunks to make hanging places. Thoughtful campers left piles of wood that they had cut and split. Sometimes this firewood was covered with an old tarp or else placed under the picnic table for protection from the rain. Many tents had to be erected using poles. These were cut at the site and usually left for the next campers to use. Boughs of cedar or balsam were cut to make soft sleeping places and these were sometimes reusable. During the winter, hunters or trappers could bring very

Camping at the Sawbill Campground in 1960

heavy items over the ice, so some campsites were equipped with a wood stove or a metal box for storing food. It was fascinating to visit each campsite and discover its unique equipment. Each campsite usually had its own dump — a place back in the woods where campers deposited cans and bottles.

During one of our first summers at Sawbill, the Forest Service decided to reopen an old route that was probably used by the native people who lived in the area before Europeans came along. It was the route from Kelso and Lujenida lakes up to Mesaba Lake and ultimately to Little Saganaga Lake. Nature is constantly reshaping itself, leaving lakes and streams as dry beds. Nature includes beavers that dam streams. A storm may cause the dam to wash out and a lake disappears. Thus, a lake to the east of the present Lujenida-to-Zenith portage had dried up, leaving a mile and a half of dry land.

In order to make this route more appealing, the Forest Service proposed to build a dam across the stream flowing into Lujenida. A man was hired to do this. We never learned his name. He camped all summer long at the beginning of the portage on the north end of Kelso Lake. He had a young boy with him, presumably his son. The boy probably helped some with the work and certainly kept him company during that long summer. They used rocks and dirt and logs lying around the woods to build a large dam. We saw them cooking over their camp fire and visited with them but, as far as I know, they never came in for food or supplies, to take showers or to use the telephone. The dam was completed during the summer and, over a period of several years, it successfully backed up the water for 30 or 40 rods so that it was possible to put the canoe in and paddle upstream, but not far. Most people continue to use the mile and a half long portage from Lujenida to Zenith. As camping equipment has become lighter, it is no longer such a formidable route and it is well used today.

By the turn of the 21st century, Forest Service policy has done a complete turnaround, the policy fueled by the wishes of the canoeing public. All the docks were torn out, although the observant traveler can still look into the water near a landing and see log cribs filled with rocks. All the signs were taken down and canoeists must depend on their maps to determine where they are. The canoe rests were removed. Since canoes are now ultralight, this is not so much of a hardship as it might seem. All the picnic tables were removed from campsites.

While the goal 70 years ago was to develop the area, the goal today is to preserve the area as wilderness with human imprint on the land kept to a minimum. The portage crews who spend the summer in the woods now do some work on trail maintenance, such as improving drainage by building riprap. They visit campsites and pick up litter that has been left behind. Any improvements which campers leave behind such as clotheslines are removed to make the site as natural as possible. Fire grates and latrines are the only amenities on campsites, both necessary for forest protection and control of pollution. Big projects for the portage crews are the occasional replacement of a latrine by digging a new hole or closing a campsite that has become worn and eroded through overuse and then building a new campsite. Most of the original artificial dams have disappeared through natural deterioration. There is considerable agitation to have all dams removed but the current thinking is to leave them alone and allow nature to take its course.

· Chapter 4 ·

─── Saga of the Telephone ───

In 1957, communication as we know it today was still in its infancy. Most nonlocal communication was by U.S. mail. True, almost everyone had a telephone and people within a community did call each other. Most calls were short and businesslike, particularly if they were long distance. At Sawbill, we were a little behind the general population. There were no regular telephone lines to connect us with the rest of the world. What there was in 1957 was an old jerry-rigged telephone line that the Forest Service had installed some 20 years earlier to communicate with the fire tower at Kelso Lake.

Fire towers at high points around the forest were the way that the Forest Service managed fire control. The fire towers were in place by the early 1930s. Kelso Fire Tower was probably built in the winter of 1927. We know that it was already in place when the Arbogusts arrived at Sawbill Lake in 1932. The fire tower at Kelso Lake was staffed during the summer months by someone who lived in a little cabin next to the tower.

If a fire was spotted, immediate communication was desirable, so the Forest Service built a telephone line from the Tofte Ranger Station to Kelso Fire Tower, stringing wire on short, rough-hewn poles or trees.

Hugo Sundling described the telephone line in detail. "The line was composed of No. 9 GI wire that was hung on split-ring insulators attached to trees with wire." The use of split-ring insulators prevented many breaks in the line as there was more available slack in the event that trees fell across it. If glass insulators had been used to hold the wire there would have been less slack.

It was necessary to put in ground wires (lightning wires) at intervals to deflect at least some of the lightning strikes from following the wire. Even so, during a severe lightning storm, it was dangerous to be following the telephone line. There were many treeless areas created by fires where no trees were available to hang the telephone line. Then poles were cut from nearby trees and dragged into place. When breaks in the line occurred, they were fixed by splicing the line. The telephone wire had to be high enough off the ground so that bull moose would not catch it with their horns.

By the time we arrived in 1957, the Forest Service had made the transition from using

Telephone service was a jerry-rigged wire from Kelso Tower to Tofte Ranger Station.

fire towers to using airplanes to spot fires. In 1957, the fire towers were still there but were not in active use. The telephone line between Sawbill Lake and the Forest Service station in Tofte had been taken over by Sawbill Lodge. The rest of the line was simply abandoned. We have a famous relic of this in our store.

In 1958, Dick Flint, one of our guides, took advantage of his day off to explore the old fire tower at Kelso Lake. As he hiked through the woods to the tower, he found the skull and rack of a moose entangled in the old drooping telephone line. He cut it out and carried it back to Sawbill. We hung it on the wall in the store and it still hangs there today. People often ask why we wrapped that wire around the moose rack! We tried to find out from the Forest Service if the moose had died of starvation after becoming hopelessly entangled in the line. The consensus was that the moose's plight was discovered rather quickly by Forest Service personnel and that it was shot and quickly put out of its misery.

So this open two-wire telephone line was still being used by Sawbill Lodge in the 1950s. Ma Bell would have nothing to do with the line, thus it was the responsibility of Sawbill Lodge and then Sawbill Canoe Outfitters to maintain it. On the Sawbill Trail between Tofte and Sawbill Lake, there were 1,385 poles. The conductors were steel wire. There were insulators on the poles. The lines ran along the edge of the Sawbill Trail for the most part but there were some long stretches through the woods. The construction of the line was imperfect originally. Then, as mishaps occurred and makeshift repairs were made, the transmission and reception became ever more uncertain.

Our new building was hooked into the Lodge's telephone line. In return, Frank began to help with the maintenance. The first thing he learned was that any twig that touched the telephone line disrupted communication. Since the line ran through thick woods, twigs and branches and fallen trees constantly touched the line, especially if there was any wind or precipitation. In some places, the line crossed the Sawbill Trail and hung low enough that a large piece of machinery being hauled on a flatbed trailer could become tangled in the line. Thunderstorms seriously affected the equipment, requir-

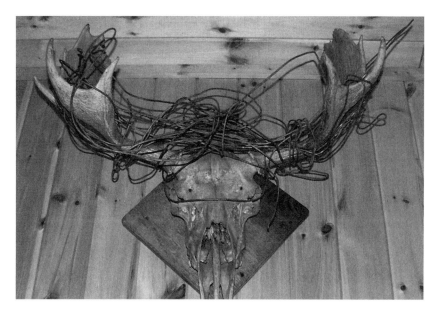

Wired for sound — a moose became entangled in the first wire telephone line.

ing the replacement of parts in the actual phones and terminal boxes. On a few occasions, lightning rode in on the wires and did serious damage to our building.

We felt strongly about having telephone service. As soon as the line was discovered to be out of order, an emergency was declared. All other activities were put aside. Dick Raiken from the Lodge, Frank, and our son Karl would load the pickup with ladder and repair kit and start out to check the line. The first part of the line ran along the Sawbill Trail so it was possible to drive along and look. About halfway down the Sawbill Trail, the line took off through the woods and the repair team had to hike, usually through mosquito-infested swamp. Once they found the problem, the fun had just begun.

Someone had to climb the shaky pole and make the repair. Sometimes, one of them got a mild electrical shock. Sometimes, the ladder slipped or the pole broke and the climber tumbled. If they were lucky, one repair would solve the problem. Otherwise, they went looking for another problem.

After Frank became involved, he installed a few junction boxes so that trouble on the line could be isolated to a mere five or six miles instead of the whole 25 miles. They carried a portable telephone instrument that they could plug into the box. They would call back to base and, if the connection was made, they knew the problem was farther down the line. Telephone repair was a labor-intensive and hazardous portion of our first years in business.

Because the telephone was shaky and uncertain, Frank joined Jean Raiken as a radio amateur or ham. Jean had become a ham as a result of her friendship with Bob Aldrich and it had, purely by chance, become a wonderful source of advertising for Sawbill Lodge. The purpose, however, was to provide emergency communication with the outside world if, or when, the makeshift telephone wasn't working.

Jean met Bob Aldrich in Chicago during World War II when she was in charge of food service for United Airlines and Bob was an airport inspector for American Airlines. They discovered that they both hailed from the same part of the state of New York and nostalgia led to friendship. After the war, Jean returned to Sawbill Lodge and Bob became the first chair of the Metropolitan Airports Commission located in the Twin Cities. Members of the commission were from all parts of Minnesota so they held meetings in various parts of the state. Bob arranged for some meetings to be held at Sawbill Lodge. When he observed the remote location, he persuaded Jean to become involved in amateur radio. As soon as she was licensed to go on the air, they began to talk every morning.

One morning in March, Bob arrived early to a meeting in Minneapolis. Jim Borman, news director of WCCO, happened to arrive early also. Jim commented that it was a beautiful spring morning with the temperature in the 40s. Bob replied, "Yes, but would you believe that there is a place in Minnesota where the temperature is 20 below this morning?" He proceeded to tell him about Sawbill. Jim said, "That's news! If that happens again, call me and we'll put it on the morning news." Bob replied, "I'm in contact with Sawbill Lodge every morning and I always get the temperature. I'll just call it in to WCCO and you can use it as you see fit."

WCCO was the preeminent radio station in Minnesota and probably in the Midwest at that time. Almost everyone started his or her day by listening to the morning show on WCCO. The announcers they heard were like beloved friends — Cedric Adams, Clelland Card, Bob DeHaven. It was the latter who included the Sawbill Lodge temperature in the morning weather report. Listeners were amazed to hear that there was a place in Minnesota so much colder than the Twin Cities. This is often the case in early spring. Because it attracted so much interest and comment, Bob DeHaven began including Sawbill's temperature on a regular basis and continued to do so over a number of years. No money was ever exchanged. This was simply an interesting piece of news that he relayed to the public. Jean and Bob DeHaven never met, never even talked. Jean did invite WCCO personnel to visit Sawbill Lodge but no one ever came, except for Jim Borman who happened to come once as part of an Associated Press conference.

Frank never needed to use his ham radio capability in a dire emergency but it was an interesting hobby and a way of making new friends. It did provide him with a knowledge base for other uses of radio. Almost immediately, Frank perceived a need to establish communication with Vi and Ken Osman who spent their summers isolated on the far western end of Brule Lake. It was decided to make use of citizen's band (CB) radio which, as the name implies, was open to everyone and did not require a special license. Harley Dinges, who had a resort near the Brule landing, was already using CB. Radios were installed at the Osmans' cabin. First thing each morning, messages were exchanged. Later, Billie Peterson, often alone at the Tait Lake Resort after her husband, Cap, died, was added to the network. No great emergencies ever arose but the calls provided a support network for elderly people living in the forest in very remote locations. A similar system is in place these days in cities where elderly or disabled people living alone call in or are called each day by telephone to make sure everything is all right.

We personally used handheld radios to stay in touch with someone out on the lakes or back roads. Sometimes, this proved more nerve-racking than reassuring. For example, our son Bill decided to go on a solo canoe trip when he was 12. He packed his gear, took the dog and a handheld radio with a call-in schedule, and departed for Smoke Lake. I had no doubt of his capability to handle the canoe trip but normal parental anxiety about a child going off alone had me in a state of tension. I could scarcely contain myself until six that evening when the first call-in was scheduled, but six o'clock came and went without a call. Tension rose but I was able to give myself rational reassurances that he was busy, perhaps away from his camp site. He had to initiate the call because his radio operated on a battery and could only be turned on for a brief period of use. I eagerly awaited call time the next evening at six. The air waves were silent. Anxiety mounted but there was little point in taking any action. Perhaps he was trying to call and the radio wasn't working. He was due to come in the next afternoon at four o'clock. When that time arrived and there was no sign of a returning canoeist, I was in a true state of panic. I enlisted a partner, jumped into a canoe and started paddling toward Smoke Lake. Not long after we passed the first narrows, a canoe came into view with a lone paddler and a dachshund perched on top of the Duluth packs. "Why didn't you call?" I demanded as soon as we were within earshot. "Call?" he said. "Oh, I forgot." Repeated similar experiences left me less than enchanted with this type of communication.

Nature continued to affect our telephone service. Although Sawbill enjoys quite stable weather, we do occasionally have bad storms in October or November. October 1968, was a time to be remembered for one of the worst of the worst. The storm probably would have been classified as a tornado except that there was no one to see it and record it, but the results were not hard to see. Maybe it was a straight-line wind such as we had on July 4, 1999. In any case, a great swath of land was cleared along the Sawbill Trail as trees were blown down. The Forest Service later placed a marker on the Parent Lake Road just a half mile west of the Sawbill Trail, designating the area as "Nature's Clear Cut."

Along with the thousands of trees blown down were a number of old and decrepit telephone poles. That was the end of the telephone line into Sawbill. It was beyond repair and it was a painful loss. We weren't sure what effect the lack of a telephone would have on reservations for canoe trips. Most of our reservations came in the mail, but some of our customers called and talked to us personally.

For several years thereafter, we had no telephone. By this time, Jean Raiken was living in her new home on the Temperance River six miles north of Tofte and we could use her telephone. One of us would stop in each day to pick up messages and make the necessary calls out. In the winter, we lived in Minneapolis where we had the customary telephone with an answering machine to handle inquiries and reservations.

Frank immediately contacted the telephone company to see if they could supply us with service. They were not interested in discussing it. Frank's study had already led him to believe that the solution to our problems was a radio-telephone and he pursued that option with great diligence during that winter. He shopped for a vendor of radio-telephone equipment. Only Team Electronics in Duluth was willing and able to supply such equipment.

The owner of the store was Bill Grazier, an amiable man with great enthusiasm and optimism, as well as a lot of engineering knowledge. He rose to the challenge and took on our telephone problems. He dreamed of installing many radio telephones in the wilds of northern Minnesota once he had pioneered the system at Sawbill. He took on the problem of guiding us through all the government regulations and licenses as well as developing the equipment to do the job. He modified a Hallicrafter radio-telephone system to fit our needs. Over the next several years, Bill became virtually a member of our family as he was continually on the scene, overseeing the installation of equipment and then troubleshooting. Needless to say, this was an expensive process and we really did not have money to spend on it, nor did he.

Our relationship with Bill Grazier began in the fall of 1971 and the radio telephone became operational for the 1973 season, but it never worked satisfactorily. By 1977, we had written off our investment and Team Electronics in Duluth was in bankruptcy. Bill Grazier held on to his dreams and his optimism, writing that this would free him up to pursue some of the other projects he had been planning. We parted company with Bill Grazier and moved on to purchase new equipment from E.F. Johnson Co. in Waseca, Minnesota.

To use radios for communication, we needed a base station at our place of business and another station on the shore of Lake Superior because there has to be transmission and reception at both ends. We had to have towers high enough for a "line of sight" transmission between the two stations. Frank studied topographic maps and finally determined that the best possible site for the tower was in Grand Marais on Maple Hill near the cemetery. Unfortunately, this land was part of the Superior National Forest, which meant we had to apply for a special use permit from the Forest Service. A lengthy debate ensued over issues such as: should Sawbill have a new special use permit for this site or should the tower site be incorporated into our existing special use permit? It took several years to resolve all the issues and obtain the permit.

Meanwhile, we also needed a license from the Federal Communications Commission (FCC) in Washington, D.C., just as any radio station does. Negotiations for this license stretched over several years. After waiting a year or so for our case to be heard, we found our application summarily turned down with the terse statement: "Part 21 does not apply." Our efforts to obtain a copy of Part 21 to determine what didn't apply were frustrated by the fact that the government was out of the document! When we obtained a copy months later, it turned out that Part 21 was a voluminous document covering all radio services under the jurisdiction of the FCC.

Another FCC argument was that we really should contact Northwest Bell to supply us with a telephone and not try to do it ourselves. Ha! Government agencies seem to move with the speed of molasses. It was at this point that we were advised to hire a Washington, D.C., based lawyer with a specialty of dealing with the FCC. We did this. Still, there was no action. Finally, when it appeared that the FCC would stall forever, we contacted Senator Walter Mondale. Frank argued that it was a matter of public safety that we should have a telephone. Thousands of people passed through Sawbill every summer and there was no way to call for help in case of emergency. Cook County Sheriff John Lyght wrote a valuable supporting letter, outlining the dire prospects for the public if we did not get a telephone.

Frank's letter to Senator Mondale spelled out our reasons for needing a telephone. An excerpt from the letter says:

> "The fact remains that we are in urgent need of an emergency permit. The experience of the personnel in your office who are unable to reach us is typical of the experiences of everyone because we are positively out of communication. During this time, we have had four customers admitted to the Grand Marais Hospital under extreme emergency conditions, all of which should have had consultation with the physician prior to transporting them to the hospital. We have had one forest fire for which it was necessary to drive several miles in order to contact fire-fighting personnel. Only yesterday, someone on Alton Lake shot a bald eagle. Even though this was reported to us, it was not until 24 hours later that enforcement officers could get to the scene because of our lack of communication. We therefore again enlist your cooperation in pressing for some sort of permission from the FCC to allow us to make operational our radio-telephone set-up."

Senator Mondale was very responsive and did intervene to get the necessary approval from the FCC. Northwestern Bell was forced to release a set of frequencies for a radio-telephone. Later, Frank learned that we were the only ones who had ever succeeded in prying loose a set of frequencies from the Bell monopoly.

In order to have a two-channel system which would eliminate the need to say "over" after each transmission, we needed a common carrier license. From the state's viewpoint, this made us a telephone company and we had to follow all the regulations the Minnesota Public Service Commission imposed. Therefore, there was still the possibility that our telephone could be rejected. One evening, we received a call from St. Paul that there would be a meeting at 7 a.m. the next morning between Bell Telephone, the State Commission, and Sawbill Canoe Outfitters. They announced that failure to appear at the meeting would cause the whole deal to be canceled. We feel sure that they thought they were calling us at Sawbill and we would be unable to make the meeting. Actually, we were in our winter home in Bloomington, and Frank was able to rush right over to St. Paul the next morning. Pure chance saved the day! He still had to put up a fight to convince the state authorities that the telephone was needed while the Bell representative argued on the other side, but Frank ultimately prevailed.

The state imposes endless rules and regulations on a telephone company so we never took advantage of our status and never had any customers. Little did the Bell Company know that we were not really a threat to their monopoly. Several other remotely located individuals or businesses have over the years taken advantage of our equipment to have their own telephone service. To avoid having customers, we simply let them put their equipment on our tower without charge. Once a year, they may make a contribution to help pay for the electricity required to run the operation. Even our own Cook County participated in this arrangement for a number of years so that the Highway Department could establish radio communication with vehicles out in remote areas.

We continued to have problems with our equipment. Radio-telephone repair was high on the list of budget items. Stress was even higher when the telephone wasn't working. In most retail operations, a salesperson stops by. Often, that is when it is determined what is needed, and the shelves are stocked. Our store depended on the telephone because no sales representative ever called at our store. And who has a repair person at their beck and call — especially if that person must travel to the wilds of Northern Minnesota? Sometimes, there was quite a wait before anyone arrived.

Once again we were saved by a friend who stepped forward to help us. Les Swanson and his family were regular Sawbill campers. Les worked for Minnegasco where he was in charge of all radio communication. Les helped Frank select the best General Electric equipment for our needs. It was a VHF common carrier business radio with telephone capability. Les and his brother-in-law, Russ Frary, installed the new equipment and it worked.

Sky Blue Waters Resort on Brule Lake opened about this time and they bought an identical system. Using radios means that there must be a receiver and a transmitter in two locations. Our remote location continued to be Maple Hill in Grand Marais, where we had a small building to house the equipment. Sky Blue Waters used our building and the tower for the few years that they were in business.

About the same time, Sawbill Lodge was being reopened by the Senty family. They also bought a radio telephone system, UHF with radio capability. They arranged to put their antenna on the new emergency medical tower in Lutsen. When they sold out a few years later, we bought their system, mostly for the purpose of acquiring the tower space and their radio frequencies. The system itself was another unreliable one but we upgraded it over the years. We used it mostly for mobile telephones in our vans and trucks. It was very reassuring to know that it was possible to call for help when it was needed.

Without communication, one needs to plan ahead with extra care when driving in the woods. We established a rule that anyone in our family or crew who was driving up the Sawbill Trail would call before starting. The arrangement was that we would allow an hour. If the caller had not arrived, someone from Sawbill would set out to look for them.

We learned this need to communicate the hard way before we had our radio-telephones. It was in the late 1960s when we had a new van that had problems with stalling due to vapor lock. Frank and I, Ranna, and Bill were on our weekend commute to Sawbill one Friday night in May. I well remember the light snow drifting down, turning the road white. We were several miles from Sawbill when the van stalled and wouldn't start again. Frank and Bill elected to walk on in with an eye to snuggling down in their own beds for the rest of the night. Ranna and I thought sleeping in the car sounded just fine. We all woke up early the next morning. In the van, Ranna and I were awakened by someone in a little red VW bug who stopped to see if we were all right. I tried to start the car and it started, so I proceeded to drive on to Sawbill. When we arrived, we found Frank gone. He had gone over to the Lodge to get Ken Osman to drive with him to where we were. He told Ken exactly where he had left us, but we weren't there. He thought maybe he was mistaken and we were around the next bend, but we weren't. Of course, they had brought their telephone trouble-shooting kit with them, so finally Frank plugged the tester in and called home. He was amazed and relieved when I answered.

Nowadays, such an emergency would be handled immediately with a radio call. One night, for example, Cindy was driving home from dance class in Grand Marais at about 11 p.m. On The Grade, near the Baker Lake entrance, a recalcitrant moose stood on the road and refused to move. It was a winter when we had a huge amount of snow and the banks along the sides of the road were too high for the moose to negotiate. This seemed to confuse them. While moose usually move quickly off the road, this was not happening this year. After trying every established trick, Cindy called home on the radio and asked Bill for help. He jumped into a truck and drove down. With a vehicle on each side of him (or her), the moose was guided to a side road and persuaded to head back into the woods. It was a much better solution than sleeping in the van all night!

As everyone knows, the technology that makes communication possible has evolved phenomenally in the past decades. At the same time, legislation making it possible to use this equipment has also evolved. Fifty years ago, Bell Telephone owned all telephone equipment and it was impossible for an individual to buy any of it or use any of it. A judicial decision in the 1960s known as the Carter case made this illegal. Until that happened, there was no way that a remote place like Sawbill could have established any private telephone service. Our radio-telephones had to hook into the Bell system at some point or they would have been useless. There was some consolation for the telephone company in the monthly "access fee" they charged for this privilege. So we have always paid the regular business telephone charge plus an additional "access fee."

A recent technological advance is the use of microwave transmission. In 1998, we replaced the telephone system in Lutsen with a microwave system that is very much more reliable. Now it is possible to have multiple lines. One line is now used for a pay telephone outside our store. Campers can access it at any hour of the day or night. This is a service that people away from home have come to expect but one we could not provide during our first 40 years.

Our storekeeper used to spend a great deal of time placing calls for customers. There were important and emergency calls, of course. There were also many lesser calls. Some years ago when the country's economy was booming, it became fairly common for a young man to rush into the store breathing heavily and declaring an urgent need to use the telephone. It would turn out he needed to call his broker to see if he should leave any buy or sell orders before departing into the wilderness for a few days. The vast majority of calls were simply to report that the party had arrived safely at Sawbill or had survived the rigors of the wilderness. In today's culture, this kind of call is customary and obligatory. It is a rare person who gives any thought to the technology that makes it possible.

The most recent development comes by satellite. So far, this is restricted to internet access but, in the near future, it will allow broadband communication which will include telephone service.

· Chapter 5 ·

--- Sawbill Lodge ---

Sawbill Lodge was born of the Great Depression, which brought great hardship to the country beginning in the fall of 1929. The vision of a North Woods wilderness resort came to a destitute family living in a rundown third-floor apartment on Laramie Street in Chicago. Being penniless was not an unusual condition in those Depression years. After the stock market crashed, numerous banks failed and endless businesses failed.

The Arbogust family was caught up in this downward spiraling economy. At the beginning of 1930, they were living in a fine new home in Upper Arlington, a suburb of Columbus, Ohio. George ("Arby") Arbogust, the head of the family, was a salesperson for Cook Porcelain Insulator Co. of Cambridge, Ohio. He was a graduate of Ohio State University with a degree in electrical engineering. Life was good, but then suddenly, disaster was upon them. George's wife died of cancer in January, leaving him as the sole parent of five children: Wilson (18), George Jr. (15), Harold (13), Jane (10), and Robert (6). In August, his company transferred him to Chicago and again the family settled into a lovely home in Park Ridge, a Chicago suburb, but their comfort was to be short-lived. By 1931, the company had failed and George was out of work.

George decided that survival would be easier in a rural setting, so he moved the family to southern Wisconsin, near Edgerton and Lake Koshkonong. Now they were living in a small, three-room house. George found a commission day job that provided a little money. He was able to feed the family by purchasing eggs at 15 cents a dozen and milk at five cents a quart from a nearby farm. They netted fish from the nearby lake. They survived the summer fairly well, but in late August, George was notified that Wisconsin authorities were planning to pick up the younger children and place them in an orphanage. George thought differently. Under cover of darkness, he packed the kids and their meager belongings into their car and drove back to Chicago. They found temporary shelter in the apartment of an acquaintance.

During that period, the oldest son, Wilson ("Nibs"), got a job selling magazine subscriptions door to door to help supplement the family income. Then he had a better idea. Several years earlier, he had vacationed with his uncle at Gateway Lodge on the Gunflint Trail in Northeastern Minnesota, and subsequently was employed at Gateway one summer as waiter, handyman, and "guide in training" on Hungry Jack Lake. Now he decided that he and his brother, George ("Chub"), would make their way north to see if they might find work at Gateway Lodge or somewhere else in the area.

Hitchhiking was their mode of travel. The first day they hitched rides as far as Red Wing, Minnesota, where they slept in a railroad freight car. Breakfast was possible because they found a bakery selling day-old bread. At the end of the second day, they were in Two Harbors, Minnesota. The next morning, their very first ride was in a gasoline tanker driven by Clarence Tofte. When Clarence heard of the boys' plans, he had the sad duty of informing them that Gateway Lodge had been completely destroyed by fire on Labor Day, just a few days earlier. That night they slept in Clarence's fish house in Tofte.

Undaunted, they continued on to Gateway Lodge and were given a ride up the Gunflint Trail by Justine Kerfoot. She dropped them at the road to Hungry Jack Lake and they walked in the last three miles. At Gateway Lodge they were welcomed by owners Jesse and Sue Gapen and their son, Don, and his wife, Betsy. Nibs was hired to help with the cleaning up and rebuilding of the Lodge, but not Chub. He managed to make his way back to Chicago. Wilson was paid $15 a month plus his room and board. Wilson recalls that the reconstruction of Gateway Lodge was accomplished that winter with a lot of hard work and determination. Norway pine logs were felled from land at the south end of West Bearskin Lake, then floated and portaged and refloated to the Lodge site on Hungry Jack. Headed by Clarence "Peanuts" Wheeler, about 10 men were on the job every day including Sundays.

Christmas, however, was the occasion for everyone to vacation — except for Nibs. He stayed alone at the Lodge with the dogs, Klondike and Kazan. Then in January 1932, he had his vacation time and he hitchhiked back to Chicago to visit his family. Chub and Harold ("Hedge") had jobs in a grocery store where part of their pay was food. Their father was still looking for work. However, he had found a new friend, a young woman named Jean Bettis. She was a graduate of Cornell University in Ithaca, New York, with a major in hotel management. She was the first woman graduate of this program. Nibs was introduced to Jean and, as the family and Jean visited together during that vacation, the idea of a wilderness vacation lodge was a frequent topic of discussion. Each of them loved the idea but they recognized the difficulties, including: no convenient schools for the children; no electric power; no running water; no telephone connections; no year-round business. How could they finance the operation? How would they attract guests? Good sense was conquered by the dream and they all agreed to plunge "full steam ahead!"

Nibs returned to his job at Gateway Lodge where he carefully observed log construction. He learned to use a compass for marking a line on logs to guide the ax when grooving lengthwise and cutting notches for corner fits. He taught himself to use the double-blade, American-style ax for notches and grooves, and the broad ax for steps and fireplace mantels. He practiced his ax skills on the discarded logs where the Norways had been cut.

The Arbogusts Travel to Tofte

Back in Chicago, Arby and Jean got married and, in April 1932, they made their first trip to the North Shore. They stopped at the Superior National Forest District Office of the U.S. Forest Service in Duluth to ask about acquiring property. The Forest Service was interested in seeing some vacation development in the central area of the Forest. The Sawbill Trail had just been extended from the railroad grade (now The Grade) up to Sawbill Lake, thus opening up a new area for camping and fishing. Therefore, the Forest Service official suggested that they go to the end of the Sawbill Trail and think of Alton Lake or Sawbill Lake as a location for their resort.

Nibs came down from Gateway that April to meet Arby and Jean at Cobblestone Lodge in Tofte and they drove up the Sawbill Trail, 24 miles on a one-lane gravel road. Jean's old Nash became mired once, but they escaped to hump and grind onward for two hours. The weather was rainy, windy and cold, as is typical of April in the North Woods. Finally, they got out of the car, walked into the forest and found a stream (Sawbill Creek). They waded down the stream to the lake and came out on the perfect lodge site on a rise of land, with hundreds of tall trees and a striking view of Sawbill Lake. Wilson reports, "We were thrilled and excited. This certainly was the right place. The name was to be Sawbill Lodge."

Arby and Jean promptly rented a cabin on Lake Superior from Andy and Gladys Tofte and moved in. Friends picked up the four kids in Chicago and drove them to Tofte. During the ensuing summer, the family lived at Sawbill Lake, tenting on the campground. Jane, now 13, and Bob, 9, stayed on the campground during the day and rented their two boats and their one canoe to occasional anglers. Jane recalls, "I fished for our suppers from time to time and I gathered firewood, carried fresh water from the guard station well, neatened the campsite, and read books. Mostly, it was fun."

The older boys guided day trips west to Alton, Beth, and Grace, north to Ada and Cherokee, and east to Smoke, Burnt and Kelly.

"We found the fishing unexcelled, rewarding, exciting beyond compare. The forest, the lakes, and rivers were unbelievably beautiful, many to be discovered and explored," Nibs remembers. The family was convinced that most of the remote lakes had never been seen, much less fished, by white men.

Fall and winter found Jean and Arby again living in Tofte and the three younger children attending school in Grand Marais. Chub had a job back in Chicago and Wilson started college at the University of Minnesota. His tuition was paid by his uncle, Oren Arbogust, owner of the advertising agency in Chicago that was to become a major resource in acquainting the public with the new resort.

At the University, Nibs met an architectural student, Hartwell Webb. Although Hartwell had never seen a log building, he looked at Wilson's sketches and measurements and studied books on log construction. He created drawings and floor plans for the main Lodge. He never found the time or money to visit the site. He drew up plans by studying Arby's survey of land levels, rock outcroppings, and prominent trees. He laid out the whole complex of future log cabins, a guest dormitory, the dock and canoe racks, crew living quarters, a power house, and a fresh water well.

The first hurdle the family faced was to obtain formally the lease of the land from the Forest Service. Although the Forest Service had suggested the location and supported the idea of a resort at this location, the final approval was a complicated process. Jean and Arby went in person to make "the pitch" to lease those "perfect for a lodge" 11 acres on Sawbill Lake, taking with them Hartwell Webb's plans. Years later, it was learned that Jean's credentials in hotel management were a major factor in winning the Forest Service approval. After months of "almost unendurable waiting," they received the go-ahead.

Lease Is Approved and Construction Begins

In June 1933, the Arbogusts moved their tent from the public campground to the Lodge site. By this time, they were totally without funds. Arby applied for a loan at the bank in Duluth, offering some stocks he still held as security, but he was turned down.

Luckily, a Chicago osteopath named Oliver Foreman offered his support and became the first financial backer and ultimately one of the first customers of the Lodge. Andy Tofte, who had a grocery store in Tofte, helped out with food on credit and was the leader of local people who helped the struggling family. Arby got a winter job with the Civilian Conservation Corps (CCC) cutting fire breaks. He earned $60 a month.

Lodge construction began. The first building was a place for the family to live. They had discovered an abandoned logging camp at the south end of Alton Lake. The main building, which was still standing, had been erected with poor and unsalable lumber, somewhat rotten and warped. There were three windows and a door. This material was dismantled and gathered into two rafts that were floated north about two miles to the Alton-Sawbill portage, carried across the portage, reassembled into rafts on the Sawbill side, and then floated to the building site. Lumber, nails, tar paper, hinges, and windows were reused. The new "tar paper shack," 16 x 20 feet, was put up on the knoll about 40 feet east of the Lodge site. It was furnished with four double beds, double-decked, a dining table with benches, a makeshift desk and chair, a wood-burning stove, air-tight heater, plus a galvanized tin tub for bathing and washing clothes. This first shelter did not cost a cent, just a lot of hard work. Fresh, clean water was carried from the well that Arby located using a willow twig. It was hand dug by brothers Nibs and Hedge. Fortunately, they did not have to go very deep.

The next task was to build the Lodge and be ready to start in business the summer of 1934. The foundation for the lodge building was made from cedar timbers set into concrete. These timbers came from a nearby swampy area. The same cedar timbers were used in the bridge that had to be built across Sawbill Creek. The Cook County Highway Department built the quarter-mile long road from the Sawbill Trail across the bridge and on to the Lodge parking lot.

During that summer, a shy, hungry-looking lad wandered into the camp with all his worldly possessions in a pack on his back. He whispered in Arby's ear, "I came to see if I could stay with you until I can get work." Arby said he would have to consult the family. He gathered them for a meeting. The boys resisted, pointing out that the family didn't need another mouth to feed. Arby pled his case. "Let's give him a week's trial," he suggested. The young man's name was Tony Logar and his story was that his parents had been convicted of beaver poaching and put in jail, leaving him stranded. Long before the week was over, the Arbogusts had all become very fond of Tony and welcomed him into the family. He ended up being a mainstay at Sawbill Lodge for many years.

Now it was time to build the Lodge. The plan was to use Norway or white pine but none was conveniently available. Jean and Arby had scouted the area and finally found stands of jack pine at the northernmost end of Sawbill Lake. The Forest Ranger went with Arby and Nibs and they selected and marked 424 trees. They were purchased at a cost of 50 cents each. They used the $500 advanced by their Chicago benefactor, Doc Foreman, to pay for the logs and other needed materials. Nibs and Tony used a 6-foot-long, two-person saw to fell the trees, cutting about 18 per day. No trees could be cut within 50 feet of the lake shore, so each tree had to be topped and limbed and dragged to the water.

Arby tried to locate a man with a team of horses to haul the logs to the lake. When this proved impossible because the terrain was considered too rough and dangerous for horses, he hired three additional men to join Wilson and Tony. The five men pulled the 424 logs to the lake, one at a time. Arby made many trips five miles up and five miles down Sawbill Lake towing six or seven logs at a time. He used one of Andy Tofte's fishing boats with a 3-horse Johnson motor. Many times, he also hauled out a disgruntled worker who found the work too difficult. Then he would drive to Duluth and hire a replacement or two.

The onset of freezing temperatures and a snowstorm on November 7, 1934, brought a halt to the towing operation. Arby made two trips that day, bringing out the men, the camping equipment, the saws and axes, and a long tow of logs. The last trip ended after dark. The next morning, they returned to find the logs frozen solid into the lake.

Each log had to be chopped free of ice and hauled out of the water

that day or they would have been frozen in for the entire winter. The logs were pulled up the hill to the actual building site with a system of ropes, powered by their old Ford truck. Then there was one more challenging task to be accomplished. Each log had to be peeled with a draw knife and marked for notching and grooving. The concrete and cedar foundation, put in place in August, was ready and the first

Logs to build the lodge were rafted from the north end of Sawbill Lake.

Log rafting froze up in November 1934.

Logs were peeled, cut, and put up during the winter of 1934-35.

of 12 rounds of logs was installed by late March.

The building consisted of a lounge that was 28 x 42 feet with a 10-foot-wide stone fireplace on the east. A 34 x 34-foot dining room, which was two steps up from the lounge, had another stone fireplace at the west end, plus an enclosed porch that overlooked the lake. Then a large kitchen and pantry, crew dining room, and an office completed the building. The fireplaces were constructed of granite boulders that were picked up along the Sawbill Trail as the Arbogusts made trips to town that spring.

As the winter progressed, so did the log building. They really needed to add another course or two of logs, but they ran out of time and materials and so they put on the roof. Anyone who ever visited the Lodge will remember that the ceilings were quite low! A 6-foot-tall person had to remember to duck whenever walking under the beams.

Next they needed cabins for guests. The first ones they built were Cedar and

Sawbill Lodge finished

Pulpwood, up the hill from the dock area. They built canoe racks and a little fish-cleaning shack at the dock. Chub built a foot bridge (2 ½ feet wide by 160 feet long) over the creek to connect the dock area to the Lodge. The cabins were primitive with no plumbing. Buckets of clear, cool water from the well were carried to the cabins each day. All cooking and eating took place at the Lodge. Each cabin had

One of the typical cabins at Sawbill Lodge, 1950

an outhouse. The shower house and sauna were near the Lodge, close to the well. Electricity came from a diesel-powered generator. A log building the size of a one-car garage was built to house this. A sign on this building said, "Sawbill Power and Light."

The next task was to attract guests. Advertising was the key but advertising costs money. Arby's brother Oren, an advertising writer, solved the problem with great creativity and produced a masterpiece of advertising. The plan was to use penny post cards, hand-addressed, saying that the Lodge was open, fishing was great, and the food was excellent. They sent a series of messages, one a week for 16 weeks, March through June. Mailings were sent to 1200 people, using mailing lists of the University Club of Chicago and the Athletic Club of Minneapolis.

Sawbill Lodge Opens for Business

Guests came. The first ones arrived in May 1935. The Arbogusts put up a wooden sign at the beginning of the lane into the Lodge saying "U NO U R at SAWBILL!" It was a simple gimmick that attracted attention and stayed in guests' minds, becoming part of the nostalgia of Sawbill. Some years later, they installed a wooden mill wheel in the creek. The flowage of the creek turned the wheel but they attached a handle and then made a dummy who stood beside the wheel with his hands on the wheel. This fellow was christened Uno. As guests crossed the footbridge going to the dock each day, they saw Uno standing there in the creek turning the wheel. This created such nostalgia! Of course, he was taken in each winter and, from time to time, got a new set of clothes. When the contents of the Lodge were auctioned off in the 1980s, no item was more in demand than Uno. Uno has since returned home and now belongs to Sawbill Outfitters.

The Lodge was thriving in the next seven years despite all the difficulties associated with being in a remote location with no public utilities. Then world events intervened and new challenges had to be faced. In 1939, war was declared in Europe. At the end of 1941, the Japanese attacked Pearl Harbor, and America joined the war. Vacations were out for the duration. Gasoline was very tightly rationed, preventing any travel by motor vehicle. Thus, the Arbogusts were forced to close the Lodge after the 1942 season. Jean moved back to Chicago where she got a job in food service management, becoming chief dietician for United Airlines. Arby moved to Duluth where he spent his last years. His life story ended in 1953 when he died of a heart attack. All the Arbogust children were in college and involved in the war effort.

Uno turns the water wheel in Sawbill Creek.

When the family split up, only Tony Logar stayed with Jean. He continued to be a major support for the Lodge for many years. The Arbogusts lost touch with Tony and are unable to determine where he is now or what might have happened to him.

Wilson worked at the Lodge during the summers through 1937 while he attended the University of Minnesota. Then he joined his uncle in Chicago in the advertising business. Wilson was not accepted into the military because of poor hearing but he went to work for Morrison Knutson Construction in the Aleutian Islands as a civilian and helped build military seaports, roads, warehouses, and airstrips. Since he was a journalism major, he was asked to plan, write, and produce a base newspaper for civilians. He shared an office with Dashiell Hammett who was the editor of the magazine, *Yank*, North Pacific Division.

Chub had enlisted immediately after war broke out in Europe and joined the Navy. He became a pilot and flew attack bombers. He remained in the service after the war and had advanced to lieutenant senior grade when he was killed in an explosion aboard the USS Bennington in 1954.

When Hedge was drafted, he chose the Air Corps and became a bomber pilot. He left the Air Corps after the war but was recalled for the Korean War and then remained in service to complete 25 years. He retired as a lieutenant colonel. Bob, too, served in the Air Corps but did not stay on after the war.

Jane also served her country. She was accepted into the very first class of WACs (Women's Army Corps) for officer's training in 1942 and served until 1946, retiring as a captain. She was in California at the time so completed her education at the University of California at Berkeley. She joined the John Hancock Insurance Agency and remained in Berkeley for 20 years before being transferred to Boston. She retired as a vice president of the company.

While Jean was in Chicago during the war, she found a homeless young couple named Cap and Billy Peterson to live at the Lodge. They went on to build a resort of their own at Tait Lake about 20 miles away in the Superior National Forest.[1]

The New Post-War Era Begins

World War II ended in August 1945, and Jean was ready to return to the North Woods to pursue her dream of operating a resort. All the Arbogusts had settled into other pursuits by this time.

Jean was faced with some formidable challenges when she returned to Sawbill, including operating the diesel to provide electricity, keeping the place warm in winter, and trying to maintain some communication with the outside world. She was 24 miles from town. She arranged some contact by taking over the very shaky, unreliable, homemade telephone line that the Forest Service had installed to connect with the Kelso Fire Lookout Tower.

Upon her return to Sawbill after the war, Jean continued to deal with the perennial problem of a shortage of operating capital. Undaunted, she set out to obtain financial backing from men who had been loyal customers before the war. She contacted a number of them and found several who were interested. Thus she was able to stay afloat and even to add some new cabins at the Lodge. Some of the prominent guests who may have become financial backers as well were Bob Hutsell of Louisvillle, Kentucky, and Herbert McCoy of Moline, Illinois, an executive of John Deere. Chief among her backers was Art Towner, co-founder of American Hospital Supply. Together, Art and Jean developed a concept that was totally novel at the time. It was the condominium. Their arrangement was that Art would finance the building of a cabin which he would own. He and his family would call this home when they were at Sawbill. The rest of the time, Jean could use the cabin for rental.

Over the years, Art was responsible for introducing Sawbill Lodge to a number of people who became regular guests. Many of them, such as "Dutch" Schultz, George Marker, Herman and Ray Schifo, were sales crew or executives of American Hospital Supply. The Towner twins, Bob and Betty, grew up, married and brought their children to vacation at Sawbill Lodge. Bob has four boys, Betty has a daughter and a son. Many of them continue to spend vacation time at Sawbill.

Besides capital, Jean needed to recruit a staff to operate the Lodge. She needed a variety of skills ranging from carpentry to guiding to diesel mechanic. Furthermore, she had to cope with long, lonely winters. Among her long standing and memorable early recruits were Kaino Rykkanen and Bud Hanson. From 1946-1951, her nephew, Phil Higley, Jr., worked at the Lodge every summer.

Bud Hanson has a fascinating story to tell. He grew up on an Osakis, Minnesota, farm. "Well," he says, "I started to grow up there." While he was still very young, his father became disabled and then died, leaving Bud and his mother to carry on. When Bud was 14, his mother decided it was time for him to go to work. They went to Duluth to assess the opportunities. There they heard of

Bud Hanson takes a break on the Sawbill Lodge dock.

Sawbill Lodge and decided to give that a try. Bud's mother cooked for the Lodge briefly before leaving Bud there. She undoubtedly felt confident that she was leaving her child in a relatively safe environment. In truth, it was quite challenging. Bud shared a room in the crew quarters with Kaino, who could be quite violent. Bud remembers Kaino as belligerent and domineering. Bud was big and refused to be intimidated. One night when Bud was lying in his bunk, Kaino threw a knife into the wall just over Bud's bed. It came so close it cut his blanket. Bud gained courage by reading his Bible and praying a lot.

Bud's first duties at the Lodge included repainting boats and preparing cabins for occupancy. When guests began to arrive, Jean asked Bud to guide. He was instructed by Bill Plouff who worked for the Pure Oil Company on Brule Lake, guiding their guests. Bud says he admired Bill Plouff greatly.

Kaino came to the Lodge along with several other lumberjacks to build new cabins. He soon became a guide and eventually a permanent staff member. The first summer, the Forest Service commissioned Kaino and Bud to cut a trail from Sawbill Lake to Little Saganaga. They had two weeks to accomplish this. Kaino told Bud, "Just leave the food to me." The first week they ate splendidly, dining on steak and potatoes. The second week they had run out of food and subsisted on roots, berries, and fish. Bud said it rained every day they were out.

Bud continued to work at the Lodge for four summers. Then he enlisted in the Navy and in the medical corps. When he was discharged, he took advantage of the GI bill to go to college and become a pharmacist, which became his lifelong career.

Other members of Kaino's family soon joined the Lodge staff. Kaino's wife, Alice, and his brother, Toivo Richard ("Dick"), became the permanent backbone of the crew. In 1952, Jean married Dick, and they shortened their last name from Rykkanen to Raiken. By 1956, Kaino had died and Alice moved to Grand Marais. The owners of the Lodge were now Jean and Dick Raiken.

Entertainment Is Provided at the Lodge

The 1950s were the heyday of the Lodge. Arriving guests were met by the cabin boy who unloaded their suitcases into a wheelbarrow and escorted them to their rustic cabin. If they arrived in the afternoon, it was soon time to walk down the wooded paths to the Lodge for a sumptuous dinner. Jean circulated in the dining room, visiting with the guests, many of whom had become old friends. She had a warm and welcoming personality. Each evening, she asked each guest what they would like to do the next day, that is where they would like to fish and whether they wanted a guide.

Card games were arranged for after-dinner entertainment, most often "Sawbill poker." This required nine people, each of whom brought five dimes to the game. The winner took home four dollars

Jean and Dick Raiken welcome guests to Sawbill Lodge.

and the second-place winner took his five dimes home. A game lasted an hour or more and guests were ready to retire to their cabins afterward. Good fishing calls for being out on the lake early in the morning.

Bears provided additional evening entertainment. The remains from dinner were placed just outside the kitchen door and a bear or two would often come to eat. Guests gathered at the windows to watch. The evening sauna was also popular. The sauna was attached to the shower house and the routine was to go back and forth between the sauna and the shower room. A wood fire heated the sauna rocks. Pouring water on the hot rocks produced clouds of steam. The most seasoned sauna-takers sat on the top benches where the steam was hottest, while novices occupied the cooler lower benches.

Jean maintained a fine library of entertaining books, mostly mysteries. A guest could read in the lounge by the big fireplace or take the book to the cabin to read.

One couple who were regulars at the Lodge were the Briggs from St. Paul. John was headmaster of St. Paul Academy and Marjorie was a concert pianist. They spent a month at the Lodge each year and she brought her full-sized piano with her. It was installed in her cabin so she could practice during the day.

Occasionally, there was special entertainment such as a slide show or a talent show. Jean insisted that everyone participate. Once each summer, all the guests were loaded into motor boats and transported to the north end of the lake for a picnic on an island known as Picnic Rock. This took place on July 15. The spot was an official campsite so it had a table,

On a rainy day, it was delightful to sit and read by the fire in the Lodge.

a fire grate, and a typical wilderness privy. There were always a lot of practical jokes in progress. On one picnic, the party started as always with drinks. By dinner time, some of the women were beginning to slip away one at a time for a trip to the privy, returning very quickly. After several had made these short forays, the matter became a topic for open discussion. It seemed that some man was occupying the privy, staying much too long, leaving other folks in considerable discomfort. Soon the true story emerged. "The man" was a very realistic stuffed dummy. Much hilarity ensued.

The dummy occupied the privy as a practical joke.

The master of the practical joke was Marge Marous, wife of Joe Marous. They were regular guests at the Lodge. One of Marge's jokes was to stretch plastic wrap over the toilet bowl under the seat in an unoccupied cabin. The newly arrived and unsuspecting guests had a surprise awaiting them. The cabin bathrooms were not brightly lit, contributing to the success of this caper.

Another of Marge's antics was to dress up as a waitress in a tight, short black dress with a white ruffled apron and a little white cap on her head. She was at least 60 years old but managed to look 16. In the course of serving, she flirted and sometimes managed to plop down on a male guest's lap, sending the other guests into peals of laughter.

The morning fishing trip often involved towing canoes with a boat and motor up to one of the four portages. The guide would then carry the canoes to the next lake. The guide found the fishing holes, baited the hooks or selected lures, and removed the fish caught. A shore lunch followed with the guide building a fire and cooking the fish that were the pièce de résistance of the meal. At the end of the day, the guide filleted all the remaining fish and placed them in the Lodge's walk-in freezer for the guests to take home with them at the end of their stay.

Sometimes, the weather turned nasty while the fishing parties were out. Jean was very much aware of each guest and what each was doing. She also knew exactly how each lake behaved. If there was a strong wind, the motor boat would be sent out to retrieve the guests so they didn't face any risk from being in a canoe in bad weather. It might be said that guests were thoroughly pampered.

Jean Raiken Is Mother Hen to Her Brood

Meanwhile, Jean took care of her crew, consisting of a front desk person, cook, cook's helper and server, cabin boy, dock worker, cabin girl, and maintenance person, plus fishing guides. In the 1950s, the front desk person was Joan Lee Hansen, a very attractive young woman from Edina. Martha Benz from Duluth was the cook. She arrived at five in the morning to prepare a hearty breakfast. She had time off during the middle of the day and then worked for hours before and after dinner. Everybody worked hard. All crew members lived at Sawbill Lodge and received full room and board. Jean drove to Grand Marais once a week where she did all the shopping that was needed for the entire crew. She decided what the "uniform" for a job was and selected the clothes for each person, such as olive drab cruiser jackets for guides. It was very rare that anyone working at the Lodge left the property during the summer, except to go out on the lakes.

Fly-In Fishing Becomes Popular

Airplanes became a "big thing" after the war. The Lodge owned or leased a plane for a time. Corinne Brown remembers her summers at Sawbill Lodge in the 1940s. As cook's helper and server, she had to arrive early to help with breakfast and to pack lunches for anglers who were flown out to their fishing spots. She had time to herself in the middle of the day and spent most of it in the lake, swimming and keeping cool. Once she challenged herself to a long-distance swim all the way to the Alton Lake portage and back. By late afternoon, she was back in the kitchen helping with dinner preparations, and then through the evening she was in the dining room serving the meals. She loved the area and remembers how sad and resentful she felt at the intrusion of airplanes on the peace and quiet of the setting.[2]

In 1949, President Truman signed an order prohibiting airplanes from flying under 4,000 feet above sea level over the Boundary Waters Canoe Area. It was a huge blow to Sawbill Lodge and other resorters — including Ray Gervais, who had a fly-in resort on Cherokee Lake, and Pure Oil Company, which maintained a company getaway on Brule Lake. Ken and Vi Osman had been flying their plane into Brule Lake where the Osman family had a cabin. After airplanes were banned, Ken and Vi traveled across Brule with a large, flat-bottomed, Chris-Craft cabin cruiser powered by two 35-horsepower motors.

During winters, Ken Osman and Dick Raiken both worked in the workshop, building furniture. Dick had a great talent for finding things in the woods which, with a little effort and a lot of skill, could be turned into something else — such as a little burl that he turned into a beaver. He fashioned coat racks, lamps, and tables for the Lodge out of tree branches with unique shapes. He made wooden platters, bowls, and trays for the Lodge dining room. Jean decorated these items by wood burning designs in them. They made their Christmas presents in this way each year. After the Osmans moved to Sawbill, Dick and Jean were able one fall to take an extended vacation in the southern part of the United States, visiting Texas, New Mexico, and Arizona.

This was the time when Jean turned over all camp store and outfitting business to the new Sawbill Canoe Outfitters. By 1960, Jean was 58 and Dick was 60 and they decided it was time to sell the Lodge and retire. She had chosen her retirement home site. It was on the Sawbill Trail, six miles north of Highway 61, where it intersects with the "600 Road." The house would overlook the Temperance River. This was Superior National Forest land and not for sale but Jean was able to negotiate a deal for a lease that would be only for her lifetime. She had no immediate heirs, so she was not concerned about the fate of the property after she was through with it. Since they needed money for the house, they readily agreed to sell their interest in Sawbill Outfitters.

New Owners Take Over the Lodge

The Lodge sold very quickly to two young couples from Chicago: Pauline and Ed Madeja and Mary and John Smith. The wives were sisters and their husbands were enthusiastic fishing buddies. Ed and Pauline had two young sons, two and five years old. Mary and John had no children when they bought the Lodge but in time had three sons. The men were sheet metal workers and had an abundance of skills needed for maintenance work, but none of the four had any experience in running a resort.

Jean agreed to stay for a year to teach them. She and Dick lived at the guard station cabin on Sawbill Lake the first summer. They started building their new home on the bank of the Temperance River. They designed it themselves and did most of the work themselves. They also took time the first summer they were free to go on a long canoe trip, exploring the wilder remote areas that were not often visited.

Jean and Dick moved into their house in 1962. They had a large workshop in the basement and they worked harder than ever on their woodcraft. Jean had a sun room in one corner of the house where she raised african violets and many other plants. She was active in the West End Garden Club and a key person in the annual flower show. They both worked at landscaping their yard. Dick planted lupines along their driveway all the way out to the Sawbill Trail. He also participated with the Forest Service in planting a stand of red pines along the west side of the Sawbill Trail just north of their house. He took care of these pines for years, trimming them and removing brush so they would grow straight and strong. Both the lupines and pines are still there, a memorial to his efforts.

In July 1970, Dick admitted that he was having severe pains in his abdomen. By October, he was dead of stomach cancer. Jean continued to live in the house but she soon became ill also. She was physically strong but extremely forgetful. For each of three years, three different young couples lived with her, watching over her and taking care of the place. However, it became evident this was not enough and she went into the local nursing home. We took her to a neurologist at the University of Minnesota Hospitals for a diagnosis. We were told it was "early senility." It was a few years later that the diagnosis of Alzheimer's came into common use. When it was certain that Jean would never return to her home, Frank, by then her guardian, sold her house for removal since the land reverted to the government. A Grand Marais couple bought the house, took it apart and hauled it to their land where they rebuilt it. Jean died in 1986 at the age of 80.

Meanwhile, the Madejas and Smiths were becoming disenchanted with running the Lodge. The men acted as hosts and fishing guides and enjoyed taking people out fishing. The women were the business executives and managed the dining room. For them, it was hard work and not much fun. After six years, they decided to give it up and the Lodge went back into Jean's hands as she held the contract for deed. In 1967, she sold it again to another family from Chicago: Robert and Gay Leali. They came to live at Sawbill bringing their eight children ranging in age from three to 17. The Osmans had moved to Tofte by this time, so the Leali's built an addition to Vi and Ken's cabin (Viken) and made this their year-round home. They were friendly and sociable people who seemed to enjoy running the Lodge but they never made enough money to support the family. After three years, they returned the property to Jean and left the county. Sawbill Lodge had a bad reputation with a number of business people because Bob Leali left with many debts unpaid. He moved to Canada, eliminating any chance of collection.

More New Owners Come to Sawbill

This time, the Lodge did not sell so easily and was closed for a summer. Eventually, in the early 1970s, Jean sold it to Charles and

Helen Case, who were Minnesotans living in the Twin Cities area. They had four children all still in school so they continued to live in the Twin Cities during the school year. They looked forward to retiring in a few years and living full-time at Sawbill. However, Chuck, who was a sales engineer with AT&T, was drawn into his career more than he ever anticipated. His last sale before his scheduled retirement was an internal telephone system for Honeywell in London, England. He became involved in installing the new system and then was hired by Honeywell to run the system. His plans to retire did not come about and running the Lodge was far too demanding while he was commuting to London. They, too, gave the Lodge back after a few years.

By this time, Jean was no longer able to handle her business affairs and Frank became her guardian. While there were some very serious prospective buyers, each of them eventually gave up the idea. The Lodge was again closed.

Very few major improvements had been made over the years, so a great deal of renovation had become necessary. When the Forest Service issues a special use permit on forest land, they impose many requirements regarding the physical plant and its upkeep. They decreed that the bridge across Sawbill Creek would have to be replaced, a new septic system installed, and all electric wires buried. These improvements promised to be quite expensive.

Finally in 1977, Frank made a deal with Al and Meg Senty from Madison, Wisconsin. He negotiated with Cook County to forgive the back taxes and with the local bank to forgive some of the totally uncollectible debt. The rationale for the county was that it would be better to have an operating business that would eventually pay taxes again. The Sentys bought the lodge at a very low price with the knowledge that they would have to invest a lot of money to bring it up to standard. Al taught at the Madison Vo-Tech School. Not only did he have a lot of skills personally but he also had access to a wide range of skills through his friends and fellow instructors. A number of them came up to help him with the lodge in return for staying there and spending some time fishing. One of the first things they did was build a sturdy new bridge over Sawbill Creek.

Not only did they need to meet the Forest Service requirements, but modernization was needed. They put in a radio-telephone system as the Lodge had been without telephone service for several years. By this time, guests expected modern cabins, meaning bathroom facilities in the cabins. Most resorts were providing guests with a choice of a housekeeping cabin or the American plan, where meals were provided in the dining room. The Sentys set about making all these improvements. Al was still teaching and they were at Sawbill only in the summer, but their son Mike had just graduated from college with a degree in forestry and was willing to take on the responsibility. He agreed to live at the Lodge full time and work on remodeling the cabins. Mike lived in Pine Ridge, which had been Jean and Dick's personal cabin, and, as a hobby, started developing a sled dog team.

In the spring of his second year at the lodge, Mike met an employee of Sawbill Canoe Outfitters, Laurie Till. Laurie was going to the University of Minnesota but decided to take the spring quarter off to work at Sawbill. Laurie loved working with Mike's dogs and, before we knew it, she loved Mike also. It was mutual and they were married that winter. Then they both lived at Sawbill all winter and worked on the remodeling. Sawbill Lodge opened for business in the summer of 1980. All the Sentys (Al, Meg, and their four children) were there and they did an excellent job of running the Lodge and the business flourished.

The Lodge Enters its Last Days

Then a new opportunity arose. The 1978 BWCAW bill, which had made the area wilderness, with motors prohibited, had a provision that resorts riparian to the no-motor lakes could ask the government to buy them out. This was a provision included in the bill as a concession to resorters in the Ely and Gunflint areas who argued vociferously that their businesses would be ruined by this new no-motor regulation. At the owner's request, the government would appraise the business and pay the owner the appraised price. The property would then belong to the Forest Service. The law required that all buildings be sold for removal and the land returned to its natural

Many people attended the Sawbill Lodge auction in 1983.

state. Al Senty consulted his accountant who advised that he sell. The government would pay cash immediately. Running the Lodge might bring in a good income but the return would be more gradual. It was a sensible business decision, and Al accepted it. The last year of operation for Sawbill Lodge was 1982.

Furnishings and personal possessions were not included in the government's appraisal or takeover. On a Saturday in the summer of 1983, the Sentys held an auction. A huge crowd attended.

Items of sentimental value such as the handmade furniture received competitive bids. Sawbill Canoe Outfitters bought some business items that most people couldn't use: the radio telephone, a small gas space heater, and a large dumpster.

Once the smaller things were cleared out, the Forest Service put the buildings up for bids. These did not go for high prices. Bill and Beth Blank, owners of Solbakken Resort in

Lutsen, were surprised to win the bid for the lodge. They hired Mike Senty to take it apart log by log and haul it down to Solbakken and eventually to reassemble it there.

Jerry Loh bought the smallest cabin, Deer, which was close to the lakeshore. He moved it intact, with Harry Johnson towing it across the frozen lake during the winter to the campground dock. There it was loaded on a truck and transported to its new location in Tofte.

Jerry Jaskowiak won the bid on several of the cabins and spent that winter tearing them down. He eventually moved them to Tofte where he made use of the materials to build his own house.

In time, the Forest Service burned the remaining cabins. They filled in the new septic tanks, fearing that they would become a hazard if left open. They tore out the new electric wiring and generally smoothed over the sites where the buildings were. They kept one cabin, Pine Ridge, for Forest Service employees working in the Boundary Waters during the summer.

Years passed and finally, in 1999, a very deteriorated Pine Ridge was burned by the Forest Service. Now, all that remains of Sawbill Lodge on Sawbill Lake are the fond memories in the hearts of many people. Nature has effectively moved in to fill the spaces where buildings once stood.

· Chapter 6 ·

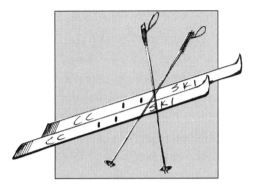

—— Becoming Full-Timers in 1976 ——

In 1976, Frank and I gathered our courage, held hands, and made a giant leap into the unknown. We retired from our jobs as school psychologists with the Eden Prairie and Bloomington school systems respectively and moved to Sawbill full time. For 20 years, we had been leading double lives. From Monday morning until 3:30 on Friday afternoon, we concentrated on our city jobs and enjoyed the work. For four months each year (April and May, September and October), we hastened to leave school on Friday afternoon to drive 280 miles to Sawbill, where we worked as hard as we could for long days and then drove back to Minneapolis, usually arriving very late Sunday night or very early Monday morning. We didn't mind the long hours and hard work or the lack of outside activities. What motivated us to make a change in our lives was the heart-wrench of leaving Sawbill each Sunday and at the end of each short summer. It was where we longed to be. Our children were through school and supporting themselves, so we were free of that obligation. Still, our business was small and certainly not producing enough income to support us. So we closed our eyes and jumped. This is when luck stepped in.

Our timing was very fortunate because our business soon increased markedly. Canoeing as a recreational activity increased in popularity about that time. Part of our increased business had to do with the fact that we were available. We began to promote May and September business. Many other outfitters were open only from Memorial Day to Labor Day. Now, 28 years later, we have strong September business. We stay open in October as well.

It was glorious to be able to stay at Sawbill at the end of the summer and the beginning of fall that first season. Tranquil it was not. Labor Day approached and we were rejoicing that we didn't have to return to the city. Then torrential rains came. Highway 61 at Tofte was washed out and Labor Day tourists were stranded on the Grand Marais side. The Forest Service closed the Boundary Waters on Tuesday after Labor Day. Our first thought was of the golden opportunity to enjoy a canoe trip but then we realized that we, as well as our customers, were banned from the lakes. We stayed at home and checked in the few people who returned from their trips. It was depressing. In a few days, the highway reopened and then the forest. We were able to go on our canoe trip and we found the waters so high that we could skip portages, floating through the streams that are normally not navigable.

During those first full-time years at Sawbill, our lives were chaotic. All the older people in our lives needed special attention. Our dear friend, Jean Raiken, was no longer able to stay in her own home. We got her settled in the local nursing home, took care of her house on the Temperance River, and then looked after the Sawbill Lodge property as it reverted back to her. My mother, who was already in a nursing home in St. Paul, moved to the nursing home (now known as the Care Center) in Grand Marais. Soon the Osmans, who were living in Tofte, were having various crises and they also had to go to the nursing home. Since their relatives were not living nearby, we took some responsibility for them. I seemed to be constantly on the road between Sawbill and Grand Marais. Frank's parents were in the National Lutheran Home in

Washington, D.C., and we made trips to the East on their behalf.

Cross-country skiing right out the door was great fun.

My greatest delight in living at Sawbill was that, during the winter, we could step out the door of our house, step into our cross-country skis and glide away. In the Cities, our skiing expeditions required an hour's drive each way. During the winter at Sawbill, I skied almost every day. In the summer, we were out on the lake. The first May that I spent at Sawbill, I went to the Environmental Learning Center in Finland, Minnesota, for a week-long course on birds. One September, Frank and I took a houseboating vacation on Birch Lake, courtesy of our Duluth friends, Wally and Hazel Niss, who owned Timber Bay Resort at that time.

We observed that most Cook County residents had never been to the end of the Sawbill Trail. We tried to encourage people to come by offering free canoe rental to locals. We also invited people to parties. For many years, we had an annual open house and potluck on a Sunday in February. It became known as the Sawbill Ski-down and Chow-down. We met many local people this way, made new friends, and had a chance to socialize.

Peace and quiet are not major attributes of our life at Sawbill. We do appreciate greatly some of the unique qualities that come with remote living, such as the moonlight and stars with no artificial lighting in the sky at night, the birds and wildlife around us, snow that stays clean and white indefinitely, living close to nature, experiencing the change of seasons, and watching the sun rise with impressive new colors and patterns each morning. It is never a boring or lonely existence. Many more people are in and out of our house than ever visited us in any of our city residences. There are always visitors and projects and activities all winter as well as in the summer.

Our housing at Sawbill was makeshift during the first year of our full-time residence. We had been living, along with some of our crew members, in a double-wide mobile home on the premises for several summers. We had hoped to build a house of our own when we moved to Sawbill full-time. This did not happen. We had also hoped to put up a wind generator to provide our electricity. The Forest Service was reluctant to accept the wind generator, arguing that it would be visually polluting to the canoe country. Our house and the wind generator were lumped as one project and we waited for approval to start construction. Our first full year at Sawbill was spent in the mobile home with our furniture and other belongings stored in an empty cabin at the lodge. We finally got approval from the Forest Service in 1977 and that summer our house was built. Doing most of the finishing work ourselves kept us occupied.

In view of the fact that we had to provide all our own utilities, Frank became a student of alternative energy. It was a time when the United States was questioning its dependence on foreign oil and there was a lot of interest in other possibilities. Frank thought a wind generator would be a very desirable substitute or supplement to our diesels. It would reduce our dependence on diesel oil and it seemed environmentally friendly. We were surprised when the Forest Service was less than enthusiastic. Wind generators were not a new idea. They had often been used in rural settings before the Rural Electrification Administration (REA) came along and made electricity more accessible in many nonurban settings. In the 1970s, the Jacobs wind generator that had been most successful was no longer made. Frank's research eventually led him to select a Dunlite wind generator that was made in Australia. We bought it and, for 10 years, it faithfully produced energy that could be converted to electricity.

An Australian wind generator produces our first alternative energy in 1977.

To utilize the wind generator, we installed a bank of batteries in our basement. When the wind blew, the batteries charged. We had a small gasoline generator behind our house that we could start when there was not enough wind. We were very conservative in our use of electricity and the wind generator took care of almost all our needs in the winter. In the summer when our business demanded laundry, shower facilities, and refrigeration, we needed to use the diesels to generate enough power. We only used one at a time but always had a second one for backup.

When we were using the wind generator, we had our new house and the mobile home wired for DC current, which is what batteries

Bill checks the diesel engine that provides backup power.

produce. We had gas refrigerators and we did not use electric appliances such as electric coffee pots, toasters, or dishwashers. Electric lights work fine on DC, but if we wanted to use the vacuum cleaner or the washing machine, we had to manually switch to AC. We had to throw a switch to make the change and then we had to remember which kind of power we were using before starting another appliance.

We managed to ruin a number of appliances by forgetting. For instance, the bathroom in the mobile home had an exhaust fan that only ran on AC power. It was immediately burned out by unthinkingly turning it on while we were on DC. We tried to improve this situation by installing special electrical outlets in our house and putting special plugs on our lamps that would only plug into the DC outlets. The goal was to make it impossible to plug the vacuum cleaner into DC, burning up yet another motor!

By 1987, we had almost figured out how to live with this system. Then a violent wind storm in the fall twisted and bent the blades of the wind generator. We needed to have major repair. To our dismay, Dunlite had gone out of business. What were we to do next?

Frank was very interested in solar power and our son Karl had by this time made solar water heating his career in California. We always shut off the diesel before going to bed each night since we didn't need much electrical power during the night. We did need it to keep the telephone operational. Therefore, when we installed the radio-telephone system in 1978, Frank had the ingenious idea of installing a small solar panel to maintain power to the telephone. It was mounted part way up the same tower that held the radio-telephone antenna and we continued to use it until 2002 when we moved the radio-telephone equipment to a separate building. Thus, we had some experience with solar power. As technological developments have taken place over the years, solar power has become much more affordable. With all these considerations, when we lost the wind generator, we elected to go to solar power.

That again took a lot of research on Frank's part to determine how best to meet our needs and where to get the best professional help. He ultimately chose Chad Lampkin, an electrical engineer who specializes in solar installations. Chad's home is in Michigan but he travels constantly working all over the country. Like our first telephone engineer, Chad moved in with us while he was evaluating our energy needs and installing and then upgrading our solar system, so we know him well. It was a standing joke that when we woke up in the morning to find someone occupying our guest room, it was most likely Chad. We knew it couldn't be a stranger or the dog would have barked.

In 1990, Chad installed 36 solar panels on the roof of our house. The energy generated could be stored in the same battery bank in our basement that we had used for the wind generator, but Chad provided us with a vastly improved inverter. Our first inverter took most of the power produced just to do its job of conversion, which was why we tried to make use of the DC power directly. Now our inverter uses only four percent of the power stored in the batteries in order to do its work. We were delighted to abandon our DC wiring and to go to full-time AC power. Solar power is a fabulous source of power — totally quiet, non-polluting, and essentially trouble free. Solar panels don't wear out or need repair. The initial investment is sizable but there are no further charges — and no monthly payments. Its development has not yet reached a point where it can compete in cost with high-line electrical power but that may happen before long.

The only maintenance the first solar panels required was occasionally brushing the snow off and twice a year adjusting their angle in relation to the sun. The batteries require minor attention to insure that they have enough water, just as car batteries need to be checked occasionally. Batteries do have a life span and need to be replaced every 10 years or so.

Chad, an ardent energy conservationist, has over the years recommended various energy saving appliances and also super-efficient wood-burning furnaces for our houses. In the 1990s, he built into our system the capability to shift from solar power to diesel power and back automatically. The trip to the diesel shed every morning and evening was eliminated. We began to have electricity available around the clock. Now we run on solar power until demand becomes too great on warm summer days or at the end of very short winter days. Then the diesel takes over to charge the batteries. Our homes operate mostly on solar power. When business is in full swing, we still need the diesels.

We were so pleased with solar power that we doubled our capacity in 1999 by adding 36 solar panels mounted on trackers. A small computer at the base of each tracker controls it and causes the panels to face the sun most efficiently. They turn gradually from east to west on sunny days. On cloudy days, they turn up horizontally looking for maximum light.

Business was increasing as we settled into full-time residence at Sawbill. The season started early in May with large church and school groups from Iowa. It was always hectic getting ready for them. Our store building was unheated so we had to wait for true

Installed in 1990, these solar panels generate a large part of our electricity.

spring weather before we could turn on the water, clean the store, get all the new merchandise in place, and get the big outfitting trips packed. Our crew members, who were college students, didn't arrive in time to help. I tried to start earlier each year in order to be better prepared but it always turned out to be a time of major stress. The arrival of crew members to take over some of the duties was greeted with the greatest enthusiasm.

Karl and Bill both worked with us during the transition years, along with their significant others, later their wives. We were heating with wood stoves and the young people spent a lot of time cutting and splitting wood. The old telephone line required very frequent maintenance. We had nonstop overnight company during the winter — extended family, crew past and present, and friends. Local visitors always stayed for meals. Things were bustling at Sawbill.

In the late 1970s, our children were going through a lot of life's transitional high points — graduating, finding careers, deciding where to make their homes, finding mates, and marrying. I remember expressing my despair when asked about our family during the summer of 1976, our first full year at Sawbill. I declared, "I don't ever expect to have grandchildren." None of our children was married or had declared any intentions in that regard.

Over the next few years, however, there were many changes. Karl moved to San Diego, California, where he stayed for the next 20 years. Ranna married and settled in Maple Lake, Minnesota, and soon had children, Marie and Marc.

Bill elected to stay with Sawbill. He married Barbara and moved to Grand Marais, commuting from there each day. In the fall of 1980, our first grandchild, Adam, was born and Ruthie followed a year and a half later. Babysitting was a happy addition to my duties and interests while both parents were working. Turmoil, divorce, and a lot more child care soon followed.

About that time, Cindy came to work for us for the summer. The following year, when she had graduated from UMD, she decided to stay on at the end of the summer. My life, although never dull or uneventful, gradually became less stressful as she began to take over some of my responsibilities for the business.

Bill and Cindy were married in 1985 and there were two more grandchildren, Clare and Carl, before the 1980s ended. As the six little ones were growing up and spending time at Sawbill, I was dreaming of the time when they would become a part of the business. I tried to include them in the various aspects of the business. I remember that Ruthie discovered that she could read when she was helping me pack food for trips. She was five that spring. Now Adam and Ruthie have taken their turns being summer employees of Sawbill and are trying to find their own life directions. In 2004, Adam, a graduate of the University of Wisconsin, Madison, became a major participant in the business. Clare and Carl are part-time crew members.

Bill and Cindy have been totally in charge of the business for a number of years, although Frank and I still live at Sawbill and watch developments with interest. Frank specializes in visiting with customers during the summer, much as always. He is very relieved that he no longer has to make major decisions and that he is not on call to deal with telephone or diesel emergencies. Since I officially retired in 1994, I have found other activities and am no longer involved with the business.

We are available to answer the telephone during the winter months if Bill and Cindy are away. We like to talk to customers about potential canoe trips and help them make reservations. We can even deal with emergencies if we must. (We have had a lot of experience with emergencies!) We are delighted that we can still live at Sawbill, our favorite place in the whole world.

Chapter 7

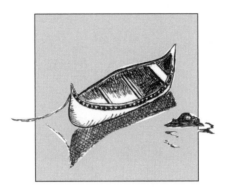

Sawbillians – The Crew

Sawbill crew members are the backbone of our business. Their contributions have made the business what it is. Most of them have returned to work several summers before going off to live "in the real world" as they always put it. Many of them, captured by the mystique of Sawbill, never really leave us but return for visits at regular intervals.

The very first Sawbill crew was recruited from the University of Minnesota, Duluth, (UMD) where Frank was teaching. He consulted with his faculty friends, particularly Fred Wolff, a political science professor and a very experienced canoeist. Fred was the leader of a Boy Scout troop and had been taking canoe trips with his Scouts for years. Together they selected four young men who were outstanding students but, more important, were personable, cooperative, and not averse to hard work.

The arrangement with Sawbill Lodge in 1958 was that we would hire college students who would be our employees but their first obligation would be to guide for Sawbill Lodge. Guests of Sawbill

Lodge expected that there would be guides available. Staying at an American Plan resort, as Sawbill Lodge was, meant that one paid a single daily or weekly amount and received living and sleeping accommodations, three meals a day, a canoe, a fishing boat and motor, plus other amenities.

Guests could go fishing on their own or, for an extra fee, they could hire a guide to run the boat and motor, show them productive fishing areas, select lures, bait the hooks, help them land the fish, and cook a shore lunch. Upon their return at the end of the day, the guide would clean the fish and package them for the guests' trip home. Some guests would engage a guide for one or two days while others took a guide every day they were at the Lodge.

Another option was to go out overnight. Then the guide also set up camp and prepared all the meals. The conventional wisdom was that fishing was better the farther you went from home base and this certainly had some merit in fact. The point of an overnight trip then was to go deep into the less traveled wilderness area. This involved portaging and it meant using canoes that could be portaged, rather than a boat and motor. It meant that the guide had the additional duty of portaging as well as a lot of paddling.

Thus it was that Sawbill Lodge was in need of a supply of strong and knowledgeable "guides," who would work occasionally, so our arrangement was very advantageous to the Lodge. Since we had no facilities for housing our employees, the Lodge provided room and board. The "guides" stayed in the Lodge bunkhouse and ate in the crew dining room. What we needed those first years was help in clearing the site and getting our first building operational. When the fellows were not guiding, they were available to help us.

It was a good job for a young man at that time. He was guaranteed a specific income. He could work outside in a pleasant environment, usually doing work he enjoyed in the company of congenial colleagues. Extra bonuses came in the form of tips but also in meeting interesting and influential people.

Guests often formed a strong bond with their guides and offered them good advice about their careers, or offered to help them in the future with recommendations or professional contacts. In today's terms, this relationship was a win-win situation for all parties.

Over the years, we have come to realize that the foremost qualification for a Sawbill employee is experience in camping and canoeing in the area. This makes it possible for the crew member to relate to the customer in the most beneficial manner. A precedent was set with the very first person hired, Tom Kubiak. Although still in high school, Tom was nominated by Dr. Fred Wolff as a very mature and knowledgeable individual. We never had reason to disagree. Tom worked for us for six years while he completed high school and college. Then he joined the Air Force and we saw very little of him for the next 30 years as he was stationed here and there around the world. He retired as a colonel and settled in the St. Louis area. Now, in retirement, he makes annual trips to Sawbill, often with one or both of his sons, as well as his brothers.

The other three of our staff members that first year were Dick Flint, Don Hempel, and Sam Overland. Sam is one crew member who has not returned to visit Sawbill. We had no information about his whereabouts until 2002. Almost 50 years had passed when a potential customer called and mentioned that he was a friend of Sam's brother, Bill Overland. Frank asked about Sam and we were delighted to receive a telephone call a few days later from Phoenix, Arizona, where Sam has been living for many years.

In his guiding years, Dick Flint was always known as "Tiger" because of his energy and intensity. He went on to law school and is now a senior partner in a Minneapolis law firm. He was our legal adviser for years until he told us that we couldn't afford him any more! By that time, we were no longer living in the Twin Cities so we transferred our business to Grand Marais. Dick has remained a lifelong friend. He got married one Christmas and I still think of Dick and Carol every Christmas as I decorate the tree with a little angel, a favor from her bridal shower.

Thinking of each crew member evokes certain memories — memories that may appear to be of insignificant things. Objects that our first crew members built or made are still with us and call up memories of them. Dick Flint decided one day, on his own initiative, to carve towel racks for our new bathroom out of tree branches. Those towel racks are useful as ever 45 years later and continue to grow in aesthetic appeal. I will always connect Bob Pike to the concept of cantilevering, which he introduced to us when he was building the front steps of our store.

Some crew members emerged as "rescuers," perhaps because of basic personality traits they possessed. Don Hempel was a rescuer of our family members. He worked on the dock the first summer when our four-year-old was continually falling into the lake. Don always seemed to be there to fish him out. He was there, too, the summer that Karl fractured his femur while water skiing. Don was the one who took charge of the rescue and tried to remedy the situation until it became evident that medical intervention was necessary. Don was a UMD student who had worked for some time for Mork's Meat Market in downtown Duluth. Clifford Mork subsequently became mayor of Duluth. Don's knowledge of meat led us to choose thuringer or summer sausage as the meat we would send out on canoe trips for lunchtime sandwiches. It was Don who knew that this was the lunch meat that would be safe for several days without refrigeration. Cliff Mork produced his own incomparable version of summer sausage and we placed special orders of that product until he retired from business.

Don also made a name for himself by his late-night excursions to Duluth to see Pat, his wife-to-be. Don went on to become a professor of economics at the University of Connecticut. He is one of four former crew members who are now deceased but still remembered fondly.

Another rescuer in our ranks was Mark Henning, who came along in 1988. Mark's reputation as a rescuer was a significant factor in his being hired. Mark had been on a canoe trip with his older brother, Lyle, and Lyle's girl friend, Caroline, when Lyle went into insulin shock. Mark's remarkable handling of the situation was reported to Cindy by Caroline, who was a good friend and former classmate of Cindy's. When Mark was old enough to apply for a job a few years later, he was at the top of the list of applicants in our minds. During the years he worked for us, Mark managed to be involved in every emergency that occurred. It must have been his caring and generous nature. If we had to look for a party to deliver an emergency message or if we had to bring someone out of the woods for medical treatment, Mark was always on the team. In fact, he acquired the nickname "Rescuer."

Mark graduated from Marquette University in Milwaukee as a mechanical engineer. He now works as a design engineer for Square D, an electrical parts and components manufacturing company. I wonder if his role as rescuer has emerged in this setting. It seems more likely that his wife, Lori, a physical therapist, might be involved in such situations. We hope no rescues are ever needed for their three children.

After several years, the first group of UMD students was gradually replaced by other UMD students: Bob Pike, Larry Snyder, Steve Hedman, John Maas, and David Quick. They continued to be "Sawbill Lodge guides on call" but they now lived in our A-frame bunkhouse that we added in 1959.

We rapidly learned that the prime service desired by canoeists was shower facilities. Dave Quick was studying architecture at the University of Minnesota. For his senior project, he designed our shower house. The outside appearance was designed to coordinate our main building and the A-frame bunk house, so the shower house has high peaks for its roofline. We already had large church groups as customers so we needed large dressing rooms where guests could change from traveling clothes to canoeing clothes before embarking on their canoe trip, and then reverse the process and reorganize their belongings afterward. So Dave's design had to include a large dressing room and a large group shower room for men, and a similar arrangement for women. We installed a pole shower with four heads in each shower room. I have checked the shower facilities at a lot of campgrounds since and have never seen a shower house anything like ours or one that could accommodate so many people at the same time. Frank knew about pole showers because of his father's connection to school physical education where such gang showers were used.

The state of Minnesota was building a lot of rest stop facilities and campground shower houses about that time, and we had access to those plans. We could have built our shower house to their specifications for $100,000 in 1960! We rejected that option and our crew built our shower house according to Dave's

The Sawbill crew pours concrete for the shower house in 1965.

plan for a bit more than $10,000. We had a lot of help from our friends on the campground. We offered the campground folks free showers for life in return for their help. Forty years later, Jim and Fran Sampson and Willard and Vivian Stevens are still camping here and making use of the shower house. Orville Dezell came in the summer of 2001 after an absence of more than 30 years and reminded our son Bill, just for laughs, that he was entitled to a free shower.

Although our crew built the shower house, we did hire a professional plumber, Clarence Hemmingson, who lived in Lutsen. Our son Karl worked with him as his helper for the whole installation and absorbed every bit of information and technique as he worked. Karl later put his plumbing skills to work for 20 years when he taught solar water heating installation in the Job Corps.

The shower house under construction, 1965

The shower house has been upgraded over the years. We added a sauna that is well used. The least successful of our amateur efforts was the concrete floor. It came out with a few bumps and holes, so we added indoor/outdoor carpeting to the dressing rooms to soften these imperfections. We have added modern refinements such as sensors that turn the lights on as one enters the room and off as one exits. The basic design proved excellent and we are grateful to Dave as well as to all the building helpers. Nothing about our business is more popular with canoeists and campground campers than our shower house.

David's career deviated slightly from architecture. He earned his PhD in architectural history. Before his retirement, he taught at Southwestern University in Springfield, Missouri. He is still the consultant restoration architect for the state of Missouri.

His parents in retirement moved from Duluth to Grand Marais and continued to spend summers at their cabin on Loon Lake off the Gunflint Trail. Now Dave and his wife, Helen, have the house in Grand Marais and the summer place on Loon Lake, which means that we see them relatively often.

I remember Steve Hedman sitting in my living room (now the store) in 1960 and telling me about an exciting new thing — DNA. He was studying biology. He went on to Stanford University for his doctorate in genetics and then returned to UMD to teach. He has since become assistant chancellor of the graduate school.

Steve's mark on Sawbill can still be seen in several of our buildings. He slept on the second floor of the bunkhouse, a small platform-like space in the peak of the building. One night, whether sleep walking or just in a drowsy dream state, Steve managed to walk straight off the platform, crashing to the floor below. His bunkmates were startled awake and were relieved to discover that Steve had suffered no permanent injuries. He probably suffered some bruises. We hastened to add a railing across the second-floor loft of the bunkhouse.

Along with our first main building, we had a garage which contained a gasoline-powered generator that provided our electricity. We had an air compressor in this building that we used to add air to tires or to blow up air mattresses. One day after using the air compressor, Steve forgot to turn it off. He left the area and the air compressor kept building up pressure until it blew up and blew right out the wall of the building. It was a noisy and shocking event but no one was injured and we quickly recovered. We nailed some boards over the hole in the building. We replaced the compressor with a more modern version that shut off automatically. Steve was a great employee and was easily forgiven but the memory still provides chuckles to all who were around at the time.

In 1962, a momentous event occurred. We added a female crew member to complement our staff of "guides." Sue Van Calcar didn't deal with outfitting in any way. Her responsibilities were to help me with the household chores and with storekeeping.

The following year saw our first, but far from last, Sawbill romance develop. Dee Sampson was my helper that year. I first met Dee when she came to our little store in Cedar Cabin to buy milk for her camping family. She was a young teenager then. When she worked for us, she was attending UMD. The mutual attraction between Dee and Steve Hedman may have started earlier when they both worked for Sawbill Lodge — Steve as a cabin boy and Dee as a server. However, the romance took off the year they both worked for us.

1960s crew members Dee Sampson and Steve Hedman shared a special honeymoon send-off at Sawbill.

When they got married, they chose a Sawbill canoe trip for their honeymoon. Our crew helped them celebrate by tying cans behind their canoe and using red produce tape to create large "JUST MARRIED" signs on the sides of the canoe. The joke became even funnier after their return when we rented the canoe out again. Somehow, no one noticed the "JUST MARRIED" decoration. Then we happened to observe two young men paddling down the lake in that canoe. We tried to imagine their reaction when they discovered the words on their canoe. The canoe was turned in a few days later without its distinctive markings and without comment.

"Small world" happenings continually amaze us. David Walker was a crew member in 1983 and 1984. His first "real-life job" was as a salesperson with Navastar. He was making a cross-country trip in that capacity when his seatmate on the airplane began to regale him with stories of a recent canoe trip he had taken in the Boundary Waters. Fortunately, he had high praise for the service he received from Sawbill Canoe Outfitters. Dave listened quietly for a while and then, to the astonishment of his seatmate, opened his briefcase and took out a brochure for Sawbill Canoe Outfitters. It so happened that Dave's picture was prominently featured in the brochure.

A similar sort of thing happened to Frank at about the same time. As a county commissioner, he traveled to Las Vegas to attend a meeting. At breakfast early one morning, he sat next to a county commissioner from North Carolina. Frank identified himself as being from Minnesota, which led his counterpart to launch into the saga of his recent canoe trip in the Boundary Waters. Frank didn't mind listening to rave reviews about the service he had received from his outfitter. When it turned out it was Sawbill Outfitters, Frank pulled out a business card indicating that it was his business that was being discussed! Frank waited impatiently until 6:30 a.m. our time before he called to tell me about this coincidence! Unsolicited testimonials are always welcome.

By the time the first two batches of UMD students had graduated and been launched into adulthood, we had moved to Minneapolis. Our children were in high school and college and new crew members came from a pool of their friends. The backbone of the crew though was Bill Kubiak, next younger brother of Tom Kubiak. Bill worked for us for seven years, a record of longevity at that time. He started the year he graduated from high school and continued all the years he attended dental school. He set up practice in Duluth and has always been a regular visitor. Bill was our "outfitting manager." That meant he was responsible for packing equipment for the customers, greeting and orienting them, and then unpacking and cleaning the equipment on their return. Bill was a night owl. He stayed up to all hours patrolling the area, reputedly looking for bears. He did a wonderful job of outfitting and was apparently successful in protecting us from bear attack. When he wasn't busy with outfitting, he could often be found amongst the sleeping bags stored on a high shelf catching 40 winks so as to be fresh for the next night's work.

Bill always expressed great interest and admiration for girls who were around the store as campers or canoeists. However, he seemed to prefer admiring from afar and never had any serious romantic attachments. When he returned to Duluth after dental school, he met Donela and it seemed to us there was no hesitation in declaring her his one and only. They were soon married. Now his favorite girls are his lovely daughter, Sarah, and his granddaughter, Paige.

We are often asked how we find our crew members. Over the years from 1957 through 2002, we had 154 different individuals, in addition to Frank and me. Twelve of these were family members — our three children and some of their spouses, our grandchildren, our niece Lydia, and our step-granddaughter, Emily Stewart. Family members have been long-term employees. When we hire a crew member, we assume that he or she will come back each summer for several years and a great many have indeed done that.

Our rule is that a new employee should be about 19 years old. This limits their tenure since most are in college and graduate in two or three years. Some of the people who worked with us for five summers or more were Tom Kubiak, Bill Kubiak, John Halvorson, Kathy Brown, Rich Huelskamp, Pam Oleson, Kathy Heltzer, Clare Heaney, Kristen Lundgren, John Oberholtzer, and Peter Glashagel. John Halvorson moved to Norway after he worked at Sawbill so we don't see him often. The others visit with some regularity.

As many as 40 individuals have been short-term crew members, working less than one full summer. As a seasonal business hiring college students, we always have a problem having enough help in the shoulder months of May, September, and October. Almost every year, we hire someone for just one or two of those months. This accounts for a number of our "one season" or short-term crew. Some short-term people were sweethearts or spouses of crew members. When we had a contract with the U.S. Forest Service to clean campsites in the Boundary Waters, we hired local residents Chel Anderson and Joyce Klees specifically for that job.

Although the great majority of our crew members have been super people, we must confess to a few mistakes. Half a dozen crew members have not been invited back due to infractions such as carelessly wrecking a vehicle or inability to do the work. Most of our crew members have returned for at least a second summer. There have been several seasons when we had so many returnees that we did not hire a single new person.

Many local businesses in recent years have had great difficulty finding enough employees. We have never had a shortage of candidates for our annual crew of 14, but we draw from a large area, not just the local community. In fact, we are reluctant to hire local students. All crew members live at Sawbill. We discovered over the years that it was better for us to have employees who couldn't "go home" easily. Although working hours are supposed to be only eight hours a day, there are emergencies when we need to call for more help. Crew members can distribute their work through the 14-hour day rather than working in 8-hour segments. We have always encouraged crew members to use their days off to take canoe trips. It's a perk of employment and also makes it easier for crew to relate to and advise customers. Crew members who come from some distance are much more likely to take advantage of this opportunity, rather than going home.

Most of the people we hire now have applied for work after going on canoe trips themselves, often with church groups. Sometimes, we ask the group leader to recommend a camper who shows leadership and willingness to contribute to the group's welfare. This has led to finding some outstanding crew members such as Peter Glashagel and David Freeman, who both came from the Chicago area and were highly recommended by their pastors.

Carleton College is a good example of how we happen to find crew members. Carleton has done large freshman orientation trips in the Boundary Waters for a number of years, renting much of their equipment from Sawbill Canoe Outfitters. In addition, Carleton College has been the source of Forest Service volunteers who work in the area each summer doing portage and campsite maintenance. They are often housed in the Forest Service Guard Station cabin at Sawbill. These contacts have brought us a succession of fine crew members, including Kurt Steffen, Dan Prince, Mike Gaud, Steve Surbaugh, Kate Ferguson, Max Wilson, and Loren McWethy. Paul Krieg was an earlier crew member who attended Carleton but he found out about us through his Chicago church group.

Most crew members have come from Midwest states, but a few have come from distant states, particularly the East Coast. Former crew members are scattered far and wide, from California to Texas to South Carolina. Several live abroad. Several have joined the Peace Corps after working here. Peter Glashagel went to Namibia. A number have spent time abroad working or traveling. Anne Strittmatter and her husband and children live in Nicaragua. Beth Pratt went to Antarctica for a season. Eric Frost was in India the year that country was devastated by an earthquake. Annie Strupeck spent a year in Japan. Our grandson Adam spent a year in Kenya.

Many former crew members visit Sawbill each summer. Some plan annual canoe trips or annual campground stays but some just drop in for a brief visit. Recently, we kept a list of former crew members who visited during the summer. In 2002, the number was 32. Otherwise, we keep in touch with most of them by Christmas letters, e-mail, wedding and birth announcements. We have a large family. We love each of them dearly and cherish the continuing relationship. We keep hoping that we will be able to hire a second-generation person to work at Sawbill, but so far that has not happened, except in our own family. Most of our earliest crew members now have grandchildren, so a new pool of crew members is growing up. Thus the cycle of life goes on.

Although we haven't hired local people, many of our crew members have become enamored of the area and continue to live in Cook County. We are very proud of the contribution each of them is making to the community. Here is the list: Karen Blackburn, Nancy Cihlar, David Freeman, John Oberholtzer, Kathy O'Neill, Barbara

Osborne, David Quick, Laurie Senty, Steve and Kate Surbaugh, Natasha (Warner) White, as well as family members, Bill and Cindy Hansen, Karl Hansen and Lee Stewart.

A few more people are here because they were introduced to Cook County by a Sawbill crew member. When we were commuting from the Twin Cities, we brought our children and their friends to Sawbill on our weekend trips. Steve Frykman was (and is) Karl's friend who used to ride with us. Sherrie Denniston came with Kathy Brown O'Neill. We are ever so pleased to claim some credit for the presence in our community of each and every one of these great people.

· Chapter 8 ·

—— Corps Values — The CCC ——

Although the Sawbill Civilian Conservation Corps (CCC) camp six miles south of us was abandoned and largely dismantled by the time we arrived in 1957, its legacy is very much with us. How often we tell canoeists about the picnic tables that used to grace wilderness campsites, built of huge half logs by the CCC enrollees. We stroll with guests down to the Forest Service guard station and admire the rock wall along the steep driveway. "It was built by the CCC," we say. Innumerable senior citizens have stopped in our store to say proudly, "I was with the Cs at Sawbill."

Although all the buildings on the site are long gone, the clearing at the intersection of The Grade and the Sawbill Trail remains as a large open field. There is evidence that people camp there. Every spring, a little wooded strip there near the Sawbill Trail is the first place to have flowers blooming — trailing arbutus.

The CCC was one of the more impressive programs ever created by the federal government. It changed the lives of millions of young men and also affected the management of natural resources forever.

Many programs have since sought to replicate the vision and accomplishments of the CCC. For example, Minnesota has had the very successful Youth Conservation Corps (YCC) for many years, modeled after the CCC.

This is how the CCC came about. Franklin D. Roosevelt was inaugurated as president in March 1933 with the clear mission of rescuing the country from the depths of the Great Depression. In 1933, 54 percent of young men between the ages of 17 and 25 were unemployed. Thirty-five days later, the CCC came into existence. It was a miracle. Legislation was written, passed, and signed; guidelines were established; and the selection process was begun to choose locations for the camps. Four U.S. cabinet departments were harnessed together to run the operation: Labor, Interior, Agriculture, and War. The expertise of the War Department was tapped for the construction and operation of the camps, which followed the pattern of Army installations. The Departments of Interior and Agriculture were in charge of finding needed conservation projects in the national parks and national forests. The Department of Labor, of course, was concerned with employment. At its peak, two years later, the CCC had 502,000 members in 2,514 camps across the country. In all, 2.9 million men served in the nine years that the CCC was in existence.

Cook County must have been a favorite place to locate CCC camps because of the wealth of forestry projects available. There were 13 camps in Cook County, Minnesota. The first camp was at Caribou Lake, followed by Gunflint and Northern Light lakes. Three different camps were built on the Sawbill Trail, although two were short-lived. The men were assigned to forest liberation, which means thinning the brush and unwanted vegetation around desirable trees. This work improved timber production and prepared sites for planting new trees. They cleared portage trails and built campgrounds and took a census of wildlife. One job was "scalping," which meant using a mattock to remove the sod and brush from a 2-foot square of turf to prepare for planting seedling trees in the fall.

Those qualified to join the CCC were young men aged 18 to 25 (later 17 to 28), single, jobless, in good physical condition, and

The CCC camp at the junction of the Sawbill Trail and The Grade in 1933

needy. They volunteered for six months and were allowed to stay as long as two years — longer if they had been promoted to leadership positions. The pay was $30 per month plus subsistence, known as "three hots and a flop." Of the cash received, $22 to $25 was automatically sent home to their families.

The Army built and ran the camps. Each camp consisted of four barracks housing 40 to 50 men each, a mess hall, a recreation building, officers' quarters, a school for night classes, and a latrine and bathhouse separate from the barracks. The boys got up to a bugler's reveille, stood morning and evening formations, and showed up on time for meals or went hungry. When they trudged or trucked to work each morning, another agency — usually the Forest Service — took over. Civilian foremen, "local experienced men" called LEMs, ran the work crews. Most of the work was manual labor. The tools were shovels, mattocks, sledgehammers, double-edged axes, and crosscut saws. The average CCC enrollee joined at the age of 18½, stayed in for nine months, and gained 12 to 39 pounds. Before joining the Cs, the average fellow had finished eighth grade and had never held a regular job. Sixty percent were from small towns or farms. Many had never lived with running water or electricity and many had not had enough to eat at home.

They went to work at 7:15 a.m. and quit at 4 p.m. with a break for lunch. GI discipline governed the camps. They had to shave, bathe regularly, keep their hair short, and salute officers. A man who threw his cigarette on the ground had to wear a butt can around his neck for a day. Every camp had a sports program — baseball and boxing mostly. There were libraries and night classes, which taught elementary school subjects, vocational training, and even etiquette. For evening recreation, the fellows played cards, Ping-Pong, or music. It was not an easy life. Many of the enrollees were grateful to be there and even came to enjoy the life. Others, unable to accept the strict regimen, hard work, and sometimes inhospitable climate, checked out. A man who was AWOL for nine days was removed from the rolls and not pursued.

The accomplishments of the CCC in our area are enormous. First, there was the personal development and rehabilitation, similar in some ways to the results of Outward Bound programs today. In addition to all the forestry projects, the Sawbill CCC camp was the main base for fish and game projects. The Minnesota Department of Natural Resources magazine, *The Conservation Volunteer* (July-August 1983) lists some of the activities that benefited the state:

1. Stream Improvement: constructed rock diversions, opened channels, and planted trout fingerlings
2. Lake Survey (winter and summer): sampled and analyzed water for acidity, alkalinity, turbidity — Planted trout and walleye by carrying in 10-gallon milk cans full of water and fish — a very hard job — Surveyed fishermen
3. Deer Census: counted and studied habitat — Jonvik Deer Yard found to be the largest deer yard
4. Wildlife Food and Cover: harvested and planted wild rice, collected tamarack cones and mountain ash berries for later planting, and put up wood duck nesting boxes.

The CCC wound down to an end in 1942. By this time, all the efforts of our country were directed toward the war. Young men enlisted or were drafted into military service. The agency issued a report summarizing its accomplishments: 46,854 bridges, 3,116 fire towers, 28 million rods of fencing, 318,076 check dams for erosion control, 33,087 miles of terracing. The CCC planted trees and grass, fought forest fires, laid pipe, improved wildlife habitat, and built or maintained thousands of miles of hiking trails. They did every conservation job that any land manager could think of![1]

Sawbill Lodge, only six miles away, was being developed at about the same time as the CCC camp. Harold "Hedge" Arbogust remembers that he was responsible for trips to town to pick up Sawbill's mail. The commanding officer of the CCC made arrangements for Hedge to ride along on the daily trips made by the CCC truck. Sometimes Hedge rode along on trips to Grand Marais or Two Harbors. Arby or Jean would drive Hedge down to the camp to meet the truck. Upon return from town, Hedge was sometimes picked up, but sometimes he had to walk the six miles back to Sawbill, alone and frequently in the dark.[2]

Olga Erickson, whose family lived at the CCC camp between 1937 and 1941, remembers Sawbill Lodge mostly because they went there for Thanksgiving dinner. Jean Arbogust would roast a big turkey and the women from the CCC camp would each bring something for the dinner. Sometimes they went to Sawbill Lake to ice skate.

Chester "Chet" Erickson, Olga's husband, was the construction foreman, one of five or six LEMs at the Sawbill CCC Camp. He was working for the Forest Service in Ely when the big Cherokee Fire broke out in 1936. Since he was familiar with the Sawbill area, he was assigned to the team fighting this fire. His wife, Olga, remembers well that they were expecting their third child that summer. When it was evident that Chet wouldn't be home for some time, Olga moved back to Grand Marais where her parents lived. Gene was born on August 24 and Chet finally got home from his firefighting duties on August 25. Chet's next assignment was the CCC camp and the family soon moved there.

Chet, like the other men of the management team, built a tar paper shack for shelter. It had a large living room and a large bedroom. Each man drilled a well under the house, hitting water quite easily. Water came into the house by way of a hand operated pump on the kitchen sink. Chet put a large barrel behind their wood burning stove and that gave them all the hot water they could use. Olga had a gasoline-powered washing machine, something the other women didn't have, but she had three children, while most of the others had none. A few couples had one child. They had a battery-powered radio with excellent reception. When the washing machine was running, they took advantage of the power to charge the batteries. They had an outdoor privy and the adults went to the CCC camp bathhouse to take showers.

Olga remembers some of the people who made up the group: the education director (Mr. Gamble); as many as three camp doctors, including Dr. Frogner, who later had a summer cabin on Brule Lake; and the machinist. There was a great deal of turnover in the staff of the CCC camp.

The women gathered for coffee every afternoon. Olga remembers this time as "some of the best years of my life." The young family did many things together. One of the highlights was picking the wild raspberries that were so thick and luscious. Olga made and canned sauce, jam, and jelly. When sugar rationing during the war put an end to canning, she still had plenty of jars of jelly stored in her root cellar.

Bears were a problem in this community and they were always around. The Ericksons had a dog that barked at the bears and nipped at their heels, sometimes successfully chasing them away. Some particularly pesky bears were shot. Still, Olga was always concerned about letting her children play outside. One time, the whole camp heard screams and then, shortly afterward, gunshots. Everybody rushed out to see what had happened. Lucy Frogner had been making candy and a bear came to join the fun. When Lucy saw the bear at her window, she screamed. Then she got the family rifle, pointed it upward and shot into the air. The frightened bear obligingly ran away.

Other fondly remembered times included dances where some of the men (including Robley Hunt) formed a band. Olga and Chet had a friend at the camp, an older single man, who would babysit for them so they could go to Grand Marais. They went to town, either Tofte or Grand Marais, every weekend for shopping.

When the CCC was over, the Ericksons moved to Tofte where Chet joined Andy Tofte in his logging and sawmill business. About that time, the railroads needed many wooden doors for coal and grain cars. Every week, Chet and Andy manufactured and hauled a load of doors to Duluth. Andy died in 1945 at the age of 41.

The Ericksons bought Cobblestone Cabins from Mrs. Martha Hubbard and lived in one of the cabins for a while. About this time (1942), Olga started running the telephone switchboard for Tofte. She could do this from her home. She and Chet soon built their own home on the upper side of the highway, across from the present-day Bluefin guest registration building. This home is scheduled for removal when Highway 61 is rebuilt through Tofte. Since Chet's death in 1991, Olga has lived in Grand Marais.[3]

Robley Hunt, who now lives in Two Harbors, was another of the Forest Service people who worked with the CCC camps. In those days, segregation was the custom, so one of the camps on the Sawbill Trail was solely for blacks. Robley was in charge of this camp one winter. Their assignment was fire hazard control. They spent the winter cutting "snags" (standing dead trees), collecting and piling all dead and down trees, and then burning them. They were cleaning up the forest! Most of the men were from Alabama and Mississippi and were totally unprepared for living and working in snow and bitterly cold weather. They were not "happy campers." The effort was abandoned after that one winter and that camp was closed.

Don Roberts of Grand Marais was involved with a CCC project that had long-range consequences. Working with a U.S. Army Reserve geologist doing lake surveys, they took depth soundings and water samples, recorded water temperatures, and studied bottom composition. They took the soundings every 100 feet. It was the beginning of lake contour mapping.

Another link to the present is Britton Peak, now a trailhead for the Superior Hiking Trail, located three miles north of Highway 61 on the Sawbill Trail. It is named for Wyman L. "Windy" Britton, who was an enrollee in the Sawbill CCC camp for two years. After that, he worked for the Forest Service as a mapmaker until he went into service in World War II. He served in the military police (MP) and was discharged as a staff sergeant. When the military contacted him and asked him to re-enlist, he went back to Germany as an MP. While serving there, he was involved in a fracas while on duty and suffered severe head injuries. He was flown back to Walter Reed Hospital for surgery, but he died. His last request was to have his ashes scattered on a favorite hilltop. His family complied and placed a marker at the spot after first gaining permission from the Forest Service. Later the Forest Service named the area Britton Peak.

Britton Peak was named for Windy Britton, an enrollee in the Sawbill CCC camp.

The CCC left a large legacy in the area as well as in the rest of the country. Many of those young men remember their time in the Cs with great nostalgia and gratitude. They didn't necessarily consider the terrain friendly or inviting. During the active days of the CCC, a joke making the rounds of the camps went like this: "The government recently tried to deed this country back to the Indians but the Indians wouldn't have it. The CCCs have now been placed here to improve the place so they will reconsider."

Chapter 9

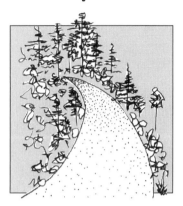

The Sawbill Trail

Hard as it is to imagine, there was a time when there was no Sawbill Trail. Today, the Sawbill Trail runs 23 miles from Highway 61 in Tofte north to Sawbill Lake. Automobiles were coming into use in the rest of the country by 1910, but there were very few automobiles in Cook County. The reason was lack of roads. It wasn't until 1925 that Highway 61 was completed from Duluth to Grand Marais. It had been built in sections. The last section around the Baptism River that presented the greatest challenge was finally completed in 1925. People started acquiring pickups and other motorized vehicles. The purchase of an automobile was big news, often reported by the local newspaper, the *Cook County News-Herald*. For example, "Godfrey Lundquist returned from Duluth Tuesday with a new Chevrolet enclosed car," or "John Anderson has purchased a Chevrolet from Midway Service Station." Cars were so important that the newspaper ran full page ads for tires. A 1920 Model A Bush Car was described as a five-passenger touring car. It sold for $1,495 which included War Tax.

118 SAWBILL

Tall pines tower over a vehicle on the Sawbill Trail in 1933.

It was about 1924 when the citizens of the town of Tofte were courageous enough to pass a bond issue for $20,000 to build what is now called the Sawbill Trail. The township of Tofte extended all the way to the Canadian border and the land was still largely owned by logging companies and was therefore on the tax rolls. This provided funds for the project or the hope of funds. The town fathers were inspired by the idea of tourism, by the need to provide jobs for young men in the area, and by the example of the Gunflint Trail, which was about 10 years old at that time. Chris Tormondsen, an early settler and member of the Tofte Town Board, along with other trappers, reported the beauty of Sawbill, Alton, Brule, and Winchell lakes and the great fishing opportunities they provided.

There was an established road from Highway 61 to the town of Springdale, now called the Springdale Road, where a number of Tofte citizens were living. This road branches off the Sawbill Trail about a mile north of the highway. In 1924, this road had been extended west to Carlton Peak to provide access to Section 16, a school section purchased for timber rights by several of the town's families. Therefore, the new road construction began at Carlton Peak, turning the road north and heading for Sawbill Lake. Cac Hussey, a county surveyor, and Andrew Tofte Sr., acting as general foreman, supervised the road crew.

Ted Tofte, son of Andrew, was one of these young men on the road crew and one who left a record of the proceedings.[1] He was just out of high school and eager to earn money for college. According to his account, the survey crew first cut and staked the center line of the road. The path of least resistance determined the route with little or no attention paid to legal right-of-way. They were followed by the cutting crew who, with saw and ax, felled the trees and cut brush for 16½ feet on each side of the center line. A team of horses pulled the stumps of the smaller trees and the alder brush. A big tractor with a cable pulled out the big stumps. After the road bed was cleaned of debris, it looked like the average Cook County garden! At this point, the tractor pushed up a berm to form the road bed. The bed was then graveled, with No. 2 shovels being the main earthmoving equipment.

Ted Tofte describes some of the young men who worked on the project. Pat Malone, who came from an educated eastern family, was the dynamite man on the project. He is remembered for his gracious way with the ladies and for his close calls with his dynamite operations. Ralph Godin was the young man who carried the cash payroll from the bank in Grand Marais every Friday. One year on the Friday following Ralph's return to college, highwaymen robbed his replacement as he passed through Lutsen. John Eide had a harrowing tale to tell of his race to the shore ahead of a fire that was "rolling like a wheel" across the forest from the west.

Wages on the road job were 50 cents per hour or $4 a day. Ted remembers walking to work until the road reached the old Jonas Nelson homestead about a mile beyond the dump road. Here, the first of many camps was established. Work on the road continued for several summers, employing many of the townspeople.

John "Casey" Tofte Jr., son of John Tofte, and Ted Tofte's cousin, worked on the road-building that first summer although he was

A bumpy Temperance River Road, precursor to Sawbill Trail, 1929

only 14 years old. He drove a road grader powered by a team of horses. It is his memory that the road building ended after just six miles because the town's money ran out. The county took over the project and built the next section up to the Temperance River bridge, about nine miles north of Tofte. They punched through the next section as far as The Grade — that is, established the right of way — but it was several years before that section was actually surfaced or graveled.

Emerson Morris, who worked for the Forest Service, recalled that it was 1930 before the Sawbill Trail reached the railroad grade and then another year or two before the county extended the road to Sawbill Lake. We know that the road did exist in primitive form in 1932, when the Arbogusts drove up to find the location for their wilderness resort on Sawbill.

Morris described one of his trips to Sawbill Lake in 1925-26. He started his day at the Forest Service headquarters in Grand Marais and had to drive his own car to Schroeder.

A fishing trip heads up the Sawbill Trail in the 1930s – left to right: Paul Stoltz, Emerson Morris, Fay McKeever, Carl Hedstrom.

"From Schroeder you went to Cramer," he said, "then took the old Alger Smith Railroad Grade from there northeast and came to the railroad tracks at what was called Camp 12 near Wanless Lake. Here you left your car and used a speeder on the railroad tracks. Fourmile Lake was 12 or 15 miles. . . To get to Sawbill Lake, we had to go on the speeder another 12 or 15 miles toward Cascade Lake until we got to the Temperance River Meadows. There was a trail cut from there to the Sawbill Ranger Station."[2]

The Temperance River Meadows was most likely the site of the Nelson Moose Camp, established by C.A.A. Nelson. One of the early arrivals on the North Shore, Nelson homesteaded in 1885 in what was to become Lutsen. He and his wife were very friendly and hospitable, welcoming visitors to their two-story home. It wasn't long until paying guests traveling north to hunt and fish were seeking accommodations. They arrived at Lutsen Resort by steamship and then needed transportation into the woods. "C-Double-A," as he was known to his friends, established a moose camp on Rice Lake, consisting of a barn, sleeping shacks, and tents, so that men could stay overnight and be ready for hunting early the next morning. To reach the camp, he hacked out a trail for horses and wagons along the Poplar River, past Barker Lake, and on to Rice Lake. (Rice Lake is just south of what is now known as Crescent Lake.)

The Alger Smith Railroad, which was part of the Duluth and Northern Minnesota Railroad owned by the Alger-Smith Lumber Company, had been punched through the forest from Knife River to Cascade, a railroad town near Brule Lake, beginning in 1898. Eventually, there were 100 miles of mainline track with 350 miles of spurs that were usually temporary tracks put in place to reach a specific logging operation. Forest Service Road 170, now known as The Grade, was built on this old railroad bed. The Grade was rebuilt about 1960 from the Ball Club Road to the Sawbill Trail and further improved west of the Sawbill Trail in the 1990s.

The road to Brule Lake which starts at The Grade is built on one of the spurs that was originally constructed to bring norway and white pine from the Winchell Lake area. The rails were pulled out and the road bed was used for many years to access Homer and Brule lakes. For years, hikers on the Brule Lake Road picked up huge spikes that had been used to hold the rails down, and left behind when the rails were torn out.

The Dinges family built Sky Blue Water Resort on a southern bay of Brule Lake in the 1980s. Even after building was complete, they delayed opening the resort for several years until the county could put in a "real" road, which happened in 1983. The resort was open for several years. In the meantime, the Boundary Waters Canoe Area Act decreed that motor size on Brule Lake would be reduced to 25 horsepower and prohibited altogether by 1990. The family objected to this, and they chose to sell out to the government.

The whole Sawbill Trail is now classified as a "County State Aid Road," which means that the county plows it in the winter and grades it in the summer. An issue that the early builders did not address is that the road passes through swampy areas. When they

A typical washout of the Sawbill Trail in May 1950

built it during the summer, it had a fairly solid and smooth surface. However, spring brings melting snow and thawing ground. The Sawbill Trail would routinely develop into a quagmire. After a few weeks, the road grader could do a temporary reconstruction and it would be passable again.

The photograph above shows a typical washout. Sometimes, this extended across the entire width of the road. Our son Bill remembers seeing a four-wheel-drive truck buried in mud up to its windows right in the middle of the road. Earl Hansen, Tofte District Ranger for the Forest Service at the time and no relation to us, believes this was the time that two culverts near each other washed out in the spring leaving a major hole in the road. This occurred only a few miles up the Sawbill Trail from Highway 61.

The bridge over the river on the 600 Road was put in by the Forest Service. Earl Hansen

A new culvert was installed on the 600 Road in 1952.

remembers that they put a huge culvert in place only to have it float downstream a few feet. It was a gigantic undertaking to get it back on the center line. "Molly," the Forest Service road grader, was instrumental in accomplishing the task, but by then she was covered with mud and a big cleanup project followed.

Earl remembers one occasion in 1950 when Louie Hootenow, Molly's driver, got off the grader for some reason. To his horror, Molly started moving ahead without benefit of a driver. Louie ran alongside her, hoping to jump on and stop her. Fortunately, she ran into the D-4 tractor that Carl Nelson was driving and that brought her to a stop. Otherwise, she could very well have rambled all the way down the hill and into Lake Superior. That would have been hard to explain![3]

The bridge over Temperance River has been replaced several times. The first bridge, built by the CCC in the mid-1930s, was made of

Temperance River Bridge on the Sawbill Trail collapsed in 1950.

green lumber and was soon well rotted. It was replaced by a steel bridge with a trestle across the top. About 1950, a pulp truck was driving down the Sawbill Trail in the spring when its loading boom struck the trestle's top cross piece and knocked the whole thing awry. The county jacked it up and replaced the beam. The present bridge was erected in the 1970s.

Driving on the Sawbill Trail continues to present problems. In 1969, we were driving to Sawbill for the weekend and had to detour by way of the Caribou Trail because the Sawbill was impassable and closed. In 1970, Tom Gerardy, a Sawbill crew member, was reporting for work in May. He made it almost to Sawbill before his car sank into the mud and he had to walk the last mile. This is not only a problem from the past but one that exists today. In the spring of 2001, Frank and I were proceeding to town when our car dropped into a crevasse of water running across the Sawbill Trail two miles from our house. We had to call for a tow to get out.

By the late 1980s, the problems of the Sawbill Trail — dangerous curves, collapsing culverts, weather closures, spring load limits — were becoming increasingly serious for us and for the numerous tourists heading for the various inland lakes. Cook County and Tofte Township had no funds to address the problems. The Sawbill Trail was officially a state-aid road but insufficient money was available for the state to deal with the needed improvements. Other roads in national forests were facing similar problems. At last, the federal government came to the rescue with money specially earmarked for upgrading roads heavily used to access national forests.

The Cook County Highway Department immediately began developing a plan to meet the federal specifications. It called for a 64-foot corridor along 15 miles. The first three miles of the Sawbill Trail had been blacktopped a few years earlier when the road to the Tofte dump was receiving heavy usage. This meant that the stretch to be improved would start at the existing blacktop and end at The Grade. They proposed blacktopping a two-lane road designed for 55-mph traffic. The cost would be $4 million to be paid out of federal and state money. Implementation, starting at the southern end of the road, began in 1990.

Immediately, a hue and cry arose. Local environmentalists protested that a paved road would lead to increased logging and increased all-terrain-vehicle (ATV) traffic. Improvement was perceived as a desecration of the wilderness. Twin Cities newspapers as well as the *Cook County News-Herald* were full of letters bemoaning the plan. One Twin Cities writer accused Sawbill Canoe Outfitters of promoting the whole project of a highway to its door to increase its traffic and profits. This writer failed to note that the plans left the last six miles into Sawbill untouched. That stretch still remains narrow and vulnerable to the weather just as it has always been. It has been improved somewhat through the skill of the Cook County Highway Department personnel who have ditched the road so that it can drain more effectively. Another writer castigated proponents of the improvements for calling the road a "trail." He claimed this was only done to win the sympathy and empty the pocketbooks of the citizens of the metropolitan areas of the state! I doubt he had any concept of the origins of the road.

People often asked for our opinions about the road. Two points put me on the side of improvement. First and foremost is the matter of dust. We drive on the Sawbill Trail every day and our vehicles are always coated inside and out with layers of dust. Without frequent rain, the whole landscape — all the beautiful wildflowers and the lovely green vegetation — is hidden under layers of dust. I also heartily endorsed the county's position that a blacktopped road would be much less expensive to maintain. I was on the Tofte Town Board at the time and, being a strong fiscal conservative, I was very much aware of the limited resources of the town and county and eager to keep spending and taxes under control.

The Forest Service was closely involved with the controversy since the improvements had been made possible by virtue of the fact that the Sawbill Trail was located within the Superior National Forest and was being used largely by Superior Forest visitors. Tofte District Ranger Larry Dawson had recently received training in mediation, and he offered to set up a committee representing both business and environmental views. He hoped to be able to resolve the strong differences of opinion. His offer was accepted and the Sawbill Trail Resolution Committee was established in 1992. Its membership consisted of Tofte residents with varying points of view: Gene Utecht, who was the West End county commissioner at the time, Greg Eide, Gary Kettleson, Joyce Klees, Chel Anderson, Ellen Hawkins, and Bill Hansen. Roger Pekuri, Forest Service engineer, and Michael Tardy, Cook County Highway Department engineer, were technical advisers to the group, with Greg Gastecki of the Cook County Highway Department attending as an alternate at times. The Forest Service was represented by Ranger Dawson as the facilitator and Patty DeShaw as the note taker.

The committee met for six months, airing their opinions and grievances about such matters as public safety, water quality, wildlife, business interests, and the unique nature of the Sawbill Trail, before reaching a compromise that nixed the idea of paving or blacktopping. The final agreement was described in the *Minneapolis Star Tribune* with Bill Hansen saying, "Let's say everyone is equally unhappy. Everybody can live with it, but nobody really likes it."

Ranger Dawson was quoted as saying, "There were no decisive winners or losers in the final decision, but it is a road design we can all live with." Dennis Carlson, a state-aid official of the Minnesota Department of Transportation, opined that the result would be an "environmentally sensitive highway that does not negatively impact safety."[4]

There was still a major stumbling block. The original design followed the federal guidelines included in the legislation. There was no provision for more restricted improvements. If the federal money was to be obtained, then Congress would have to pass legislation modifying the guidelines. This miracle did occur after 11 months, during which the Forest Service lobbied for it. The final plan approved by all agencies called for a 28-foot-wide road including the shoulders, with a provision that trees would be cleared for 10 additional feet on the ditch slopes on either side of the road. It was felt that the dust could be controlled with the application of calcium chloride.

The road design was for 45-mph traffic and a nine-ton road bed. This eliminated the need for the seasonal load limit. The first three miles going north that were already under construction were completed in 1993. The remaining 12 miles were scheduled for rebuilding between 1994 and 1996. The worst curve near Plouff Creek, known as Dead Man's Curve because of the many accidents that had occurred there, was eliminated by relocating the road in that area, a step that also cut the total distance by about a mile.

We look upon the new road as very satisfactory in terms of safety and ease of driving. The gravel surface is very good. From Sawbill going south, once we get past the first six miles to The Grade, we no longer drive with bated breaths or white knuckles, fearful of meeting a logging truck. The road is now wide enough to allow any two vehicles to pass each other safely. The clearing along the sides makes it far less likely that a deer or moose will jump out unexpectedly. We now rarely find the road blocked by a fallen tree. We are pleased to be able to drive faster and to reach our destinations in a few minutes less time. On the other hand, the dust problem is still with us. Applying calcium chloride does a wonderful job for several weeks before it wears off. The county cannot afford many applications. The last six miles into Sawbill Lake are not included in this dust control.

When the road was completed, we had many people from the metropolitan area arrive at our store bewailing the desecration of their beloved Sawbill Trail. I am sympathetic with this nostalgia. I also love a shady trail through the woods with branches meeting overhead. I love driving across the Honeymoon Trail or the 600 Road (side roads off the Sawbill Trail) especially in the fall. However, I don't think it is sensible or practical to have the Sawbill Trail be that kind of road in view of the amount of traffic it carries during the vacation months.

Some landscaping was done by the road builders. I love seeing the variety of ferns that appear in June and the lupines along the sides of the road in July, and the black-eyed susans in August. Other wildflowers lining the Sawbill Trail are daisies, asters, goldenrod, and joe-pye weed.

· Chapter 10 ·

—— Neighbors at Sawbill ——

It's 8 o'clock on a Friday evening in 1960. Once again, I've emptied the cold dishwater out of my sink, replaced it with warm water, and resumed washing the dinner dishes. I have been interrupted three times to go around the corner from our house into the store to make a sale. First, some new arrivals stop in to buy fishing licenses and to pick up another package of leaders and some slip-bobbers. At their request, I have reported on the recent fishing experiences of other customers. "Where they been gettin' 'em? Any size to 'em? What were they usin'?" Two youngsters come in to buy candy bars. They are bored because their parents down at the campsite are busy cleaning up after supper so they wander through the store looking at everything, touching things, and picking up some things. They don't talk because the age difference between 10 and 30 is just too great, but I have to stay in the store as long as they are there. After they leave, I get two plates washed and I'm back in the store visiting with a couple who came to buy milk and bread for breakfast the next morning. I listen to their reports of their day's activities.

It's not the city. No one comes in, makes a purchase, and leaves immediately. The store is a place to hang out and to have a visit. Frank and the guides are over at the Lodge visiting with those guests and planning their next day's expeditions. My young children help out a lot during the day but doing dishes after dinner is not one of their chores.

Now it's 8:30 p.m. and the beer drinking group arrives. We never intended to have a bar but the nicest furniture donated to us for store furnishing was the handmade pine-paneled bar with six matching bar stools that Dick Raiken made. Small neighborhood bars were common all around the North Country in the 1960s but Frank and I were unaware of this as we had never stepped foot in one. So we have a bar, and the beer drinkers arrive. Tonight, it is a pleasant and peaceful group from Duluth who are on the campground for the weekend.

Theoretically, our store hours are 7 a.m. to 10 p.m., but clearly the group at the bar has no intention of leaving at 10 p.m. I start debating with myself. How can I tactfully get them to leave? I don't want to offend any customers. We need every customer and we need every possible dollar and nickel to keep our little business afloat. I'm tired and sleepy. I have to be up at six in the morning to have the store open by seven and ready to rent canoes. My customers buy another round. It's close to midnight when they happily depart.

We are back on the job the next morning, selling some bait and sending a few people off with canoes when Charlie Niemi arrives in his pickup. He is one of our neighbors, a lumberjack living in a shack in the woods not far away. Charlie is an elderly Finn who can barely speak English. His speech in any language is slurred due to an earlier stroke. One side of his face sags and the eye on that side looks glassy. His body is round and soft but there must be muscle hidden there as he works in the woods all week with his ax and saw, chopping down trees, limbing them, and cutting them into 8-foot lengths. His demeanor is equally soft. He comes as a good friend but with a flat wallet. He probably spent the evening before in the bar at Tofte. Now Charlie needs a six-pack on credit. He has brought his rifle and offers it as security that he will be back later to pay his bill. His word and his credit are good. Frank accepts the rifle because that's the way Charlie wants it. It will remind him that he needs to come back with money.

Sunday morning about 10 o'clock, another lumberjack comes in. Cook County decrees that no alcoholic beverage will be sold on Sunday until after noon, but Eino doesn't want to wait. He comes begging us to sell him a six-pack now. He pleads, "I'm thirsty." Finally, he goes away angry but not belligerent.

Later that day, the Wisnewskis stop by. They are our nearest neighbors, living at the old CCC cabin six miles from us. Stan Wisnewski is the exceptional lumberjack in our experience. He is young, clean cut, and sober. He and his wife, Joan, bring their little ones, Carol and Kenny, for a visit.

During these early years, the logging business was changing. When we first arrived at Sawbill, there were no longer any big lumber camps. Only a few men continued to live in the woods and cut trees by hand. The Hahn Harvester had been invented and logging had become mechanized. The old lumberjacks then gradually disappeared, moving into retirement and dying.

Stan Wisnewski continued to work in the woods but the family moved to Grand Marais and he drove to work. By this time, cars and pickups were commonplace, gasoline was relatively cheap and plentiful, and it became accepted practice to drive considerable distances to work.

The Wisnewski's story is a sad one. One winter day, Joan was sledding on a hill near Grand Marais with her children, five of them by that time. As she flew down the hill headfirst on her sled, she lost control and hit a tree. She had a concussion from which she never woke up. She was in a coma for about 10 years before she died. The beautiful young family suffered many hardships in those years.

One morning at 4 a.m., we were awakened by loud pounding on our door. It was anglers who wanted to buy bait. This incident brought us to the realization that as a small family business we could not be all things to all people. We posted signs on our doors saying that our hours are 7 a.m. to 10 p.m. and we disciplined ourselves to be firm about this.

Another awakening occurred one morning when a church group of young teenagers came into the store, getting ready to start out on a canoe trip while a couple of bleary-eyed lumberjacks were sitting at the bar. It dawned on us that we had to make a choice. We moved the bar out of the store, and didn't renew our on-sale beer license.

It is 10 o'clock in the morning when Emma jumps out of her pickup and rushes into the store in a state of agitation. She says she has to use the phone to call Philadelphia. We think perhaps there is a family emergency but she explains that the government owes her $10,000! Emma is a Native American married to a Finnish lumberjack, Gust Lehto. Apparently she has just found out about some treaty provision that entitles her to a cash payment and she needs the money! We sympathize with her and stifle our strong suspicions that she is not going to hear, "The check is in the mail."

Emma and Gust have three young children. Johnny, the oldest, is already in school. The two girls are preschoolers. When Johnny comes to the store with his mother, he makes a beeline for our classic comics. Comic books are at the height of popularity at this time — Mr. Marvel and Superman — but we don't stock those in our store. We do have paperback books for sale and Classic Comics for children. Typical comic book titles are *Ivanhoe*, *Tom Sawyer*, *Hamlet*, *Hansel and Gretel*, and *Romeo and Juliet*. The stories are gripping and presented in typical comic book format. Johnny has some spending money that he has earned peeling logs for his father and he wants to buy a comic book instead of the candy most youngsters crave. We help him out by creating a sort of lending library. When he comes again, he can trade his comic in on another one at a bargain price. During the summer, Johnny manages to read all the comics, some of them several times.

Several years later, the assistant superintendent of schools in nearby Lake County was visiting schools in the remote reaches of the county. He posed the question to the students, "What did you read over the summer?" He was totally amazed when one young Native American boy held up his hand and reported that he had read *Hamlet*. The incredulous administrator said, "Well, maybe you could tell us the story." Johnny gave an excellent summary. "Well, who wrote the story?" Johnny knew that, too, because a short biography of the author was included in each comic. He also named some of the other books he had read over the summer. The amazing story of a backwoods Indian boy with a remarkable taste in literature circulated throughout the state. We were the only ones who recognized that he was reading from a very limited selection of comic books, obtained from our store.

   Johnny Lehto graduated from college and became a teacher. He undoubtedly has an unusual appreciation of English literature that has served him well in his educational and professional career.

   Emma came in often to buy groceries, usually on credit. One day she brought with her two older women relatives who were visiting her. They spoke very little English, but they had some birchbark creations to show us, which we admired very much. Several weeks later, Emma brought me a gift of a birchbark basket. It is like a vase with a handle and has "Mary Alice" painted on it. I have treasured it ever since.

   In the fall, Emma introduces us to the custom of wild ricing. She proposes a deal whereby she will "rent" a canoe for several weeks and pay with wild rice. Most of our canoes are not in use at this time of year so we don't mind letting her use one. She tells us that the rice is growing in certain nearby lakes and that only Indians are authorized to harvest it.

   The rice ripens in early September and is harvested by paddling a canoe through the beds, bending the stalks over and knocking the grains of rice into the boat. It takes two people in the canoe. The "poler" stands in the back of the canoe and poles the canoe back and forth through the shallow water. The "knocker" sits in the bottom of the canoe and uses a pair of sticks called "knockers." One stick is used to hold the stalks over the canoe while the other stick knocks the grain off. The knocker works first one side of the canoe and then the other.

   Back at home, the rice is laid out on a tarp to dry for several days. Then the rice is put in a huge cast iron pot and cooked slowly over a low fire. It needs to be stirred or turned constantly so that it does not burn. Parching takes about half an hour.

The next step is to remove the hulls in a process called "dancing the rice." In the old traditional way of ricing, a shallow pit was dug and lined with leather. Poles were set over the ricing pit for the dancer to hang on to so that he could dance lightly on the rice with his new moccasins. This loosened the hulls and then the rice would be placed in ricing baskets. The rice would be tossed gently in the air and the wind would blow most of the hulls away.

I don't know how precisely Emma followed the traditional methods of preparing the rice but the rice we received in payment for the canoe was excellent. She made some money selling her rice to stores around the area. Like all the other lumberjacks, Gust Lehto and his family moved away after a few years and this exciting aspect of our lives at Sawbill came to an end.

In our first years at Sawbill, it was possible to follow a very definite road from the north end of the campground east through the woods almost to Burnt Lake. One day when Bill was quite young, he and I hiked down this road for several miles and came to a dilapidated shack in a small clearing. There was a

Emma and Gust Lehto taught us the traditional way of wild ricing.

rusting cook stove and the remains of an iron bedspring plus the usual pile of old tin cans and broken glass bottles. Bill was delighted to find a rusty child-size wheelbarrow that he pushed all the way home. Frank sanded and painted it and we still had it around the place after Bill grew up. A family must have lived in this shack in the woods at one time.

Another time, I was walking in the woods on an abandoned logging road and came upon a patch of sweet william in bloom. There was no other remnant of human habitation, but a family must have had a shack at this location and planted those flowers, which became the last survivors.

In the first half of the 20th century, the accepted procedure for disposing of unwanted cans and bottles was to have a private dump site in the woods. It would be conveniently close but hidden from view. Consequently, there are still many locations well away from the beaten path where a pile of cans and bottles can be found. It was also approved practice to sink cans and bottles as well as old motors and other hardware in the middle of the lake where they would be out of sight and gradually disintegrate.

Over the years, most evidence of people's occupation has disappeared from the woods. Any buildings left in the BWCAW were purposely removed. Outside the BWCAW, the buildings and other artifacts have returned to dust or rust.

During our first 20 years at Sawbill, our most significant neighbors were the various people who owned and operated Sawbill Lodge. We were always happy to have this relationship and it was sad to have it end.

After that, our only neighbors living on the Sawbill Trail were those at Pancore Lake, which is halfway between us and Highway 61. Several houses were built there but only one has always been a year-round home. This belongs to our good friend Ellen Hawkins, now married to another good friend, Rick Brandenburg. Rick and Ellen both work for the U.S. Forest Service. Their household includes superkid Willy. Willy is a delightful person, very friendly and always full of enthusiasm about his current activities and his new adventures.

About 1998, a developer was able to buy a section of private land at the intersection of The Grade and the Sawbill Trail, across the trail from the old CCC site. He divided the land into smaller plats and installed one-room prefab log cabins on two of the plots. These are vacation cabins or hunting lodges, intended for occasional use. The big Fourth of July storm of 1999 knocked out most of the trees in this area, leaving these "cabins in the woods" standing nakedly on a bare knoll of land. These cabins were purchased and the owners might now become our nearest neighbors. Actually, the cabins do not seem to be occupied very often and we have not become acquainted with the new residents.

Over the years, our neighborhood has expanded in area. I think that is true for most people, regardless of where they live. We used to live so remotely that we didn't go anywhere and local people didn't want to drive all the way to Sawbill. Driving some distance for work or to attend community activities has become much more the norm. We never feel alone or isolated at Sawbill because so many people drive in here even in the winter. At the same time, we have expanded our activities to a much larger area. We drive 50 miles to Grand

Sweet william, sometimes the only remnant of an old homestead

Marais to attend church each Sunday and we often go there during the week to attend a meeting or event. We drive at least as far as Tofte several times each week. It is part of our routine and we don't give the long drive a second thought. We are surprised from time to time to discover how fast the mileage builds up on our car.

· Chapter 11 ·

Wild Animal Tales

One of the attractions of Sawbill is that it is a great natural wildlife preserve or, one might say, a free, open-air zoo. Animals roam without restriction.

Mammals commonly seen while driving down the road are moose, deer, black bear, red fox, coyotes, wolves, fisher, pine marten, weasels or ermine, snowshoe hare, red squirrels, chipmunks, porcupines, and woodchucks. Beaver, otter, and mink are spotted splashing in the water along the shores of the lakes.

Many people come to the North Woods with high hopes of seeing wildlife and many of them do. Others go home disappointed. Most of these animals are very shy and will make themselves scarce at the first sound of a car or of voices on the lake.

We who live at Sawbill often play a game of keeping a mental list of the wildlife we see on a trip to town and then reporting the count when we get home. We usually see a couple of animals and sometimes half a dozen or more. From our experiences we can offer some tips for increasing the likelihood of seeing animals in the wild.

Suggestions for spotting wildlife are the following:

1. Look for animals around dawn or dusk, rather than in midday.
2. Look for animals near water — creeks, streams, shorelines, and swamps with standing water.
3. Be quiet, especially out on the lakes.
4. Scan the area at the first opportunity to spot a creature before it has a chance to spot you.

Some people come to the North Woods hoping against hope that they won't see a bear. It is a very reasonable attitude. Bears can be a great nuisance. While they have no interest in eating people, some bears have a very strong interest in the food people bring with them. It can be very difficult to persuade them to leave a campsite and sometimes the only solution is for the campers to move to another campsite. On one occasion, two women camping on Alton Lake had a visitor. They stayed up all night guarding their food. The bear was not aggressive but it refused to leave. In the morning, they identified the problem. There were two little cubs up a tree, afraid to come down while there were people around. Mom was not about to leave without them. Usually, though, food is the issue.

It should be noted that the bears in the BWCA are black bears as opposed to grizzly bears. Grizzlies are dangerous to people but it is extremely rare for a black bear to pose any threat to a person. They are, however, highly interested in campers' food. For example, during one year when bears were particularly pesky at wilderness campsites, a bear was so bold as to walk into a camp where several men were cooking dinner. The bear advanced to the fire grate and began to help himself to the goodies. It was unfazed by the shouting and banging of pots and other human threats, so the campers decided to try fire. They arranged some wood immediately behind the bear and lit the fire. That convinced the bear to give up its feast but did not inspire any retaliation on the bear's part. It lumbered peacefully away.

Historically, the bear has a big name in the Tofte area because of the popularity of the Tofte dump. The dump was an open pit just two miles north of the highway at the base of

Carlton Peak. Until the late 1970s, Tofte's garbage was dumped there and, of course, the bears came to feed, immediately followed by onlooking people, both locals and tourists. The dump became famous as a tourist attraction. Pictures made the newspapers in the Twin Cities, and most North Shore visitors included the Tofte dump as one of their main sight-seeing attractions.

There was a large parking area in front of the dump so people could sit in their cars while watching the bears. Of course, it was a great photo opportunity. Cameras snapped as people captured pictures of the bears. Some folks were not content to have a picture of a bear alone but tried to capture the bear with a

"Saturday Night Live" at the Tofte dump became a famous tourist attraction.

person. Parents would lure a bear to stand next to a child by having the child hold out food. One man persuaded a bear to get into his pickup and sit in the passenger seat. We actually observed these things at the dump. They made memorable pictures. It was all good clean fun with seemingly no thought of possible consequences.

We have firsthand knowledge of a Forest Service employee buying Holloway "Black Cow" suckers to feed the bears. He would lure a bear to his car, hand a sucker out the window, and then watch with great amusement as the bear got its jaws stuck in the soft caramel. The bear would roll and writhe on the ground pawing at its mouth while the spectators laughed. This kind of human behavior would be looked upon with much less tolerance today. Some folkways do change and most people no longer find enjoyment in watching an uncomfortable animal. In the early 1980s, in response to federal and state efforts to clean up the environment, Cook County closed its open dumps and people had to find new sources of entertainment.

We have seen a complete turnaround in people's attitudes toward animals over the years. In the 1950s and 1960s, most people still were operating in the pioneer mode. They thought of wild animals as dangerous and as competitors, and the goal was to eliminate them. The state paid a bounty for wolves and other "undesirable" animals. Bears were not bountied, perhaps because their antics have always made them so entertaining.

In 1971, the DNR classified black bears as big-game animals. Before that, they were considered varmints and could be shot on sight without a permit. Bear hunting season now occurs around the first part of September each year and an average of 3,500 bears are taken. This keeps the population stable with northern Minnesota claiming about 2,500 bears in residence during the winter.

In the 1950s, Sawbill Lodge offered a "bear show" to the guests every night. After dinner, the chef put food out behind the kitchen and the guests peered out the windows while the bears feasted. Most bears ate politely but occasionally one would become impatient and try to tear into the shed where garbage was stored. Then the gun came out and that bear was shot. It wasn't until years later

Guests would feed bears behind Sawbill Lodge in the 1950s.

that students of wildlife taught that this was unfair to the animals.

A gradual evolution in the attitude toward animals came to our attention about 1964. Bears are mostly nocturnal, rarely appearing in the daylight. Thus it was that Karl, carrying his 12-gauge shotgun, was roaming the campground late one Friday night looking for a particularly troublesome bear. The DNR had given us blanket permission to deal with bear problems. The bear made its routine appearance and Karl thoughtfully waited until it was near the water's edge to shoot it. Disposing of the body was a major problem that he planned to solve by tying it to a canoe and towing it up the lake to some remote location. So he left the dead bear at the water's edge and went home to bed. Very early the next morning, he returned to the scene and proceeded to tow it away but he wasn't early enough. Some canoeists were already at the landing, setting out on a trip. By Monday morning, we had several telephone calls telling us about a scathing article in the *St. Paul Pioneer Press* regarding the callous cruelty of destroying wildlife at Sawbill. It turned out that one of the Saturday morning canoeists was a woman reporter for the *Pioneer Press* and she did not endorse the idea that the campground needed to be made safe for campers by eliminating bears. After that, we insisted that the game warden take over personally whenever we needed bear control.

Not so long ago, Yellowstone National Park was widely known as a place where bears would gather along the road as people drove through the park. The bears were there to receive food. As the number of visitors to the park increased, this got out of hand. Now, all national parks have strict prohibitions against feeding animals. They also have ingenious garbage cans that animals can't get into. In the Superior National Forest now, most animal feeding is unintentional but still undesirable. All campers receive detailed instructions about protecting their food.

Campers were not the only ones who had trouble with bears making off with their food or destroying their equipment in the search for food. After the dump was closed, we acquired dumpsters and deposited our garbage there each day, to be picked up by the local garbage service once a week. It was a common and unwelcome sight on many a beautiful summer morning to find garbage scattered all around the dumpster on the parking lot, with a bear being the perpetrator. Frank was usually the first one on duty in the morning and the one to discover and clean up the mess. Being the idea man that he is, he soon began developing schemes for preventing this mess. Each new scheme would be touted as the final answer to a frustrated outfitter's prayer and each morning he would discover that he had been outwitted by the bear. It became quite a joke to see who was smarter.

One morning, crew member Becky Heltzer, pursuing her job of taking the trash to the dumpster, returned hastily to the dome to report that there were noises in the dumpster and she didn't dare to open it. Bill accompanied her to the dumpster. There was indeed huffing and puffing inside. They stood behind it and carefully opened a lid. Out popped a young bear that beat a hasty retreat across the parking lot into the woods. Bill finally put chains with padlocks through every lid of every dumpster. It didn't take long before the bears discovered that dumpsters were no longer a source of food and they no longer hung out around the campground. The chains are still on the dumpsters but they are rarely used. It's a rare occasion now when a bear makes the rounds of the campground at night, although there are a few episodes each year.

When there is a problem, the DNR conservation officer (game warden) comes with a baited live trap. Once the bear is caught, he loads the trap on his pick-up and drives it to another area of the woods at least 20 miles away — to an area usually unused by people. There he tranquilizes the bear and puts a tag in its ear before releasing it. With luck, Mr. or Mrs. Bruin establishes a new territory. On occasion, this does not work and the bear is back before the game warden can get back to his base. Then the process is repeated. It is extremely rare for a private individual to shoot a nuisance bear these days, although the DNR will still exterminate a particularly troublesome animal.

Bears frequented the Sawbill campground in our early years. I saw my first bear in the wild as I walked through the campground during my first year at Sawbill. I was on the road above the lake and the bear was wandering along the edge of the lake, less than 50 feet away. We both kept walking. I know I was holding my breath.

Our daughter Ranna at age nine also saw her first bear that summer. She was on her way at dusk to take a sauna at the lodge when she came face to face with a bear on the path. In this case, both child and bear hastily changed direction. A few years later, the parents of one of our guides were staying on the campground. Mrs. Snyder was standing at one end of the picnic table working at her Coleman stove to prepare dinner when she glanced up to find a bear seated at the other end of the picnic table. She reported later that her heart stopped and her body began to tremble. By the time she recovered her composure, the bear had decided to stand up and move on.

Once, when the children were still young, we were camped on an island in Ogishkemuncie Lake. After breakfast, we were out in the canoes when a group of Girl Scouts approached. They pointed to the shore behind us where a large bear was pacing the hillside. We paddled back to our camp to see about protecting our food. In those days, we packed canned bacon. After we had eaten our bacon that morning, I had poured the leftover grease into the empty can. We secured our food and then I carried the can of bacon grease down to the water's edge and left it there. When we returned from fishing, the can was licked clean but nothing else was bothered.

We were not yet hanging food packs in those days, so whenever we left a camp for the day the procedure was to take the food pack with us. This is still the best possible plan. I will never forget the emotional reaction I had one time when we had left our camp for the day and returned in the late afternoon to find that it had been ransacked. We had left all the cooking and eating gear on the table, neatly stacked and covered. There was not a crumb of food in the camp, but it was evident that the bear had been there and checked out every pot and pan. Nothing had been harmed in the least, but there was this distressing emotional reaction of having been violated. I experienced the same feeling when our buildings were robbed several times. Nothing of great value was ever lost, but the idea that an unknown person had come into the house and sorted through things was painful. I am amazed that an unwelcome bear can cause the same feelings.

Knowing this, we could perhaps have been more sympathetic to a family camped on Alton Lake one summer. Bill and I were also camped on Alton. As we were headed home on our last day, we saw the family pull out from their campsite and paddle across the lake to fish. When we paddled past their campsite, Bill spotted a bear. We paddled right over to their campsite where Bill jumped out of the canoe, ran up to the site, and chased the bear back into the woods. He found all kinds of food spread out on their picnic table and he knew the bear would be right back. Their canoe was in sight but across the lake at some distance. We tried to signal to them to come back but they pretended not to see us. So we paddled across the lake to give them the message. They didn't want to be friendly with strangers but when we finally got within earshot and yelled,

"There's a bear in your camp," they gave us their full attention. They were amazed at the news because they said they had carefully put their bread in the food pack and hung the pack. For some reason, they thought bread was the only thing the bear would want. Having delivered our message, we proceeded on our way. Back at Sawbill a few hours later, we heard that a family from Chicago, who had been camping on Alton, had rushed in with their rented gear in great disarray. They said they were ending their trip after only one night out and heading straight home because a bear had come to their camp!

In our early years at Sawbill, Frank and I sometimes went on an overnight camping trip. Since we had to be back to open the store at 7 a.m., we got up early. One day, we were walking up the road from the Sawbill landing at 5:30 a.m. when we saw a bear walking ahead of us. It walked faster than we could but we caught up with it in a metal shed behind our store where we had cases of food stored. He or she had just taken down from the shelf a carton of 50 packages of "pancake mix for four." It was frightened by our appearance and departed in haste. If we had discovered the misdeed a split second later, we would have lost the whole case of food and had a horrible mess to clean up. We called the game warden and received authorization to shoot this bear. Karl, our designated bear hunter, set up a bait station but the bear never returned.

Another time, we found a pickup camper on the parking lot with its back door torn loose. Inside were large muddy paw prints all over the beds and the kitchen counter. Cupboard doors had been opened and food was scattered everywhere. It was the kind of mess that only a bear can make. Besides, he left his calling card of footprints. We don't know how it happened that the bear was able to open this door but we certainly felt a lot of sympathy for the owner of the pickup.

Bears do not always leave so promptly when people confront them. The current recommendation is to chase them away by making noise or by throwing rocks. Frank and I and our grandson Adam were camped on a small lake near Snowbank Lake a few years ago. Frank had gone to bed and Adam and I were playing cards on a big flat rock overlooking the lake. I glanced down toward the shore and saw a black animal walking there. At the time, we had a large black dog and my first thought was, "There's Hazel. Did we bring Hazel with us?" Then there was a moment of truth. It was a bear! Although we yelled, Mr. Bear proceeded right up to our camp site and began to circle the tent where Frank was sleeping. We threw quite a few rocks before it very slowly withdrew. We weren't frightened because every bit of our food was in the food pack hung high between two trees.

Once a group was sitting around our living room about 10 o'clock in the evening when we heard a noise on the front porch. We looked out and found a bear lying on the deck lapping up dog food from a dog dish we had left out. After that, we kept the dog dishes inside.

Most campers never see a bear at their campsite or anywhere else out in the woods. One bit of wisdom that every camper should know is that bear problems are very cyclical. Just as the grouse population varies from year to year — apparently on a 10-year cycle — bear problems follow a cycle. The conventional wisdom is that bears don't bother people in "good berry years." I don't understand how this could be the true since bears get up from their months of hibernation about April 1 and berries don't become available until midsummer. Normally, we never see a bear around our buildings or around the campground until July. One year, however, bears arrived in April and destroyed every bird feeder we had as they frantically ate the sunflower seeds. Something unusual in nature was going on that year. Bears, like grouse, undoubtedly vary in the size of their population from year to year, and certainly there are years when bears show no interest in people food. Then there are years when bears seem frantic for food and are very much in evidence. This is a subject that could use more research.

Bears are fun to have around and very entertaining to observe, partly because of their human-like behavior. It is no longer acceptable to have caged bears on display for tourists' benefit or to torment bears for people's entertainment. For years, business establishments along the North Shore would obtain a cub from Canada at the beginning of the summer season. It was kept in a cage and tourists enjoyed watching it drink pop out of a bottle just as a human would. Unfortunately, at the end of the summer, the malnourished animal had to be destroyed.

The Forest Service recognized people's fascination with bears when it made Smokey Bear its mascot and educator to impress forest users with the need to protect the woods from fire. However, when Smokey appeared at Fourth of July celebrations, he was not a live bear but a person in a bear costume.

Smokey Bear and Woodsy Owl hug Mary Alice at a Fourth of July celebration.

Moose are the animals that tourists hope to see in the wild. We have a great many moose around Sawbill. There are not so many deer as moose since deer do not usually inhabit the same territory. Deer have a problem getting around in deep snow so they regularly move out of the woods in the fall and gradually make their way down toward the shore of Lake Superior where snow cover is much lighter. In the spring, they gradually move

We often see moose standing in the water.

north so that some deer are seen in the canoe country. Usually, they are seen at the water's edge drinking water. Deer are beautiful but they do not inspire the awe that moose do.

Moose also are usually seen at the water's edge or in the water. I was camping on the north end of Alton Lake with two friends, Alyce Monten and Marion Calph, just a few years ago. We were sipping our morning coffee when we glanced up and saw that we were being observed from about 20 feet away. We all remained motionless momentarily. Then Marion reached for her camera causing Mrs. Moose to turn around and walk away. I followed her at a discreet distance as she walked down to the lakeshore and right to the place where our canoe was pulled up. For a moment, I had visions of a canoe with a very large hole in the bottom, but she stepped gracefully over it and continued on her way.

We saw our very first moose on the Sawbill Trail as we headed home to Duluth in our Volkswagen microbus in 1958. The moose was standing on the road and Frank stopped to give it the right of way. It was a cow that chose to examine the microbus. We were in a very unique vehicle for its time and it inspired a lot of stares from people but we didn't expect that kind of interest from a moose. It walked up and peered into the side window, then walked slowly all the way around the vehicle peering into each window. All the occupants of the car sat frozen, staring back. We evidently passed inspection as she walked away and let us continue on our way.

The first baby moose I ever saw was on the shore of Kelly Lake a few years later. As my daughter, Ranna, my daughter-in-law Nancy, and I came over the portage from Burnt Lake, we saw this animal standing in the water on the other side of the lake. It was the size of a deer and the color of a deer but it was not the shape of a deer. None of us had any idea what it was. When we came close enough to get a clearer view, we could identify it as a young moose.

It's not unheard of for moose to come right up to our house. The first time I saw a moose just outside my window was on Easter morning. The children were still young and I had gotten up early to hide the Easter eggs inside the house and store. Just outside the west windows of the store stood a moose! Another time in the middle of the day, we were experiencing a violent thunderstorm. I looked out the window and saw a moose standing in the yard right outside the window. Apparently, the open area seemed safer in the storm. Still another time, I was walking home from the store after dark followed by our Samoyeds, Aurora and Borealis, two very mellow dogs. Suddenly, Boris pushed ahead of me growling and snarling. In a few more steps, even I could see that there was a moose standing in the driveway right in front of our house. It responded to Boris's complaints and left promptly.

We see many more moose in the winter than we do in the summer. They can be a nuisance on the road in the winter. It was the winter of 1995-96 when we had a record amount of snowfall that we also set a record for "moose-on-the-road" troubles. One morning, we were held up for 45 minutes as we tried to make our way to Grand Marais over the back roads. We rounded a corner to see two moose standing on the road. One immediately headed into the woods as they usually do but the other one started walking down the road ahead of us. We had a long lesson in moose behavior as we followed this moose cow down the road. She stopped to nibble at branches. She crisscrossed the road, apparently looking for a good place to get off. At times, she stopped for a period of meditation. Honking the horn would startle her into action but only to walk down the road again. There were side roads that looked like possible points of exit to us. She examined and rejected each of them. I think the problem had to do with the separation from her companion. We were between them and she couldn't figure out how to get past us just as we couldn't figure out how to get past her.

Unlike bears, moose are usually perceived as peaceful and non-threatening. I have come upon moose a number of times when I was cross-country skiing. They didn't run away but neither did they go after me. They stood their ground and I went on my way. Only in the fall during mating season do moose pose a threat to people. They have been known to chase and stomp people at this time. A hunter in the woods in the fall may need to get behind or up a tree to escape from a belligerent bull moose.

Bill had an experience not many years ago that inspires a bit more caution. He was driving home in our Subaru station wagon late at night after a meeting on the Gunflint Trail. He had just turned on to The Grade when he saw a scrawny cow moose in the road ahead of him. He cautiously pulled off to the side and turned off his headlights, thinking he would give her every opportunity to do her thing and get off the road. She dithered and dawdled, going from one side of the road to the other. Finally, she turned and started back toward him on the other side of the road. When she seemed set on her course past him, he turned on his lights ready to proceed on his way. Evidently this startled her. She turned toward him and attacked, bringing her front hooves down on the windshield of the car. Bill tried to duck but the seat belt he was wearing held him

tightly in place. The windshield was shattered but fortunately the safety glass held the pieces together and the deadly front hooves didn't come through, but they did smash the front fender and damage the side of the car. Although his view through the windshield was seriously impaired, Bill managed to drive home. The insurance adjuster whom he talked to on the telephone the next day was flabbergasted. "You were attacked by what?!!" The insurance company is accustomed to claims resulting from people hitting deer or deer jumping out on the road and hitting cars, but this was something else.

Moose are fairly gregarious creatures — at least in the winter. They rarely travel alone and we have seen as many as five bulls with huge racks hanging out together. Moose drop their racks each January. In the spring, new racks appear and grow very fast. Each year, another prong is added and the new rack is a little larger than the last one. It seems a terrible drain on a living organism to produce such a large appendage so quickly.

A moose attacked our car and smashed the windshield — while Bill was at the wheel.

Winter snow provides a great record of animal activity. Footprints in the snow show clearly what is happening. In stormy weather, animals tend to hole up and no evidence of them is seen. As soon as the weather clears, footprints are everywhere.

Fox walk in such a way that one foot is put down directly in front of the other, making an absolutely straight line of little prints. We see lots of fox prints as we drive down the road and often see the actual fox at night, crossing the road or walking down the shoulder of the road.

Another animal that runs across the road, particularly after storms, is the fisher, the larger relative of the weasel and pine marten. There are a number of animals in the weasel family. One of the smallest is the animal generally known in its summer dress as a weasel. In the winter, it turns all white except for the tip of its tail, which is black. It becomes a beautiful animal, known as an ermine. We would welcome some ermine for their beauty and also because they are known as good mousers. Sawbill Lodge once claimed to have a resident weasel living under the refrigerator in the kitchen all summer, controlling the mouse population. However, we see these animals very rarely.

The next larger animal is the pine marten. It is about the size of a house cat and has a cute puckish face much like a cat. Martens are the most active animal in the woods. In the winter, their tracks are everywhere, not because there are a lot of individuals but because one individual covers a lot of territory. We see them often, bounding across the snow in our yard. If a marten feels cornered, it bounds up a tree, often going to the very top of the tree. We do not put out food for the marten and they have little interest in the sunflower seeds that we have for the birds. They do like suet and will tear a suet feeder apart, so we don't put suet out for the birds.

The fisher is the next largest of the species. It has very dark brown, almost black, fur. This is the animal also known as a sable.

Fishers are rare and are never seen anywhere near human habitation. Other members of the family are otters and mink. The largest member of the weasel family is the wolverine, which is essentially nonexistent around here, and seen only in zoos.

A beautiful ermine darts across our woodpile in the hunt for mice.

It must have been late April 1959 when we were up for the weekend to start getting the place ready for summer. Around dinner time Saturday evening, our good-natured, friendly game warden, Earl Nelms, dropped in. He was flushed and grinning from ear to ear. He said he had heard rumors that there were some beaver poachers camping on Kelso Lake and he proposed to hike up there to look for them. The ice had already pulled away from the shore of the lake and I wouldn't have stepped out on it for a million dollars, but after a short visit he set out. I'm not inclined to worry much, but I worried a lot that night. I was just sure that he would fall through the ice. I probably should have worried that his poachers might prove belligerent! He found them camped up on Kelso Lake with about eight otter pelts, a much more serious offense than trapping beaver. Otter were very scarce at that time. I was very relieved when he returned safely.

We see wolves very rarely. We are fortunate enough to hear them occasionally. One of our first years at Sawbill, we camped out on an island in north Sawbill. During the night, I listened for a long time to a chorus with many voices so synchronized and beautiful that it made me think of a symphony orchestra. I assumed that it was loons but learned years later that it was wolves. Wolves were extremely rare at the time. They were declared an endangered species in 1966. At that time a total of eight wolves had been counted in our area by wildlife specialists. There was also a protected population on Isle Royale.

One September in the early 1970s, we were at Sawbill for the weekend. Business was very slow so we had time to socialize a little and we had invited friends for dinner. It was almost ready when they called to say they couldn't make it due to a family emergency. Within the hour, a tired, cold, and bedraggled couple appeared at the store. Frank suggested that they take saunas and he invited them to join us for dinner.

They were Ewan and Jennie Clarkson, who had come from Devon, England, to do some research on wolves in preparation for a book Ewan had been commissioned to write. He has written a number of very successful novels featuring animals that inhabit the coastal waters near his home. The first of his books was called *Halic: the Gray Seal*.

The wolf book was to be nonfiction and he wanted to have some firsthand experience with wolves. While still in England, he was advised to visit Isle Royale. Therefore, he and Jennie had flown to this country and arrived in Michigan ready to go to Isle Royale, only to find that the island closed down after Labor Day.

In Michigan, they happened to meet a Forest Service employee who had once worked on the Tofte Ranger District. He suggested that they go to Sawbill. They found that they could take a bus around the west end of Lake Superior as far as Tofte. But then it was still 24 miles to Sawbill with no apparent transportation, so they hiked! They would have accepted a ride but no one came by to offer.

They had brought their camping gear for Isle Royale so they were prepared to camp and they stopped halfway up the Trail at the Temperance River Campground where they spent the night. They arrived at Sawbill at the end of the second day in a cold rain.

Long saunas and dry clothes, followed by a substantial dinner in a warm house, revived their spirits as well as their bodies. Besides, it was one of those rare occasions when you know immediately that you are destined to be friends. The next morning, they purchased appropriate food from our store and set off on a canoe trip. They went for a fortnight, as they put it. Two weeks is a long trip and the weather was not pleasant that September, but they stayed out the whole time and were good sports. However, they were very disappointed by the fact that they still didn't see a single wolf.

Frank knew that most wolf study goes on in the winter so he suggested that they come back in the winter. Bill was living alone at Sawbill that winter, so there was plenty of room for them to stay in our house. They decided to accept the offer and, the following January, they flew into Minneapolis. They stayed with us in Minneapolis and then we drove them up to Sawbill. The following morning, we were all up early. A pickup with two or three very excited men pulled up to the store. They said, "Come quickly. There are wolves getting drinks out of Sawbill Creek. We just saw them as we drove by." I dashed off to alert Ewan and Jennie and we all rushed down to the creek. We saw by the tracks in the snow that the story was true but the wolves were gone.

During the month Ewan and Jennie spent at Sawbill, they tried every conceivable method to observe wolves. Back in England, someone had taught Ewan to howl like a wolf. He was afraid to try it in the neighborhood around his home but he practiced as he drove on the motorway, attracting some puzzled looks from passing motorists. While at Sawbill, he contacted the game warden and other local nature experts and tried everything they suggested. Ewan and Jenny learned to cross-country ski and spent time in the woods every day. Finally, the month was almost over and desperation was setting in. Ewan's howls brought responses from wolves on Alton Lake but no viewing. The game warden was persuaded to participate to the extent of providing a fresh road-killed deer, which Ewan and Bill hauled to Alton Lake and put out on the ice. They made frequent trips over to check it until they could see that it had been discovered and was being eaten. Then they built a blind for themselves on the shore so they could watch. Although the wolves evidently came and ate during the night, the humans were never able to see them. Ewan did get a wonderful picture of a bald eagle feeding. Finally, their time was up and they flew back to England.

Ewan wrote the book. In it, he admits frankly that he never saw a wolf. Nevertheless, it turned out to be an excellent book. Ewan went on to write more novels featuring animals. Our friendship continued over the years. They came back to visit Sawbill one summer, and we flew to England to visit them during an Easter vacation.

Shortly after Ewan's study, Dr. David Mech came to Ely and began his research on wolves, spotting them by airplane, capturing them, and equipping them with radio collars so they can be tracked. In 1965, Minnesota stopped paying a bounty of $35 for each wolf killed. An average of 300 wolves had been killed annually and the population was almost extinct. Wolves were included in the *Endangered Species Act* passed by Congress in 1966 and again in 1973, protecting the remaining animals. By 1989, a wolf population survey estimated a statewide wolf population of 1,550 to 1,750 animals. By 2004, the population had become quite stable, and the wolf will probably be delisted from its endangered classification.

Footprints in the snow show us that we have a lot of snowshoe hare living around us but we rarely see these neighbors during the day. The ones we do see are hopping along the road at night. Headlights seem to confuse and distress them and they run frantically from side to side. There are numerous smaller rodents such as mice and shrews. They live in holes also and their habits are made evident by tiny delicate footprints in the snow.

We live in the midst of small animals and birds. Chipmunks hibernate during the winter but we see red squirrels every day. Their antics are entertaining as they chase each other up and down trees, sometimes across the snow, sometimes jumping from tree to tree. Try as we will, we have not yet found the answer to keeping squirrels out of bird feeders. Squirrels live in holes in the ground and their natural food seems to be found in pinecones. They strip the scales off the cones of the white pine to get to the seeds. Piles of stripped cones are often seen on the forest floor. One year, a squirrel took up winter residence in our store and left a huge mess of stripped pinecones on top of the maps on the map table.

Our most exciting rare animal sighting occurred in 1992 on a Sunday at high noon. As we drove down The Grade, we saw an animal standing in the road. As we drew closer, we saw that it was a large cougar or mountain lion. It looked just like the female lions we have seen in zoos, only slightly smaller. As we approached, it moved on across the road very slowly and ambled down to the river to get a drink. Of course, we didn't have a camera with us. In recent years, there have been a number of cougar sightings plus evidence of reproduction.

Seeing the animals in our great open-air zoo is one of the great joys of living at Sawbill. The wild animals make our long drives on the Sawbill Trail and other back roads into a continuing source of entertainment.

· Chapter 12 ·

——— Animals, Not So Wild ———

Sawbill is such a treasured and beloved place to many people. By now, we know a number of families who have three generations with strong attachments to Sawbill. Sometimes we feel loved, too, just by virtue of being in this place that inspires such affection.

But often, it seems that "man hath no greater love" than the love for dogs. Why is it that we all love our dogs so much? Is it because dogs love us unconditionally? We often are impressed by the attachment people have for our dogs. Many times, our dogs are greeted by name by people who have no idea what our names are. Children rush in looking for the dogs they remember from the year before, and they ask anxiously for them if they are not immediately in view.

The history of Sawbill would certainly not be complete without recalling the dogs that lived here. At Sawbill Lodge in the 1950s, the cocker spaniel named Tucker was king of the hill. Tucker achieved worldwide fame when he tried to protect his owner from a bear.

Dick Raiken was out in the yard raking leaves off the paths when a black bear appeared. Tucker saw it first and went for it. Dick thought the bear was going to hurt Tucker so he drove the bear off with his rake. The story made the news and was copied especially in the newspapers that went to our armed forces around the globe. Letters came back to the Lodge from the far corners of earth with the clipping enclosed.

At Sawbill Outfitters, our favorite breed for many years was the dachshund. When we first came to Sawbill, we had a black dachshund named Sieglinde or Siggy. Our children were always great animal lovers and Ranna promptly adopted and tamed a chipmunk that lived in her bedroom. The animals co-existed contentedly for the most part. Then one day, the chipmunk raced through the house with Siggy in hot pursuit. The chipmunk dove through a crack between the floor and the logs but its tail remained in Siggy's mouth. All of us were very upset by this performance, especially the chipmunk — who didn't return.

Bill had a special pet in the house also, a small garter snake. The only problem was that the snake disappeared without fanfare and we didn't know for the whole summer if it was still in the house or not. Probably it wasn't. Years later, a snake lived in the utility room next to the laundry under the water heater. Bill's children loved to visit it during the summer. It was a preferable home for it.

The last and most well-known of our dachshunds was Freue (pronounced "Froya"), a small red dachshund that was at Sawbill from the latter part of the 1960s through the 1970s. She lived for 17 years and she certainly was convinced that she owned the place and was in full charge.

She was an enthusiastic canoeist and skier. One winter, she won a Kodak medal for skiing 50 kilometers! (Actually, she didn't wear skis, but she did accompany skiers for that distance and undoubtedly expended more effort than the skiers.) They skied on the frozen lake a lot. She not only followed but made extensive side forays to check out scents which only she detected. Anyone who skied that far during the season could send their documentation to Kodak, so Karl sent her name in along with his own. He filled in her age on the

Freue, our medal-winning crew dog, settles in for one of many canoe trips.

proper blank, six years old. Kodak didn't question this accomplishment and sent out her medal.

In the summer, she went along in the canoe as often as she possibly could. She would climb on top of the softest pack and make herself a comfortable nest while her people paddled. When the canoe approached shore, she would perch on the bow of the canoe and jump out before the canoe touched land.

She adored fishing, becoming very excited by the mere sight of a fishing rod or even a lure. When a fish was caught, she really went into high gear and she stood guard over any fish placed in the bottom of the canoe.

A memorable escapade occurred when she went for a hike with some family members and friends on a trail between Sawbill Lodge and Alton Lake. The path ended at a campsite where they stopped to rest and visit. When they were ready to depart, Freue was nowhere to be found, so they hiked back, thinking she would find her own way home. She didn't, but several days later, a canoe pulled up to the landing with a familiar figure riding high on a pack. Two campers who were strangers to us had moved into the campsite and found it equipped with a dog. Freue was content to camp with them so they let her stay. Later, they brought her back to civilization with them, where she was recognized and returned home.

Freue was the great protector. She would sit for hours in front of a woodpile or a hole in the ground waiting for a chipmunk or a squirrel to reappear. She also chased bears. One day, Powell and Babbie Krueger were at our house sitting in the dining room having a glass of iced tea. We heard Freue barking and looked out the window to see a bear shinnying up a tree with Freue barking at the bottom, her front paws up on the trunk of the tree. Powell was the chief photographer for the *Minneapolis Star and Tribune* during his working career and he declared the sight of a dachshund treeing a bear one of the prize shots of his lifetime. Of course, he didn't have a camera with him at the time.

In the 1970s, our allegiance to a breed changed to Samoyeds. Tim Norman, who works for the Forest Service, had a Samoyed that had puppies that were subsequently distributed around the area. We fell in love with these big, fluffy, white dogs. They are natives of Siberia and thus ideal candidates for enjoying our cold winters. They also tend to be very friendly and loving, a requirement for any dog living at Sawbill in the summer.

Our first Samoyed was a male named Howlin' Wolf ("Wolf" for short). He was named after a favorite jazz singer of Karl's. Wolf loved to go camping. He not only went with us but he tried his best to go with anyone else who would have him. He particularly enjoyed winter camping. We first discovered this when we left him outside while we went to Grand Marais to attend church one Sunday morning. We were panic-stricken to find him gone when we returned home. Several days later, a young couple came in from their winter camping trip and Wolf was with them. They had been simply delighted to have him along and kept in touch with us through the rest of his life, checking on his well-being.

After that, if we were aware of people departing on a winter outing, we shut Wolf in the house for several hours. He was not easily deterred but sometimes followed their tracks or scent once he was let loose. He went with two young men up to Zenith Lake on one occasion. They loved having him and reported that they didn't mind sharing their food. However, they all emerged from their tent after an afternoon siesta to find a wolf standing on the ice some distance away. The fellows dove into their tent for their camera but Wolf promptly chased his fellow canine away. His camper friends were not pleased about that.

Wolf was such a great and lovable dog but he became very ill in his third year and finally was in such distress that he had to be put down. We consulted vets in the area and even contacted the University of Minnesota School of Veterinary Medicine but to no avail in identifying his problem.

A year or two after we moved to Sawbill as full-time residents, a pair of Samoyeds came to live with us and Freue. We wanted to give them Russian names and also names that would denote the fact that they were brother and sister. We ended up naming them Aurora and Borealis ("Boris" for short). Once again, at about three years of age, Boris developed health problems. First, he lost his eyesight and went through the winter almost totally blind. When I went skiing, Boris followed along by hitting the back tips of my skis with his front paws. It slowed me down a bit. Otherwise, he let Aurora lead the way and he followed her.

One day, he went with me as I walked over to the Lodge. When we crossed the bridge over Sawbill Creek, he missed the bridge and fell into the water. He couldn't get out because he couldn't see which way to go. He was too big for me to pull out so I had to get Mike Senty down off the roof of the Lodge where he was working to help pull Boris out of the creek. By spring, he began to lose his fur and to yelp in pain just as Wolf had done. Still we could get no diagnosis and consequently no remedy for his problems and he had to be put down.

Aurora and Boris, a happy pair of Samoyeds on the ski trail

Aurora stayed healthy and lived for 17 years. When Aurora and Boris were young, Boris was the protector and Aurora always followed quietly behind him. When he was gone, she took over as guard dog. She spent the summer stretched out on the cool tile in the store and never twitched when customers came into the store as long as there were a lot of people around. However, when she and I were alone, she became very alert and was clearly looking after me. If a bear put in an appearance anywhere in the area, she was after it in an instant and chased it away. For several years, she made sure there were no bears in the campground at night.

When Aurora slept in the house at night, she usually slept right next to our bed. Early one morning about 4 o'clock, she suddenly jumped up barking loudly and ran out of the room. Frank jumped out of bed and followed her to the little greenhouse attached to our kitchen. He was just in time to see a bear backing out through the torn screen door with Aurora calling the shots. What if the bear had gotten all the way in?!

All our dogs tend to gain weight in the summer. It is our rule to feed them only dog food, a practice recommended by veterinarians. During the summer, however, it is not at all uncommon for campground residents to come to the store in the morning, proudly announcing that they have shared their French toast or pancakes. Our efforts to discourage this sort of thing were rarely taken seriously. Occasionally, we heard that campers had shared involuntarily but that was rare or else the campers were too nice to tell us about our dogs' transgressions. What really amazed us, though, was when campground returnees would come into the store asking for Aurora because they had brought her a present — a steak! This happened more than once.

Aurora really disgraced herself and us one October during moose hunting season. I awoke early one morning and headed for the kitchen. In the dim light of an autumn morning, I saw a strange dark spot on our new dining room carpet. At first, I thought someone had dropped a jacket on the floor in front of the closet door but fortunately I hadn't yet touched it when I could see that it was a disgusting mess rather than a piece of cloth. Quite some time was devoted to cleaning it up, whatever it was. No one confessed to making the mess. However, when we opened the store that morning, we heard from a successful but somewhat distressed moose hunter that he had carefully removed the liver from his moose and left it in a canoe at the dock and now it was gone! Uh oh!

A happier story was told by a young woman camper shortly after that. There was a campsite just adjacent to the parking lot at the time. This young couple had arrived late in the evening after our store was closed. Noticing this convenient campsite, they set up their tent. It was a very cold night and the young woman fell asleep comfortably aware of the warm body in a sleeping bag next to her. When she awoke in the morning, she was startled to find that there was a warm body on each side of her. Moving as little as possible, she ventured to put out a hand and felt fur. She was too frightened to scream, but eventually she dared to raise her head and look. A big white dog was sound asleep next to her. Aurora woke up, too, and quietly exited the same way she had come in.

The next canine resident at Sawbill was Bill and Cindy's beloved dog Hazel. She was all black in color but part black Lab and part golden retriever in breed. Like the male Samoyeds before her, Hazel became ill at an early age — about four. The onset of her illness was very sudden. She was in a car accident and hit her head on the windshield. Her troubles started shortly after that. She was still alive when the vet realized that she had blastomycosis, but it was too late to save her. This is a fungal disease of unknown origin. The fungus can live in the body without causing any serious trouble but a severe blow can activate the disease. Theories are that dogs may acquire the fungus by digging in the ground or digging and scratching in rotting wood.

After that, Cindy acquired a large full-breed golden retriever from a friend who guaranteed a dog with an especially laid-back and mild-mannered personality. Gust was born in the spring of 1990. He lived up to his guarantee and scarcely ever became excited in his whole life. After four years, Bill and Cindy felt that Gust needed a companion and they purchased a full sister named Sunny. Bill and Cindy have named all their dogs after area lakes — Hazel (in the Lady Chain), Gust (on The Grade Road), and Sun High Lake (near Wonder Lake). The winter that Sunny was three, she also contracted blastomycosis. By now, Bill and Cindy were able to recognize the symptoms immediately. They interrupted their Christmas celebration to rush her to the vet in Duluth and thus saved her life. She had months of expensive medication and had to have one eye removed but otherwise recovered completely.

In the fall of 2000, an opportunity arose to buy another golden retriever. This one is not related to the first two, but his ancestry is well known in the area and it seemed safe to assume that he also would be friendly and laid back. He was christened Homer for the lake near Brule.

By this time, Gust was showing his age. He had a white muzzle and was moving with difficulty. It appeared that he had arthritis in

Homer, a laid-back golden retriever, joined our crew in 2000.

his back legs. He balked at climbing stairs and also at walking on bare wood floors where his legs tended to slip out from under him. One evening in April 2001, the dogs were not around home at dusk as was their usual habit. Soon Sunny came home alone. Bill immediately went out looking for Gust. With Sunny leading the way, they walked down to the lake that was beginning its spring breakup. There was open water at the mouth of the creek and it was there that they found Gust. The dogs had evidently jumped into the water, a common practice for them, but Gust had been unable to get himself out and had drowned. It was a tragic ending, bemoaned by many friends who got the news on the Sawbill web page.

Cats have been much less outstanding at Sawbill as they tend to be reclusive. Still, many people will remember Tamarack. She came to Sawbill because a summer employee, Laurie Till, had seen a "bad mouse year" at Sawbill the previous summer and she decided we needed cats to cope with the problem. She called just before arriving for the summer and said a friend's cat had just had kittens and could she bring a pair of them with her. They came, already named Spruce and Tamarack. Those kittens caused far more damage that summer than the mice ever had.

More to the point, Laurie's plans changed during the summer and she could no longer keep a cat, so we put up a sign in the dome, "Free Kittens." Spruce very quickly found a home but Tamarack stayed with us. She matured into a fine black cat and became a valued member of the family.

When she was quite young, she often slept on top of the cash register that gave off a bit of heat or under the counter on top of the towels we had for rent to shower customers. She loved that spot and we had to make special arrangements for her bed so that the customer towels were kept clean. Occasionally, she roamed through the campground and then she would often be brought back to the store in the arms of a small girl who thought she had found a stray. When we went for walks in the winter, the dogs were always eager to accompany us. Tamarack invariably declined the invitation but she would manage to be outside and would trail behind us at a respectable distance.

There was no doubt she was a cat. Her chief hobby was playing hockey. We provided her with a small flat object and she would dribble it from one end of the house to the other until it finally would be knocked "out of bounds" (i.e., out of her reach).

She always got along well with the dogs. She liked to curl up for a nap with Freue, but she liked to tease Aurora. She would lie on the piano bench near the front door. Aurora quickly learned that walking by to get to the front door meant that a paw would suddenly shoot out at her. I am sure Aurora was never actually touched but she would studiously avoid this situation for long periods. Tamarack undoubtedly savored her power. She lived to be 16 years old, not showing her age except possibly by becoming less active. One night, she went out as usual and soon afterward I heard a loud wail such as only a cat can make. We never saw any sign of Tamarack again. Perhaps she was carried away by an owl.

We vowed not to have any more animals as we were traveling and away from home a great deal. We actually stuck to that resolu-

Teva watches a pine marten on our deck railing.

tion for several years. Gradually, we began talking more and more about how nice it had been to have a cat and reminiscing about how Tamarack had entertained us with her antics.

Then fate intervened. (Maybe there was some human intervention, too.) Our granddaughter Clare called us from Duluth with a touching story about a kitten whose owner had become ill and couldn't keep her. The woman had given the kitten to Clare's accordion teacher, who couldn't keep her either. Clare asked if she could bring the kitten home for a one-week trial period to see if we might like to have her. She telephoned each of us separately and each of us very tentatively agreed that we would give it a try. Eight-month-old Teva arrived at our house later that day. We don't know anything about her heritage but she bears a close resemblance to a Maine coon cat.

Teva's trial period probably lasted an hour before we were convinced that we wanted her to stay and she seemed to feel the same way about her new home. She has proven to be a great pet for older people, friendly and affectionate but relatively quiet and sedate from the very beginning. Like a dog, she always meets us at the door when we come home. She doesn't disguise her interest in going for walks with us, but of course follows at some distance, never walking with us as a dog would. We continue to be pleased to have Teva living with us.

· Chapter 13 ·

Feathered Friends

Birds are a never-ending source of entertainment at Sawbill. When we first visited Sawbill in the winter of 1956, Vi and Ken Osman introduced us to the joys of bird-watching. They sat in front of their picture window by the hour watching the birds at the bird feeder. At night, they illuminated the feeder with a floodlight and the show continued with flying squirrels sailing down.

Our feeders always have a good number of black-capped chickadees and a few red-breasted nuthatches. We have an occasional white-breasted nuthatch, which is a larger bird and one much more common a little farther south. The white-breasted nuthatch is generally seen marching up and down the trunk of a tree on patrol for insects. It may be joined by brown creepers, little birds that never come to a feeder but walk down tree trunks in search of food. When they reach the bottom, they must fly back up to the top of the runway and start over.

Our most colorful birds are grosbeaks of various types, so named because of their large bills made for seed cracking. They are large birds, almost as big as blue jays.

Evening grosbeaks are bright yellow with black and white markings. They come through in waves all year round, stay for a few days, and then move on. They are often seen in the summer on the gravel road where they sit in flocks of one to two dozen eating the gravel that is necessary for their digestion. They make a spectacular display.

Pine grosbeaks are here only in the winter. They are described as ground feeders and have only in the past five years started coming to our feeding trays. They are basically gray birds with their colors subtly blended into their overall appearance. Males are mostly red on the upper half of their bodies while females have a subtle yellow-orange blend mixed into the gray. We love having them.

Rose-breasted grosbeaks come to the feeders only in the spring and fairly infrequently even then, but what a treat they are. The male wears a sharply defined black tuxedo with a bright rose shirt while the shy female wears all brown. They are somewhat smaller than the other grosbeaks but larger than the purple finches.

One of our least-known birds, at least to visitors who live south of us, is the Canada jay. It looks a bit like a giant chickadee and has a beautiful flight pattern. In our area, it is at the southernmost edge of its range as one might guess from its name. It is a very friendly bird, also known in Ojibwe as "wiiski jack" or translated, camp robber, because it will come readily to a picnic table and partake of the goodies or it will eat out of a person's hand. Once when we were camping, Frank stretched out full length on the ground and placed a peanut on his chest. The Canada jay residing at that campsite came right in for the peanut.

Our neighbor, Ellen Hawkins, carried food in her pockets one winter and the jays were quickly conditioned to follow her as she

A Canada jay flies in for a peanut.

walked or skied, waiting for her to bring out the refreshments. Our granddaughter Clare has trained the jays to eat from her hand on her front deck.

We have a lot of blue jays as well, a species unrelated to Canada jays. Blue jays are not popular with some people but we find them well-behaved. These birds, along with the various red birds that come to our feeder, provide a delightful color contrast in the white snow.

For red birds, we do not have cardinals but we do have a lot of purple finch. Audubon described them as birds that look as if they have been dipped in raspberry juice. A similar looking bird that passes through in large flocks during the winter is the red poll. It is smaller than the finch and has a red spot on its head. Like the finches, the males appear to have been dipped in raspberry juice.

Bald eagles, like wolves, were once almost extinct in this area. Research showed that DDT sprayed around the area to kill mosquitoes was getting into the food chain and causing eagle eggs to have soft shells. The eggs were laid but almost never survived to become new birds. Once DDT was banned, eagles began to make a comeback. In our first years at Sawbill, we often visited the Osmans at Brule Lake where they spent their summers. Eagles build huge platform nests near the tops of tall white pines and the same pair uses a nest year after year. So we watched the Brule eagles with great interest and saw the babies being fed, later sitting at the edge of the nest, and then being taught to fly. Later, a pair of eagles built a nest on Alton Lake on the point just south of the portage and returned year after year. It is no longer uncommon to see eagles when one is out in the BWCA, but it is still a great treat for most people.

Various kinds of woodpeckers can also be seen in the area. Flickers are the most ubiquitous bird of the summer, flying up along the side of the road as one drives by. They have beautiful coloring but move too fast for most people to see that.

Yellow-bellied sapsuckers make their presence known in May when the male advertises for a mate. He does this by pecking on metal at dawn, which is about 5 a.m. There is very little metal available to him at Sawbill as most buildings are wood, but two of our crew's living quarters provide the requisite metal on their roofs. The slow but loud rat-a-tat goes on for perhaps half an hour. Crew members who are here in May tend to be very early, if grouchy, risers. In a few weeks, the mate has been located and approved and the sapsucker is usually not seen or heard from the rest of the year. They are the birds that drill a whole series of small holes in a tree. A tree that looks like a natural colander is the work of a sapsucker.

In the winter, we have hairy woodpeckers around our house and at our feeders. These are large, beautiful, black-and-white birds with a red spot on the head of the male. However, they do not

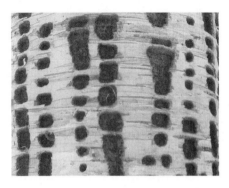

The distinctive pattern on this birch tree was pecked by a sapsucker.

endear themselves to us when they hunt for insects in the cedar siding of our house. They do not drill their holes at random but all evenly spaced and at exactly the same height, leaving a girdle of sizable holes all around the house. We don't find it attractive decoration and we doubt that they are finding insects, but their patience and persistence is endless. It sounds exactly like someone knocking loudly at the door. It has fooled me more than once.

Downy woodpeckers are clones of hairys in appearance but half the size. They are much more common in the woods but do not come to our feeders at all.

We also have pileated woodpeckers, huge birds mostly black with red heads. They peck out holes in trees about the same size they are, as much as 18 inches high, leaving piles of wood chips on the ground under the tree. We don't see pileated woodpeckers often, but there was one working on a tree just opposite my office window a few years ago. For weeks, I could watch as I sat at my desk. Just a few years ago, we found that a grouse hunter had shot a pileated woodpecker on a trail near our house. It's the kind of thing that can give hunters a bad name.

Grouse are interesting birds. They usually move very slowly, allowing observers plenty of time to examine them. During spring

A ruffed grouse moves slowly through the brush.

evenings, one often hears the sound of a motor being started. That's a male grouse sitting on a log and drumming for a mate. He makes the noise with his vocal chords. During the summer, many grouse may be observed sitting by the side of the road. Usually they don't move as a car drives by. Only occasionally, one will fly up to a tree. The numbers of grouse are cyclical. Numbers seem to reach a peak at 10-year intervals and then drop off over the next 10 years. It is entertaining to guess where we are in the cycle by counting the number of grouse sitting along the road during the summer. In the fall when hunting season opens, grouse seem to know that they are in danger and are rarely seen on the road. They are most interesting during the winter. We always have some living near us. They feed on bushes in our backyard. This very large bird will make its way slowly down a very small branch, eating buds as it goes until it teeters on the end of a slender twig.

In the winter, grouse live in brush buried under the snow. If they are disturbed, they do not move slowly but burst out in sound and fury just like an explosion. It's enough to give an innocent hiker or skier a heart attack.

Of course, our most famous bird is the common loon, which was officially declared the Minnesota state bird in 1961. Loons spend their summers on the northern lakes of Minnesota, Wisconsin, and Maine. In the winter, they go to the Gulf of Mexico or the warmer waters of the Atlantic coast off southeastern United States. In the summer, they are very territorial and each pair establishes its own area. A small lake may be home to one pair of loons. A larger lake such as Sawbill has some natural divisions due to islands that effectively cut off a section of lake. Each section becomes a loon territory. When migrating or preparing to migrate, loons gather together in sizable groups. While they are in the south, they lose their distinctive plumage and abandon their distinctive vocalizations so, at that time, they are not very interesting birds. As winter changes into spring, the loons acquire their black and white feathers and begin to fly north. As spring slowly develops in the North Country, they gather on Lake Superior. Scouts fly north to check the condition of the ice on their inland lake destinations. The day the ice goes out, the loons arrive.

Loons are considered the most primitive of bird species or the earliest to appear in the evolutionary cycle. They are magnificent swimmers and divers but have considerable difficulty walking on dry land because their legs are so far back on their bodies. Consequently, they build their nests at the water's edge and come ashore only to lay and tend their eggs. They also have difficulty raising their 8- to 9-pound bodies off the water to prepare for flight, but once in the air their flight is swift and powerful. This is particularly remarkable in view of the fact that their wing area is among the smallest in comparison to their body weight.

Loons mate for life and share equally in taking care of the one or two olive brown eggs in the nest. The loon on the nest calls and the

other one comes to take over the incubation. The chicks hatch after 29 days, which usually occurs in the first two weeks of July. They are covered with black down except for the belly, which is white. After two to three weeks, this first down is replaced by a second downy plumage that is gray. The drama of each season is the race with the clock. Will the little ones be mature enough to migrate when the waters of their first homes freeze over? Toward the end of August, the adult loons begin to gather together. After a few days, they take off for their winter homes. The chicks, now able to fend for themselves, stay behind for another month or so until they gain enough strength to make the long trip. Young loons do not attain full adult breeding plumage until the third summer. It appears that they stay in the southern waters full time for several years until they reach maturity.

The common loon, Minnesota's state bird, is a summer visitor at Sawbill.

Loons eat fish, crayfish, and some aquatic vegetation (salad?). When the chicks leave the nest, they spend most of their time riding on a parent's back. They practice swimming and diving, using both wings and feet for dives. Adult loons use only their feet when they dive. Loons can dive to 200 feet or more and can stay submerged for several minutes. They are able to go to such extraordinary depths because their bones contain no air as do most birds' skeletons. Consequently, a loon can expel air from its lungs, air sacs, and feathers to achieve a specific gravity almost the same as water. A loon may dive with great sound and fury or it may sink from sight almost imperceptibly.

Once I was walking over the portage between Weird Lake and South Temperance Lake. As the always welcome sight of water appeared, I saw a loon just a few yards out standing up on its tail with about 10 inches of wriggling northern pike protruding from its mouth.

The most endearing thing about loons is their vocalization. Loons have four different calls: the tremolo or laugh, the yodel, the wail, and a one-syllable coo. People rarely notice this last soft sound that loons use when they are near each other. It is the other calls that spell wilderness. Especially in the evening, one can hear a single impressive wail answered by a similar wail in the distance. Perhaps one loon is warning others of approaching bad weather. On other occasions, several loons seem to form a chorus. In the summer, we hear loons flying over our house in the morning, calling together.

One warm July afternoon, two baby owls were found by a camper on the path along the lake. At that time, we were being encouraged by naturalists not to rescue baby animals or birds that seemed to be abandoned but to leave them alone and let nature take its course. So that was the advice I offered: "Just leave them alone." I could see that my advice was not well received. My kind-hearted, nature-loving camper was eager to help. Within the hour, another camper and her child arrived in the store and presented us with a laundry basket containing the two baby barred owls.

Now what were we to do?! Our thoughts turned immediately to a young man, Bill Lane, who had been working in the area for a number of years doing research on boreal owls. We weren't sure if he was around but we called the Forest Service in Tofte and they were able to contact him immediately. He arrived quickly with climbing equipment and his pockets stuffed with mice. He took a look at the babies and gave them a little food — mice. The little fluff balls appeared in good shape. Crew member Will Decker and I accompanied Bill Lane to the campground where we tried to show him just where the owls had been found. Bill scouted the area for likely owl nesting trees, then shinnied up a tree to take a look. On the third try, he reported success — a nest. He carried the babies up and deposited them in the nest. He told us that the nest, being high in a tall white pine open to the sun, was an advantage on cool days but uncomfortable for these well-insulated infants on such a hot, sunny day. It was his theory that they jumped out to escape the unbearable heat.

The rescue was successful as we saw and heard the owls in the campground the rest of the summer. The two young barred owls were often observed sitting side by side on a branch

This downy, baby barred owl was rescued and safely put back in its nest overlooking Sawbill Lake.

and we would hear them call, "Who cooks for you? Who cooks for you?" Maybe it is one of their descendants who can still be heard in the campground in the evening or early morning.

· Chapter 14 ·

Emergencies

Whether you live in a large city or a small community, you take support services for granted. Should you have a fire, you would call the fire department. In a medical emergency, you would hasten to the nearest hospital, which would not be far away.

At Sawbill, everything is distant. The nearest help in case of fire is 25 miles away. So far, we have not had a serious fire, but we took precautions early to deal with fire. We bought fire hose and a small pumper so that we could get water out of Sawbill Lake if necessary. We installed many fire extinguishers around the place. We accepted the Forest Service's offer of a key to their cache of fire-fighting equipment at the Sawbill guard station. When smoke detectors came into popular use, we put them in every building.

After the severe blowdown of July 4, 1999, fire danger markedly increased due to all the fallen trees on the forest floor. Business and cabin owners all over the forest are taking additional steps to protect themselves. We cleared brush around our buildings and installed metal roofs and sprinklers on the roofs of each building.

The South Temperance Fire burned 4,100 acres in 1996.

Although there have been several forest fires nearby, none has ever been a serious threat to us. The closest forest fire was in 1996 at South Temperance Lake. At first, the Forest Service thought this fire was a good candidate for the "let burn" strategy, but it rapidly flared out of control. It was fought hard for two weeks, ultimately burning 4,100 acres. Included in the multitude of fire-fighting equipment that was rounded up were two huge yellow Department of Natural Resources (DNR) tanker trucks from St. Paul. While they were waiting around on standby, the drivers stopped in for morning coffee at Sawbill. At the height of the fire, we discovered one morning that we had no water in our system. The water pump had collapsed from old age and we had used all the water in the storage tanks before discovering this. Bill McKeever of McKeever Well Drilling promised to come immediately to install a new pump. Nevertheless, we faced hours without water and suddenly felt like the emperor riding in the parade in the buff. Just then, the DNR truck drivers stopped in. They offered to fill our storage tank from the water they were carrying on their trucks. They could quickly drive to the lake and refill their tanks. We gratefully accepted their offer and the potential for disaster was averted.

There have been several fires on Sawbill Lake. Two were near the guard station. This is a group of log buildings just north of the campground that was the original Tofte Ranger Station. The Forest Service uses it to store equipment and to house summer volunteers. Years ago, Tofte rangers and other high level officials sometimes vacationed in the cabin.

One of these fires occurred in May 1960. I was alone at Sawbill while Frank and the kids were still in school. We had outfitted two young men from Ohio. By the greatest good fortune, Tofte Ranger Jim Reed was staying in the guard station cabin for a few days. He stepped outside in the afternoon and saw smoke on the island at the first narrows. He jumped in his canoe and paddled over. The fire was still small enough to control and he was able to put it out. Our young campers had selected this island to make camp although there was no campsite there. Then they had gone out fishing, leaving their campfire burning. A breeze came up and fanned the fire. It leapt easily to the nearby trees. The fire burned all their personal gear and all the camping equipment rented from us, plus a strip of land about 50 feet wide across the narrow part of the island. Forty years later, it is still easy to see the opening in the trees, a sort of passageway across the island.

Of course, the fire was under control before I heard about it, but it certainly left me trembling with "what ifs?" racing through my head, along with enormous gratitude for my good fortune. The young men were chagrined and embarrassed and faced with a lot of problems, not the least of which was how to drive home to Ohio without money or identification. They were a pair of customers who never returned to Sawbill.

Another Sawbill fire occurred at the guard station in January 1993. A returning winter camping party from the University of

Minnesota stopped in on Sunday afternoon to report that one of the buildings at the guard station was on fire. Frank tried to drive our snowmobile up the lake but got stuck in deep snow. I skied out and found the burning building. It was a small, primitive wooden building that was built to be used as an ice house. It was virtually gone by the time I made my way through the trees. One tree next to it was on fire. The hardest part of this fire was getting to it. The snow was too deep to walk through and there were too many trees to go in on skis. Since I had already struggled through all these obstacles, I decided to try to put out the fire that was creeping up the tree. I batted at it and threw snow at it. When I got home again, we called the Forest Service and Ranger Larry Dawson himself drove right up to check out the situation. By the time he arrived at the scene, the fire was out and he did not feel further action was necessary.

It was very clear how the fire had started. All the evidence lay in the snow. There were the remains of a campfire about four feet in front of what had been the door of the building. Half a dozen small trees completely burned at one end were pushed up to the edge of the fire ring. It had been 40 below zero the night before. Some unknown winter campers had understandably sought shelter in the little building and built a fire to keep warm. Rather than chop wood, they found long pulp sticks that they kept pushing forward to keep the fire burning. Morning came and the campers hastened to leave their makeshift camp, leaving the fire still smoldering. Undoubtedly, they had had great difficulty keeping the fire burning during the night and naturally assumed that it wouldn't continue to burn without their continuing attention. However, during the day, the wind came up and the picture changed. The campfire flared up and the logs burned all the way back to the building and caught the building on fire. Once again, disaster was averted by the sheer good fortune of a responsible party passing by. Otherwise, the whole complex of buildings and the woods around could have burned with no one around to notice it. The building that did burn was not in current use but was valuable as a historic relic.

Medical emergencies and rescues occur more frequently than fire. However, the danger of being out in the woods is immeasurably less than many anxious people — such as wives who wait at home while their husbands are on canoe trips — imagine. Over 40 years, we have averaged about one full-blown emergency per year, a minute percentage of the number of people who are out on the lakes. It is a record any city might covet. Still, it is a very serious matter as the nearest clinic and hospital are 50 miles away.

In anticipation of possible medical problems, Frank and Bill both took Emergency Medical Technician (EMT) training. In 1975, Bill helped to establish the Tofte Rescue Squad, a community service that cuts in half the time it takes to get outside help to Sawbill.

The first medical emergency I remember occurred on a peaceful, rainy morning in mid-August, some time in the early 1960s. Two boys in their early teens walked tentatively into the store, waited politely while I talked with a customer, and then said, "We were up on Cherokee Lake this morning and we were struck by lightning." Red alert! Immediately, all sources of help were contacted.

The full story was that the boys and their fathers, outfitted by us, sat up in their tent early that morning and were zapped by lightning, which came down a tree and then up through the floor of the tent. At least the older men and perhaps also the boys lost consciousness. When the fathers woke and assessed the situation, they dispatched the boys — who seemed uninjured — to get help. They had paddled back to Sawbill in about three hours.

We were able to get the Forest Service "Beaver" airplane based in Ely to fly into Cherokee Lake to pick up the men. Later that afternoon, we learned that one of the fathers was in the Ely hospital being treated for burns. Later we heard that he was able to go back to work. He was a professor at a college in Manchester, Indiana.

We were informed that all our equipment had been picked up and loaded on the plane. We worried a lot about the victims of the lightning strike and we also wondered and speculated about the tent. We assumed that it would be burned beyond repair. Several months later, the equipment was delivered incidental to some Forest Service errand between Ely and Sawbill. We hastened to examine the tent. It seemed to be undamaged. Finally, we found a 3-inch slit in the canvas floor, a neat cut with no charred edges.

A Forest Service Beaver is called in for rescue and medical emergencies.

The best news came several years later when a relative of the injured man came on a canoe trip. With great apprehension, I inquired about Fred, the man who had been hospitalized. Not only was he fully recovered from the experience, but his nephew said that he had suffered from arthritis for some years before the lightning strike but had had no symptoms since then. This may sound like fanciful thinking, but it is a fact that arthritis was in the past successfully treated by electric shock.

On another occasion, two teenage boys came into our store, visibly distraught. They said they were camping on Alton Lake and their father had had a heart attack. It turned out that their father was a physician from Fargo, North Dakota. He had diagnosed himself very accurately and knew what to do. They had finished breaking camp when he realized that he couldn't go on so he lay down and sent the boys to get help. Luck again played a large role. The Forest Service plane was already on Alton taking water samples. We called the Forest Service in Tofte who radioed the plane on Alton and the victim was picked up in no time. We also called the hospital in Grand Marais and they arranged for the ambulance to meet the plane at Devil Track Airport in Grand Marais. The man was in the hospital within half an hour where he received appropriate care and eventually made a full recovery.

One of the most tragic occurrences befell a group of seven young men from Omaha. They had gone out on an ambitious week-long trip. About two days into their trip, we received a telephone call saying that the wife of one of the men had been killed in a small plane accident. We knew exactly what route they had selected and even approximately where they would be camping each night. So, with great confidence, we promised to go find them. Two of our employees volunteered to make the trip. Two days later, they returned defeated. They had followed the seven-day route checking campsites carefully as they went but they had not found the group. It turned out that the men had gone off on a little side exploration at just the critical moment that our rescuers went by.

This experience was a big lesson to us in the futility of attempting to deliver emergency messages. The area is just too vast and complex to track people. When the party returned on schedule, we had to deliver the message to call home for a family emergency. I just couldn't bear to be in the room when he made that call.

About 10 years after that, we got a frantic call from a very authoritative-sounding individual in Schenectady, New York, demanding that we go out to look for a young man who had gone on a canoe trip out of Sawbill. His father had had an accident involving a fall from a ladder and was unconscious in the hospital. The family wanted the young man to come home immediately. We had no idea who this canoeist was, who might be in his party, or where they might be. We had no record of his renting anything from us. The caller could give us no information about the other people in his party or about their vehicle. We simply could not envision how we could be of help, but they were not easily dissuaded.

Our local sheriff and the Forest Service received similar calls and in turn contacted us. None of them could get a handle on a rescue procedure either. Over the next several days, we received calls from the Minnesota Highway Patrol, the American Red Cross, and the national offices of IBM demanding that we find this young man. Clearly, the rationale was that if they could find a responsible and competent agency, the problem could be solved. It turned out that the injured man was an IBM executive and the callers were probably fellow executives who were accustomed to solving problems this way. One caller had the solution. They would send an airboat up from Florida that could be used to cruise the area quickly in order to find him! Frank persuaded him that an airboat would not negotiate portages very well. They did send a corporate jet to the Duluth airport to await the son and to fly him back to Schenectady. They arranged for the sheriff to drive him Code 3 (siren and flashing lights) from Sawbill to Duluth.

The efforts to locate him finally turned up a description of the car. We found it in the parking lot and blockaded it with one of our vehicles so that the group couldn't leave without coming in to get the emergency message. It turned out that the young man had been at a party in St. Paul. On a spur-of-the-moment whim, some of the group who were not close friends decided to go on a canoe trip. The car had been recently purchased by one of them and was not yet registered to its new owner. They had not rented anything from us or gotten their Boundary Waters permit from us. This group had not left much of a trail. Of course, it had not occurred to them that anyone would want to find them with an emergency message in the few days that they were out.

Although a given individual may be hard to find, canoeists themselves do not often get lost. There are certainly times of confusion and there may be times when it takes hours to locate the next portage but it is very rare that anyone is more than temporarily lost. Usually the problem arises from a camper wandering into the woods away from the portage or campsite.

I was lost once on Java Lake. Frank and I had gone on a day expedition to explore and fish. We found a nice grassy spot on an island for lunch. After our picnic, Frank wanted to take a nap and I wanted to paddle around and fish. Other people whom we knew were also on the lake. Soon, I caught a little northern pike. While I was struggling to get it off the hook, a wind came up and whipped my canoe around in a circle. I easily regained control of the canoe but I no longer knew which direction I had come from or which direction I was going. I looked around for the other canoes but to my great dismay, they were all gone. Java is a small lake and I knew I had been in one of the arms, so I set off paddling toward what I hoped was the middle of the lake where I had left Frank. Instead, I soon found myself in one of the other arms where there was a camp site. To my great relief, there were lots of people there. It turned out to be a church group of young people whom we had outfitted, led by Rev. Jim Davenport. I paddled over and explained my plight and they were most accommodating in helping me find my way back to Frank. By this time, he had had more than enough time to wake up from his nap and to wonder why he had been abandoned on an island. What could he conceivably do to help himself? Needless to say, he was happy to see us coming.

We thanked our rescuers and headed home with no ill effects from the slight deviation in our plans. However, I was dismayed and embarrassed the following winter to find that my little misfortune had been written up in a Presbyterian church newspaper which was circulated all over the country. Somebody thought it was hilarious that they had to rescue their "outfitter." I didn't think it was good publicity at all!

One of our employees had a happier ending to an experience of being lost. She and her boyfriend were on a canoe trip. After making camp for the evening, they decided to bushwhack through the woods to get a better view of the night sky. Then the moon disappeared under some clouds and the night became very dark. They started walking through the dark woods and finally reached the lakeshore but they had no idea where to go from there. Since it was a warm summer night, they just curled up and went to sleep. When they awoke in the morning, they could see their campsite not very far down the shore. It was both amusing and embarrassing as they were both expert campers. The happy outcome was that it was after this experience but before the end of the trip that they became engaged to be married. A wilderness canoe trip is a good test of the compatibility of two people who might be considering living together. Being lost overnight must be the ultimate test.

We were involved with a truly lost person one of the first years we were in our own building at Sawbill. This was not a canoeist but a trout angler on Plouff Creek. His wife came to our store in tears, begging for help. Her husband had put on his high rubber waders, donned his hat, taken his trout rod, and set off down Plouff Creek that morning, leaving her in an RV nearby. When evening came and he hadn't returned, she was justifiably worried and upset. He was a man in his sixties, in good health, as far as she knew.

A massive search party was organized for the following morning. At first, all Sawbill men (Frank, Karl, our employees, and every able-bodied man from the campground) plus the local sheriff went looking for him. The women made hundreds of sandwiches in our kitchen for the rescuers to have for lunch. First, they looked up and down in the creek. Then they combed the woods, marching in formation with each person about six feet from the next person. This was extremely difficult since a straight line through the woods includes huge rocks, thick brush, and soggy swampland.

When this didn't yield results, the National Guard was called in. Big Army trucks brought in a hundred or more men in uniform. They set up a base camp with a camp kitchen as well as radios and bullhorns. They searched for days. Finally, they brought in a big Army helicopter that flew over the area. They expected to find, if not the man himself, at least his hat or his fishing rod, which would float if he had drowned in the creek. Finally, they gave up. Members of the family came up from time to time over the next several years and conducted private searches. It is unbelievable but no trace of the man was ever found.

Another airplane search was conducted when a woman paddled into Round Lake Resort all by herself. She reported that her husband and two young sons had gone into the woods from their campsite on Frost Lake the night before and had not returned. This

family was from Chicago and had driven their motor home to Sawbill and parked on our parking lot. They rented canoes and started on a canoe trip at Sawbill Lake. Judging by the fact that she appeared small and frail and had stylish purple hair, we suspected that she was not a well-seasoned outdoor person.

It must have been a terrible night for her alone on Frost Lake. She didn't even have the consolation of knowing that the others were together. One of the boys had gone into the woods from their campsite to look for firewood and had not returned. The other boy went to look for him. When he did not return, the father went to look for both of them. By this time, it was dark. She must have painted images for herself of each one meeting a separate horrible fate.

In complete despair and totally alone, she got in a canoe at first light and started paddling out to get help. She met a canoe party coming into Frost Lake, and they portaged her

The National Guard mounts a search for a lost angler in 1959.

canoe over the rather difficult portages between Frost and Long Island lakes. They pointed her in the direction of Round Lake, a route that required very little portaging, although it must have seemed a very long paddle.

The Leeds of Round Lake Resort called us mid-afternoon to ask on her behalf if the others had returned to Sawbill. That was the first we had heard of the problem. We called the Forest Service and they promptly sent a plane. The first thing the pilot did was to fly over their campsite on Frost Lake. Lo and behold, there they were!

The father reported that he had met up with the boys and they had tried to return to their camp but they couldn't find their way in the dark. They lay down and rested and then, at daybreak, continued to hike until they came to a stream and ultimately to a portage sign that gave the distance to the next lake. This oriented him and they were able to make their way back to their camp. Of course, by the time they arrived, after a long and difficult hike, Mother was gone. The Forest Service pilot waited while they hastily packed their gear. He then flew them back to Sawbill for a happy reunion with Mother, who had gotten a ride back to Sawbill from someone on the Gunflint Trail.

After World War II, the troops came home and settled into their old neighborhoods, got married and had children, went to school with the help of the GI bill, and established careers. Then there was time to think of having a good time pursuing recreational activities. One of these was canoeing in Northeastern Minnesota, and canoe outfitters went into business to provide canoes and camping equipment. Bill Rom dreamt of doing this as he lay on a beach in the Pacific, and he came home to start Canoe Country Outfitters in Ely. However, canoeing was a recreational pursuit that started very slowly and grew gradually.

At the same time, the Forest Service was taking note of wartime technology and making the change from staffed fire towers to airplane patrol. Airplanes flew regular fire patrol over the forest, weather permitting. When there were only a few canoeists, and fire patrol planes were flying anyway, the Forest Service got into assisting with rescues. As the number of canoeists grew in the 1970s, they

realized it was not an appropriate use of their equipment and personnel.

The rule now is that rescue operations are directed by the sheriff's department from the appropriate county. If a Forest Service plane is required for a rescue, there is a charge for its use. The party being rescued is responsible for this charge. Hiring a plane is, of course, quite expensive. Local rescue squads, which now perform most emergency services, are made up of volunteers from the community. Their expenses for equipment (which are considerable) are paid for by local taxes. There is no charge made to rescued parties. Often, however, individuals who have been helped express their gratitude by sending a donation. Rescue squads are, in turn, very appreciative.

An autumn rescue operation illustrates the new Forest Service procedures. It was late October and we had sent out our last canoe trip of the season — a group of six men. Several of them were from the Twin Cities and several were from Arizona. They started out

Fire patrol by small airplanes replaced the use of lookout towers.

on a Thursday morning for a trip to Cherokee Lake, planning to return on Sunday. The weather was chilly but bright and sunny when they left. As the days went by, the temperature dropped. When the men awoke Sunday morning, they saw ice beginning to form around the edges of the lake. When they checked the Cherokee River, through which they would have a long paddle, they found it frozen solid. They decided to stay put and wait for rescue.

Meanwhile, back at Sawbill Outfitters, everyone who had rented canoes came in and departed for home. The parking lot was empty except for the Blazer that had brought the six men from Minneapolis. (When the parking lot is empty, we know the season is over.) The leaves had all fallen and there were no more tourists driving around looking at leaf color. Frank waited anxiously at the front desk all through the day, hoping that any minute he would see them walking up from the landing, but night came and they didn't appear. The rest of us were busy with the last details of closing the place down for the winter. About midnight, one of the wives waiting anxiously at home called to say that they were overdue. Frank promised to take action in the morning.

Monday morning was a bright clear day. By chance, the Forest Service was flying a small plane with a researcher who was counting moose. When they flew over Cherokee, they saw a large orange X on the ice indicating that there was trouble. By this time, the Forest Service had been notified of our missing party and radio communication established that they had been found. The plane was too small to bring any gear but the pilot airlifted the men back to Sawbill one by one. They called home to say they were safe and then departed hastily.

They had thoughtfully packed all their gear into packs and placed the canoes over the packs and marked the spot. They left us a map with the location marked. Some of the gear was ours and some belonged to the six campers. The Forest Service promised to bring the gear out with their dog team, which patrols the area during the winter. Unfortunately, it was a winter where heavy snow came before the ice on the lakes was solid. This meant there was slush under the snow and conditions were not suitable for taking a dog team out until late January. By this time, the cache was buried under a lot of snow and was difficult to find. When it was uncovered, it was apparent that animals had discovered it first and much of the equipment was torn to shreds. There must have been a bit of food or at least the odor of food that attracted some animal, perhaps a pine marten. The canoes were returned to us largely undamaged. They were dragged over the ice and snow behind the dog team. All the losses and expenses were covered by the campers.

Winter emergencies are more dramatic and potentially life-threatening than summer ones, and we have had a number of them. We wonder how it is that we don't hear of people outside our rescue area losing their lives or being in big trouble. There seem to be vast areas where people can go by ski, snowmobile, or snowshoe where no assistance is available. We often provide emergency-starting for frozen-up cars. What if they were parked on a back road where no one lived?

We moved to Sawbill in 1976 as full-time residents and moved into our new home there in the summer of 1977. It was that very year that another late fall emergency occurred. Two young men were camped on the Kelso Bay campsite halfway up Sawbill Lake enjoying a last foray into the wilderness before winter. While they were at the edge of the water loading their gear into the canoe, they slipped on the frost-covered rocks and fell into the icy lake. Falling into the water with clothes on is always uncomfortable but, in the summer, one soon dries out. These two campers were already wearing all the clothes they had brought so they had no choice but to paddle about an hour in wet clothing. It was cold, in the 30s, and they were soon on the verge of hypothermia. They made it to our house where they shed their wet clothes and took warm showers while we ran their clothes through the dryer.

Another midwinter camper was much further into hypothermia before she arrived at our house. A group of young women, students at University of Minnesota Duluth (UMD) were on a winter camping trip to Alton Lake. In the evening, they were gathered around their campfire, visiting, when they noticed that one was not doing so well. It turned out that she was wearing enough clothes but all cotton clothes — jeans, cotton shirt, cotton windbreaker, cotton socks, and tennis shoes. She didn't want to be a spoilsport by complaining but she was feeling more and more miserable. When the others became aware of her symptoms of hypothermia, they put her on the toboggan and pulled her back over the frozen lakes to our house. We called the doctor on duty at the emergency room at the Cook County Hospital and followed his instructions for checking her condition and treating her. We put her in a tub of warm water and then to bed under a heap of blankets. One of the others stayed with her all night. By morning, she was recovered enough to head home with the group. It had been a narrow escape.

The week after Christmas is a popular time for winter camping. One of the first years in our house, our family and guests were gathered to celebrate New Year's Eve. Our chief entertainment was cross-country skiing and, at that time, we had a ski trail that started on the Sawbill Trail two miles south of us, followed an old logging road through the woods to Wonder Lake and then to Alton Lake and back to Sawbill Lake, a loop nine miles long. It was about dinnertime when one man from a party of three who were out skiing on this trail knocked on our door. He said he had become separated from the other two and now that it was getting dark he was very concerned that they had not returned. They had set up a base camp on the campground. He had been waiting there for some time but his companions had not come.

At first, we counseled patience, but he came back in a few hours and reported that they still had not returned. The temperature was dropping. It went to 30 below before the night was over. We were very concerned and started calling for help. At the Forest Service, the ranger himself was the only one around. Obviously, no employees were on duty in the evening on a winter holiday weekend. He suggested that the only sensible thing to do was to use a snowmobile to look for them. So we started looking for a snowmobile. Today, it seems everyone has a snowmobile, but in 1977, we could not readily think of anyone who owned one. The sheriff had one but hadn't used it yet that year and he said it was buried under a lot of snow. He promised to come in the morning. He didn't think it was practical to mount a search in the middle of the night. We all spent a very unfestive evening worrying, stewing, and debating whether to attempt a rescue in the middle of the night. Bill and his wife, who lived in Tofte at the time, finally left for home right after midnight. They were so concerned that they stopped two miles down the road and again seriously considered trying to ski the nine-mile trail in the dark to search for the lost couple. Instead, Bill came up very early the next morning and set out on his skis across Sawbill Lake to Alton. Not too far out, he heaved a deep sigh of relief at the sight of two skiers coming down the lake toward him.

They had gotten lost on the woods part of the trail and wisely decided to turn back and try to get back to their camp the same way they had come. When they reached Alton in the dark, they couldn't find the portage to Sawbill so, again very wisely, they stayed on their feet and kept moving all through the long cold night. If they had given in to fatigue and allowed themselves to sit down to rest, they surely would have dropped off to sleep, possibly leading to very serious trouble. They were warmly dressed but did not have matches to build a fire. As soon as it was light, they were able to find their way back to Sawbill. They were a very tired pair.

Another close call occurred in January 1981. Our friendly computer technician had driven up to help work out the many bugs in our first computer. A lot of support was part of the package in the early days of computers.

It was the one day of the winter when the temperature hovered at 40 below zero all day long. When he left, we urged him to follow our routine procedure and call us when he reached the highway. We told him that if his car broke down on the Sawbill Trail, there would be no one by to help that day and this could prove disastrous. He was self confident and didn't agree to call. However, he came to appreciate our warning.

Halfway down the trail, he found two couples in a stalled car. They were staying at a resort on the North Shore and had driven up the Sawbill Trail that morning without informing anyone where they were going. They found a logging road where they could ski. When they returned to their car very tired from a long ski, they couldn't get the car to start. They hunted for wood to build a fire but deep snow covered everything. They had just about reached the depths of despair and had decided to tear the upholstery out of the car to use as fire-building material when our repair technician came driving up. He delivered them to their resort.

The following week, he forwarded to us a thank you note from one of the women. She said that they were immensely grateful for the rescue from a near-death experience. Then she added, "Our four children send their thanks as well"!

In 1991, Frank and I were away in the fall when the famous Halloween snowstorm occurred. Quite unexpectedly, snow began and continued until 40 inches piled up. Cindy barely made it home from picking up her children at Birch Grove School in Tofte before road conditions became treacherous. The first snowstorm of the year is always the worst for driving. A logging truck slipped on the icy road and jackknifed just past the intersection of the Sawbill Trail and the road to Crescent Lake. Usually, the Sawbill Trail is plowed immediately after a storm but this storm kept the snowplows occupied for several days. When they did come up the Trail, they were blocked by the stalled truck. This led to the very rare circumstance of keeping the family at Sawbill snowbound for days. Finally, the road was cleared and Bill set out for Grand Marais, intending to go via the back road by Crescent Lake. It was now the evening of the third day after the storm.

He had just turned on to The Grade when he saw a pickup truck stuck in the ditch. Two young men popped out to enlist his help. They had been at their cabin on Jock Mock Lake about 20 miles away. Unlike many people who seem unprepared for North Woods conditions, these two were caught by overconfidence in their excellent preparation. They had a new four-wheel-drive pickup. They had a full complement of emergency supplies but didn't bother to put them in the truck for this short trip. They thought it would be no problem to make a quick run to town for supplies. Icy conditions caused their vehicle to slip off the road and the very deep snow made it impossible to budge. They had waited in the car for three days and three nights for someone to come along. Bill put them in his car and radioed Cindy that he was bringing them home. They hadn't eaten for three days. When they came into the house, Cindy said to them, "Would you like some soup?" They apparently had not reached a state of any kind of desperation yet or maybe one was somewhat irrational as he replied tentatively, "What kind?"

The disaster of the century here occurred on Sunday, July 4, 1999. Frank checked the barometer that morning as he does every morning and noted that he had never seen such a low reading. Still, it was a clear sunny morning and we set off on our weekly trip to town to attend church services with no further thought of the weather.

After church, we headed back to join in the Tofte Annual Fourth of July celebration that begins with a parade at 1 o'clock. As we approached Tofte on Highway 61, we saw that we were heading into a storm. The sky darkened and then took on a strange green cast. Suddenly, there was a downpour of rain so thick that we just couldn't see to drive, so we pulled into the museum parking lot to wait it out. In less than five minutes, the rain ended. As we started out on the highway again, we were flagged down by a very bedraggled young couple who asked us if we would drive them back to their car. They had been hiking on the Superior Hiking Trail when the storm hit. After delivering them to their car, we decided we were no longer interested in celebrating the Fourth. We called home and Natasha, on telephone answering duty, immediately said, "No one is hurt but you can't come home. There are trees down across the road." Shocked and dazed, we could only think of driving home immediately to see what was happening.

As we drove north on the Sawbill Trail, we encountered an occasional tree across the road. We were able to get through easily until we arrived at the intersection of The Grade and the Sawbill Trail. There we saw down trees piled one on top of another in crazy array. A number of cars were there ahead of us, parked, with their occupants out milling around.

Frank called 911 on our car phone. The dispatcher asked, "Is your power out?" She had been receiving many calls about downed power lines on the Gunflint Trail. Frank tried to explain quickly that we didn't have power lines so that wasn't our problem.

The big problem was that it was Sunday on a holiday weekend. County road equipment operators would not be working or even at home. Forest Service personnel were not working. We were fortunate enough to find the McMillans at home. They had established a tree trimming and removal business based in Schroeder just a few years before. They were just the experts we needed. They came up immediately and started cutting trees off the road. The county road crew pitched in on Monday morning although that was officially the Fourth of July holiday. Later, independent loggers were hired to widen the road and haul the downed trees away.

The storm that had passed through was designated a straight line wind reaching a velocity of 200 miles per hour at its leading edge. It affected a swath of roughly 10 miles. In this area, not all the trees were blown down. No tamaracks were blown down as far as I could observe. There was already a great number of dead spruce and balsam resulting from the spruce budworm destruction that had peaked a few years before. Unfortunately, those dead trees were not blown down in great numbers. Pine and birch, alive and leafed out, were the primary victims.

Meanwhile, at Sawbill, our crew mobilized to cope with the disaster. The first mission was to check the campground to see if anyone was hurt. Fortunately, no one was. Adam Hansen and Nathan TerBeest were the crew members who undertook this duty. They found hundreds of trees down in the campground. They also found a camper who had a chainsaw that they could borrow. For the next eight hours, the two of them used our chain saw and the borrowed one to cut trees in the campground that were blocking the roads there. Then they started clearing a path down the Sawbill Trail wide enough for a car to go through.

The two Forest Service portage crew volunteers happened to be at home in the guard station. On their own initiative, they set out to inspect the campsites in the area. They paddled from lake to lake checking to see if anyone had been injured or needed help. Lives were undoubtedly saved by the fact that it was midday and campers were not in their tents when trees fell across the tents. No injuries were suffered in the Sawbill area. There was only minor damage to our buildings, although a number of big trees cleared buildings by only inches as they fell.

The most fortunate victim was a customer who was driving to Sawbill pulling a canoe trailer with his two aluminum canoes bought from Sawbill 10 years previously. He was on the stretch of the Sawbill Trail between The Grade and Sawbill when the storm struck. As he saw trees falling ahead of him, he tried to back up, only to find that trees were falling behind him as well. A tree fell across his trailer, smashing his canoes. The insurance settlement he received for the loss of his canoes enabled him to buy a used Kevlar canoe, a very nice upgrade.

Most people who were in the Sawbill area that Sunday hastily packed their gear and departed as soon as a path was cleared. By Monday morning, new parties were arriving ready to start out on canoe trips. We even acquired some unexpected business when the Forest Service allowed a few groups who had planned to be outfitted by businesses on the Gunflint Trail to start their trip at Sawbill Lake instead. There was more damage to buildings in the Gunflint area and the impact of the storm was far greater because their electricity was knocked out. The Gunflint Trail was closed to all but local traffic for about a week while they dealt with the disaster.

Back at The Grade Road intersection that Sunday afternoon, Frank talked to our son Karl, who was working at Sawbill. Karl asked us to check his house in Grand Marais because his alarm system was indicating some damage there, perhaps a door blown open. We turned around and drove back down the Sawbill Trail and then to Grand Marais. We were very fortunate to be able to spend the night at Karl and Lee's house because there was "no room in the inn" that night. Facilities, already quite full with holiday visitors, were stretched to the limit by campers coming out of the woods.

We attended a wonderful Fourth of July fireworks display in Grand Marais — a first for us. About 10 o'clock, it started to rain and the crowd dispersed to shelter. I remember lying awake all night long listening to pouring rain. It added up to about four inches and did a lot of damage to Highway 61, to feeder roads coming down the hill to Highway 61, and to driveways leading into houses and businesses on the lower side of the highway. Basements of buildings below the highway were flooded.

We started back to Sawbill early on Monday morning. Highway 61 was deserted but we observed the washouts and other damage such as a foot bridge at Cascade Lodge that was uprooted and carried downhill by the heavy rain. Just before we reached Tofte, we heard on the radio that the section of Highway 61 we were on was closed to traffic. No wonder it had seemed deserted. At The Grade intersection with the Sawbill Trail, we found a path had been cleared just wide enough for a car to drive through. The landscape was so drastically changed that it was unrecognizable.

The Forest Service moved quickly to clear roads. First, a path was cleared just wide enough for a car to drive through. Then, loggers were hired to clear all the trees off the roads and out of the ditches. They loaded the debris with the booms on their trucks and hauled it away. By the end of the week, driving seemed normal again.

The landscape, however, will never be the same. Cleanup of blowdown back in the woods continued into 2002. Still, there are enough trees remaining, so the change in scenery due to the great storm isn't readily apparent to someone seeing it for the first time. There have always been a lot of fallen trees in the forest and there still are. How many will miss the beautiful big white pines that they have never seen?

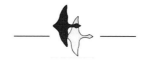

· Chapter 15 ·

Fire in the Woods

The very thought of fire in the woods strikes dread into all hearts. With an endless supply of fuel, an unchecked wildfire could burn the entire forest. Ever since the Superior National Forest was established in 1909, forest fire has been a major concern of the U.S. Forest Service. Of course, fires did burn unchecked for centuries before that but the whole forest never burned at any one time.

Fire burned various sections so it is a very rare tree that is more than 200 years old. Eighty percent of the virgin timber in the Boundary Waters wilderness is 150 years of age or less. Dr. Miron "Bud" Heinselman, the leading researcher of this matter, has estimated that, in pre-settlement times, major fires burning 50,000 to 100,000 acres at a time occurred about every 25 years in what is now the Boundary Waters Canoe Area Wilderness (BWCAW).[1]

Major fires were documented in 1595, 1692, 1801, 1863, 1875, 1894, and 1910. In the immediate Sawbill area, large-scale fires occurred in 1929, 1936, 1948, and most recently the South Temperance Fire in June 1996. Between 1981 and 1995, 57 percent of fires were caused by lightning strikes; the remaining 43 percent from human causes.

The response to fires has evolved and changed markedly over the years, as have the precautions taken to prevent fires. In the 1920s, fire lookout towers were installed at strategic locations throughout the forest. These were designed to spot fires at the earliest possible time and thus to provide a "rapid response." At this time, the Forest Service did not own vehicles to transport its personnel. Emerson Morris, who worked for the Forest Service in the 1920s, said the workers checked into the office morning and evening to see if there was a fire reported anywhere. If there was one, the Forest Service had to rent vehicles to transport personnel and equipment to the site, which did not make for a rapid response. Sawbill Outfitters at one time had a signed agreement with the Forest Service to rent our vehicles in case of fire. Major changes in fire fighting occurred in the late 1930s when the Forest Service added airplane reconnaissance, used bulldozers to build fire lines, and constructed emergency "tractor roads" and emergency telephone lines.

By the 1980s, forest ecologists realized that complete fire suppression is not totally desirable. Fire is necessary for reproduction of certain natural species. Jack pines, for example, require fire for their seeds to germinate. Jack pines live up to 200 years. Absence of fire for 200 to 250 years would eliminate jack pines from the area.

Without fire, spruce and balsam fir move in to take over the forest. Therefore, in 1987, the Forest Service adopted "prescribed natural burning," which gives knowledgeable personnel the option to determine whether a fire can burn naturally without posing a threat to human safety or resources. Thus, a lightning strike in the wilderness may be allowed to burn itself out.

The plan allows up to 15,000 acres in a decade to be burned in this fashion. In the first decade, 10,000 acres were burned in 36 separate fires. No fire exceeded 500 acres until 1995, when the Little Gabbro Fire burned 3,000 acres. One year later, this record was broken when the Whitefeather Prescribed Natural Fire burned almost 5,000 acres.

The Whitefeather Fire was an example of a highly successful prescribed natural fire. It was deep in the interior of the wilderness area so it posed no threat to human resources (buildings). It opened the

area to jack pine reseeding. The operation was successful economically with its cost being only six dollars an acre compared to an average cost of several hundred dollars an acre for wildfire suppression.

Another fire that occurred at the same time was managed entirely differently. Since it was close to the border of the BWCAW, it posed a threat to improvements (such as Sawbill Canoe Outfitters buildings, and dwellings at Gust and Tait lakes). Therefore, it could not be designated as a prescribed natural fire.

This was the South Temperance Fire of 1996. Since the fire had started near a campsite, it was assumed that it was camper-caused. However, after the fire was out, a lightning strike to a large spruce tree near the campsite was discovered and became the designated cause.

The fire started on June 14. By June 19, more than 100 personnel were fighting it. They used planes to drop fire suppressant and built a fire

Forest Service fire policy now allows some fires to burn in the wilderness.

line on the ground. The fire line was constructed by clearing a strip of brush around the perimeter of the fire and then dropping napalm to start a fire. This removed the fuel in the path of the wildfire and stopped its spread. The Forest Service information officer reported with some confidence that the fire was now under control. However, the fire got a dreaded assist from the weather and it began to spot and crown. These are technical terms that mean the fire was jumping from treetop to treetop, fanned by the wind, and starting more fires out ahead. Another 1,700 acres burned and it took an additional week before the fire was truly under control. Finally, on June 27, just after the fire was declared controlled, heavy rain poured down.

This fire burned 4,450 acres. Its suppression, by 262 individuals, cost one and a half million dollars. A lot of this money stayed in the local community, most of it as salaries paid to local firefighters. Owners of grocery stores and restaurants experienced a sudden growth in their businesses as they provided food to the many additional people in the area. Canoe outfitters provided canoes and life jackets to the firefighters. The command center was set up at Birch Grove Community Center, which meant that unused schoolrooms were rented for the summer. The unexpected income was some consolation for the anxiety and heartache of having a major fire raging.

Forest Service records show the great concern for the safety of the firefighters. A daily bulletin issued to the firefighters said, "Safety is the number one priority... If it can't be done in a safe manner, don't do it." The safety officer listed some of the hazards: "Crisscrossed dead trees, waist high, and standing, dead balsam fir; extremely low fuel moisture of both dead and green vegetation — not a good place to be!!... Hazardous footing due to fuel conditions; eyes are in danger due to so many dead branches at eye level, especially if one should fall; numerous rocks and logs in the water, may need to designate a lookout in each boat."

While the occurrence of fire in the wilderness is unchanged, human response has evolved and developed markedly. The Forest Service is certainly a key player in this history.

The Superior National Forest was established in 1909. In 1910,

Fire in the Woods 209

John "Ed" Mulligan, surveyor extraordinaire, began his employment with the Forest Service as the Tofte ranger.

In a 1975 interview done by Grand Marais Ranger Earl Niewald, John Mulligan, Ed's oldest son, recounted some of his childhood experiences working in the woods with his father.[2] Before the 1920s, discovering fires seemed to be mostly luck. Most fires were caused by lightning strikes. John said that if someone working in the woods found a fire, that person hiked out to report it. One of the early strategies for fighting fire was to build tool caches along the portages so that workers who discovered a fire could take quick action to control it. The tool caches contained shovels and axes, which were the fire-fighting tools of that day.

Forest Service crews in those days were putting in portages and docks to make travel easier. They were using canvas-covered canoes weighing as much as 120 pounds. The canoes were easily punctured, so they needed the docks and the canoe rests that they built. Portages followed old Native American trails that were not necessarily the shortest distance between lakes but wound through the easiest terrain. Tourists had not yet arrived on the scene in any number but the Forest Service was thinking of that possibility for the future.

The next step in fire control was installing lookout towers. The first fire lookout tower, located at Pine Mountain, was built on a wooden scaffold.

In the late 1920s in the Sawbill area, four towers were built: Kelso, Brule, Cascade (just north of Lake Superior), and Honeymoon (halfway between the North Shore and the Sawbill area). The Kelso Tower must have been one of the hardest to install as its location was almost inaccessible. The story is told that Ranger Leslie S. Bean enlisted the services of Horace Stickney — a logger and shop owner in Schroeder and later a county commissioner — to help him haul the 100-foot steel tower sections to Kelso Lake. Stickney was an expert in handling horses, which were used to drag the steel sections of the tower nine miles through the woods after they were unloaded from the General Logging Railroad that ran on what is now known as The Grade Road. This difficult expedition took place

Brule Lookout Tower in 1929

in January, probably in 1927, and took 10 days to complete.

The lookout towers were staffed throughout the possible fire season. Similar to the life of lighthouse keepers, individuals were employed to live in the little cabin near the lookout tower and to be on constant watch from the tower throughout the daylight hours. Tower locations were carefully chosen to be high points. It was quite a climb through the woods from Kelso Lake up Kelso Mountain. The first tower person was Julius Baske. Later, Vivian Johnson of Schroeder staffed the Kelso Lookout Tower for years. She had to haul in all her own supplies. This involved going by canoe across Sawbill Lake, then over the portage into Alton Lake, then back into the canoe and across Alton, then over another portage, and finally up Kelso Lake to the trailhead for the fire tower. Having hiked up the mountain, she had to climb the 100-foot tower.

Her task was made somewhat easier by the fact that there was a small gauge railroad track on the portage between Sawbill and Alton lakes and one between Alton and Kelso lakes. The small flatcar was powered by a person pulling the car over the tracks by an attached rope. That was easier than portaging a heavy load. After the fire tower was abandoned, campers continued to use the cars for many years to transport their boats and gear over the portages. Unfortunately, campers occasionally let the car slip off the tracks into the lake and it had to be rescued with consider-

able difficulty. Finally, the iron wheels deteriorated. Since there was no repair facility left that could handle this sort of thing, the cars had to be abandoned. Many campers remember these rail portages with great nostalgia.

The most serious fire in the Sawbill area occurred in 1929 near Brule Lake. At that time there were no automobile roads in the forest area. However, the General Logging Railroad stretched across Cook County from Fourmile Lake (just over the Lake County line) all the way up to Rose Lake near the Gunflint Trail. Sparks from the stacks of the locomotives that were pulling carloads of logs through the

A railroad portage was used from Sawbill Lake to Alton Lake until 1965.

woods were a serious fire hazard. This was especially true on uphill grades where they poured on the coal to build up power, causing fire to pop right out of the stack. Although there were rules about screening the stacks, the practice was not always observed. The General Logging Company, a branch of Weyerhauser, was cutting the last of the big white pine stands, with hundreds of lumberjacks working. The area was littered with white pine slash, (branches and other residue left on the forest floor after cutting timber). Frank Kelly, the General Logging Company's superintendent in charge of the operation, had formerly been with the Forest Service and was very much aware of the fire danger and totally cooperative in trying to prevent fire. He had a speeder patrol follow each logging train to watch for stray sparks, and he had arranged to have slash removed from the right-of-way and from other hazardous areas. Slash removal was also the subject of a Minnesota state law but it was not being consistently followed by all loggers.[3]

In spite of all precautions, at 11 a.m. on July 22, 1929, the Cascade Ranger Station received a call that there was smoke along the railroad spur near Star Lake, just south of Brule Lake. Five minutes later, the Pine Mountain lookout also called in to report the smoke. The ranger and two other men immediately left by speeder, arriving at 11:30 a.m. They found a camp foreman and 30 lumberjacks fighting to control the blaze, which, fanned by west winds, had already jumped to the east side of Star Lake. The ranger, recognizing how serious the situation was, made his way up to the lumber camp and called back to Cascade for more help. He was able to get the message through just before the camp's telephone line burned out. The Grand Marais ranger got the message and immediately ordered a substantial fire-fighting crew to be sent to Brule.

The difficulties of transportation prevented a speedy response. Firefighters from Duluth and Ely had to drive long distances to the intersection of the railroad and the Sawbill Trail. There, a logging train was waiting to take the first 70 men another 16 miles to the scene of the conflagration.

Meanwhile, 186 more firefighters from the logging company's camps at Swan and Flour lakes in the Gunflint area came south by railroad. By evening, a substantial fire control force was assembled.

On the fire lines, things were going badly. About 4 p.m., the wind shifted to the northwest, threatening another logging camp and the company's main base at Cascade Lake. At 5:30 p.m., the clerk at Camp One called headquarters in great alarm asking that an engine be sent immediately to pump water. The superintendent, who was at dinner, did not feel the situation could be all that serious and failed to take action. At 6:10 p.m., 40 minutes later, a second desperate call came through saying that the whole camp was in flames. Fortunately, all personnel escaped before the camp burned.

The attack on the fire began in earnest at 3 o'clock the next morning with more than 200 men on the fire lines. Although the crews worked 18 hours a day, the fire continued to spread west and north during the next three days, jumping Homer Lake. On July 26, 70 more firefighters were sent from Duluth. A seaplane, which arrived from Ely with supplies, was used to scout the fire. Nevertheless, it burned over two more square miles to the north, to Juno Lake.

On the night of July 27, the wind shifted again, threatening the town of Cascade. Superintendent Kelly directed a dramatic fight to save the village, but elsewhere the fire raged out of control. Two small logging camps on the south shore of Brule were destroyed. Lumberjacks from one of these camps were being evacuated by barge when the barge caught fire out on Brule Lake. They were rescued by an alligator boat and death was averted.

By July 31, the fire was completely in Forest Service territory and they assumed full charge. The situation was complicated by a spot fire two miles north of Brule Lake that necessitated shifting crews back and forth across the lake. Seventy more firefighters arrived from Duluth on August 1. In response to pleas for help, other Forest Service personnel arrived along with equipment from the state of Minnesota and other agencies.

Still the fire raged on and was only brought under control when a substantial rain fell on August 7. Workers spent four more days grubbing out fire lines around the area to prevent further spreading. Over 25,000 acres burned and the cost to the government was estimated at well over $50,000 in 1929 dollars.

Three years later in 1932, Franklin D. Roosevelt became president and established the CCC. Through this program, hundreds of young men began forest development work in the area. They built roads, docks, and portage trails, planted trees; and were available for fire fighting. Weather conditions were conducive to fire in the 1930s since most of the summers were exceedingly dry. Logging was in its prime.

In 1936, there were three serious fires in the Sawbill area, devastating nearly 10,000 acres. The afternoon of Saturday, July 11, was exceptionally hot with large thunderheads in the sky. Shortly after noon, a light shower began, preceded by heavy flashes of lightning somewhere north of Sawbill Lake. The tower person at the Kelso Tower reported several lightning strikes a few miles northeast of his post, but no smoke was visible. At 3:45 p.m. the next day, he saw a gray-white plume rising to the northeast and notified the Sawbill CCC camp of his discovery. Simultaneously, the Brule Lake Lookout Tower reported the smoke. A cross-reading placed the fire near the portage between Gordon and Cherokee lakes. D.M. Williams was the Tofte ranger who immediately requested help from Grand Marais, Ely, and Duluth.

Reaching the fire was a difficult matter as all those canoeists who have made the trip to Cherokee and Gordon lakes can attest. Two principal routes were used. The shorter one involved a truck trip to Sawbill Lake, a canoe trip up Sawbill through Ada and Scoop lakes, and then through the Cherokee River and Cherokee Lake to the scene of the blaze. This entailed making three or four portages as well as paddling miles across the lakes. The second route was by truck and logging railroad from Grand Marais to Brule Lake. From there, motorboats, barges, and canoes transported people and equipment through North Temperance and Sitka lakes to Cherokee. This trip, including two difficult portages, took about 11 hours compared to four or five hours from Sawbill.

Ranger Williams was the first on the fire, arriving by seaplane about three hours after receiving the report of smoke. The blaze already covered about 60 acres and was threatening the Cherokee Ranger Cabin. Williams immediately sent the plane to Seagull Lake

for a fire pump. By 8 p.m., he and a mechanic had it in operation. They saved Cherokee Cabin and a few virgin white pines. Fire crews came in from Sawbill and worked all through the night to build fire lines.

Progress was good until Monday morning when a 20-mph wind arose from the northwest. As the day proceeded, the temperature soared into the 90s. With little warning, the fire roared out of control, jumped across the east bay of Cherokee, and went racing down the eastern shore of the lake. The 295 firefighters who had arrived by this time were forced to take refuge on the islands. By late afternoon, the magnificent white pines of North Temperance Lake were engulfed and the fire was rolling toward Brule Lake. By 3:30 a.m. on Tuesday, the firefighters were back in action, building fire lines around the lake.

Once again, it was primarily the heavy rain — which arrived on Tuesday night — that became the deciding force in stopping the spreading fire. It took four more days and a

The Cherokee Ranger Cabin was saved from wildfire in 1936.

total of 619 men before the fire perimeter was completely trenched and declared under control.

The Cherokee Fire burned 3,200 acres of forest and was responsible for one death. G.H. "Jerry" McDonald, superintendent of the Sawbill CCC camp, disappeared on Friday night, July 27, during the final stages of the battle. His body and his overturned canoe were found on Sitka Lake the following Sunday. Apparently his canoe swamped and he was too exhausted from a solid week of fire fighting to save himself.

Roger McKeever, now of Schroeder, was an enlistee of the CCC Sawbill Camp. He ran the speeder between Cascade Lake and the Sawbill CCC camp where someone else usually took over and took it on to Wanless Lake. Sometimes Roger made the whole trip.

When fire broke out on Cherokee Lake in 1936, the CCC men were enlisted to fight it along with other recruits from Duluth and elsewhere. Roger remembers that they walked all the way from Sawbill to Cherokee on a rugged path through the woods. This was known to locals as the Hudson Bay Trail because it supposedly went all the way to Hudson Bay. It was used by local trappers. Roger's job on the fire was to make sure the pumps were running.

When the fire was out, everyone was expected to hike out and each one was expected to carry a tool, perhaps an ax or a pulaski. The plane that had been used to dump water on the fire was ready to take off when Roger asked the pilot if he could have a ride back. The pilot said he wasn't allowed to carry any passengers, but that if someone stowed away behind coils of rope in the back of the plane he wouldn't be likely to see that person. The pilot then walked away and Roger climbed in. Back at camp, Roger received a tongue lashing from the ranger. As punishment, he was told to report immediately to the Gunflint Trail area where another fire was in progress on an island. When he got over there, he found they had a big boat capable of carrying 25 men but no one could get the brand new motor to start. Roger offered to try, and was able to turn it over in short order. As a reward, he became skipper of the boat that delivered the firefighters to the island. After it was all over, someone asked Roger how it was that he always got these good driving jobs.[4]

The exceptionally hot summer of 1936 contributed to a record number of fires all over the forest. On July 18, there were 30 small fires in the eastern part of the Superior National Forest. On August 6, another large fire broke out north of Timber Lake. Reinforcements of men and equipment were brought in from Duluth and by August 11, that fire was under control. Further trouble developed the next day. On August 12, a smoke was reported at Frost Lake. Three Forest Service workers who were already nearby were dispatched to take initial action with reinforcements promised. Everything went wrong. The first three decided not to wait for the reinforcements but they got lost in the dark on unmarked, difficult portages.

By the following evening, the fire had already burned 250 acres. Troubles increased as strong winds kept changing direction. On August 18, a fire camp on Long Island narrowly escaped destruction when the wind suddenly shifted and flames surrounded the camp. In the end, 3,400 acres burned, leaving only charred rubble between Gordon and Long Island lakes. Eight hundred men helped to fight the fire at a cost of $25,000 plus a timber loss of $46,000. Equipment transported into this remote area included 13 pumps, 41 canoes, four boats, two radios, and a portable telephone.

The Plouff Creek Fire in 1948 crossed the Sawbill Trail, stranding guests at Sawbill Lodge for several days. For the next 40 years, the gap in the vegetation was very noticeable to anyone driving on the Sawbill Trail. Ten years after the fire, there was still a mostly bare swath. The Forest Service placed a marker there telling a bit about the fire. Then the jack pines that had reseeded as a result of the fire began to be evident. It looked like a big plantation. By 2000, the trees were mature enough to blend in with the rest of the forest and the site is no longer obvious.

Like most wildfires, the Plouff Creek Fire burned in a mosaic pattern. In some places, the fire burned so hot that it consumed the forest floor duff and the organic material in the soil. In other places, it moved through the forest understory and left the big trees untouched.

A stand of red pine next to a swampy area survived the fire. Bruce Giersdorf, a Forest Service fire technician, measured some of the trees in 1998 and found them to be 85 to 90 years old. The pattern of growth that can be read in the rings of the wood showed that the trees had experienced a growth spurt after the fire. This is because the fire released a burst of nutrients into the soil.[5]

This all started on June 11, 1948, when careless smoking ignited a blaze two miles northeast of the former CCC camp located at the intersection of the Sawbill Trail and The Grade Road. The blaze was quickly attacked and brought under control but it led indirectly to the main disastrous fire. A logger on Plouff Creek, who had sent his regular bulldozer to fight the first fire, continued to haul logs with a spare tractor. This machine, which had no exhaust pipe, apparently dropped sparks into the dry undergrowth, quickly resulting in flames. Fire was soon racing south along the Sawbill Trail.

The efforts of 200 firefighters with five bulldozers and a dozen pumpers were ineffective in stopping the fire. Urgent appeals for help were answered by the Duluth office of the Forest Service and by neighboring forest agencies who sent 852 more people, 21 bulldozers, and 29 pumper units. In two days, 20 miles of fire line had been built and the flames had been checked. Even so, 1,200 acres were burned.

This fire was notable for the developments in fire fighting. Large-scale resources were quickly brought to the scene and damage to the forest was limited. The ability to control fire was well demonstrated, but this type of fire fighting was becoming increasingly expensive, with costs to the Forest Service on this occasion topping $100,000.

Since the Fourth of July blowdown in 1999, fire has become a more serious threat to the BWCAW because of the abundance of fuel now lying on the ground. Lightning strikes are more likely to cause significant fire, and the fire will burn with much more intensity. Studies predict that area fires will now be much more difficult to control.

The Forest Service has alerted people who own property near the BWCAW, urging them to be vigilant and to take additional steps to prevent fire damage such as installing metal roofs on buildings. They are encouraging campers to use stoves instead of building campfires. They have hired loggers to clean out the blowdown outside the BWCAW in order to decrease the fuel available in case of a fire. They have increased their own vigilance and have brought in extra personnel for the times when fire danger is usually highest.

These efforts helped prevent major fires for five subsequent fire seasons — much to everyone's relief.

Chapter 16

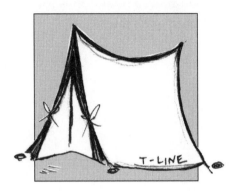

Customers Remembered

There are many lessons to be learned in the course of meeting the canoeing public. One we have noted is "Don't make hasty judgments about people," or, "Don't judge a book by its cover." It is unintentional but natural to draw some conclusions about people as one visits with them. Judgments may often be based on a person's attire. However, camping is a great leveler and dirty grubs become the standard clothing. This leaves very little room for pegging a person's financial or occupational status. It is not unusual that the grubbiest among our customers turns out to be most distinguished in his or her workaday world. When people give their names at Sawbill, they most often use nicknames rather than their formal first names, and they omit titles. Thus, we might know Jerry Olson, who, in his professional life, would always be Dr. Gerald P. Olson. Lacking these common clues, we frequently discovered that we had misjudged an individual or at least failed to appreciate how distinguished a person was.

One season, I became somewhat annoyed with one of our regular customers who made a reservation early in the year, then canceled at the last minute, promptly made another reservation and again canceled, and once again repeated this procedure. In September, three sad-looking young men came to rent a canoe. They confided that they were headed for Cherokee Lake to scatter the ashes of their friend who had loved the BWCAW so dearly. They named him and it was the person who had been making reservations and canceling all summer. He had died of AIDS. He had been hoping to make one more canoe trip but then would find that he was too ill to make the trip. All summer, I had assumed that he was being irresponsible.

During our earlier years at Sawbill, it was common for people to camp on the Sawbill campground for extended periods or to return repeatedly during the summer. There are still a few families who come every year and stay for a week or more, but that happens much less often now. The reason for this is related to the fact that motors are no longer permitted on Sawbill Lake. Many of our friends of earlier days fished every day with their small motorboats. When motors were banned, many of them found other places to camp. Now the Sawbill campground is primarily used as an overnight camping spot before and after a canoe trip.

The Sampsons were one of the families on the campground in 1957 when we had our business in Cedar Cabin, just above the Sawbill Lodge dock. I remember very clearly the teenager who came to buy milk and eggs from me. It was Dee Sampson, the second of five children in her family. A few summers later, Dee got a job at Sawbill Lodge. The next year, she was one of our crew members. Dee's parents, Jim and Fran Sampson, moved from Duluth to Pennsylvania and subsequently retired to Florida, but they still camp at Sawbill. Since 1999, they have been campground hosts at Sawbill during the month of August.

Another family camping on the campground our first summer were the Millards: Edwin and Lizzie and their two children, Lee and Richard (known then as Speedy because his initials were RPM). The Millards, who lived in Chicago, returned every summer and we quickly became close friends. Their children were about the same age as ours and played together constantly.

In 1958, Lizzie and I deserted our families and took a three-day canoe trip, doing the Cherokee loop. In those days, women very rarely went on canoe trips without men but we were not ones to abide by convention. We did weaken at the last minute, though, and took 10-year-old Karl with us. He was a great help, too.

When the Millard children were a little older, the family started taking long canoe trips and spending less time on the campground. They routinely took one or more of our children along. One year, we all went with them. That was the year we explored the Verne River. Looking at the map, it appears that there is an easy route between Verne Lake and the Temperance River route from Kelly to South Temperance — but appearances deceive. I know we have saved many customers a miserable trip by warning them away from that route. We spent one entire afternoon wading in the treacherous river, pushing or pulling our canoes and hanging on to them when we went over deep holes. It was not a navigable stream then and it still is not.

In time, the Millards moved to New York. For several years, they still returned for their annual canoe trips. However, the years went by and the kids grew up, went to college, started their careers, and got married.

Lee Millard, especially, continued to stay in touch with us. She brought her family to camp at Sawbill several times. She and her three daughters attended Sawbill's 30-year celebration in 1986. Lee and Ranna were always special friends and Lee came from New York to attend Ranna's wedding in 1983.

Lee and Karl had discovered a romantic interest in each other as early as eight and nine years old. This close relationship extended into their teens, but then each went their separate ways. In 1997, some friendly telephone calls between Lee in New York and Karl in California led to a rekindling of romantic interest. On New Year's Eve 1999, they were married at the Sawbill Campground. Now they make their home in Grand Marais.

Several families who camped regularly at Sawbill stand out in my mind. One is the Geving family of Duluth. There were six children in this family, all boys except the oldest, and our children spent much time playing with them. A favorite activity was to sit in a circle on the ground and play "spoons." As adults, the Gevings are scattered across the country, but each of them returns to Sawbill Lake from time to time.

The Jensens, from Silver Bay, were another fine camping family. There were three boys and a girl in the family. One of the boys, Tom, eventually became a Sawbill crew member. His hiring was unique. He was spending the summer camping alone on Alton Lake. As he came in to reprovision, he began to do odd jobs around the place just because he thought they needed to be done. Eventually, he made himself so useful that he was put on the payroll. He earned his RN some years ago and now works in St. Cloud as a neonatal nurse. He has never lost his love of camping. His brother Bill, who still lives in Silver Bay, is also a regular winter visitor as he comes to ice fish.

When we started Sawbill Canoe Outfitters, we were living in Duluth. By 1961 we had moved to Bloomington, a suburb of the Twin Cities. Several of our regular customers were from Bloomington. One particularly memorable family was the Wales, who had 10 children. (Camping is a good vacation choice for people with large families.) When Don Wales

Snow drifted down as Karl and Lee were married at the Sawbill Campground December 31, 1999.

heard that we were moving to Bloomington, he quickly offered to help us get settled in the community. (A similar offer came from Chuck McCann, the father of another camping family with five children.) The Wales had only boys when we first met them but two little girls eventually completed their family. They invited us to dinner at their home and helped us get acquainted in the community. This story has a tragic ending in the fact that they lost one of the little girls. One spring, the children were playing in their yard on Nine Mile Creek. The little one fell into the creek and the hazardous rushing waters carried her away despite the fact that several members of the family jumped in to try to rescue her. We still see several of the sons who bring their own children for canoe trips.

When Frank was working in the Eden Prairie schools, he became friends with Patricia Bell, one of the high school English teachers. She and her husband, Don, were interested in canoeing. One summer, the four of us took a canoe trip together. Pat subsequently started her own publishing company, Cat's Paw Press. One of the first books off the press was *Roughing It Elegantly*, a fine how-to book on wilderness canoeing and camping. The book sold well and was responsible for introducing the Bells to additional canoeing adventures in Maine and Florida. Pat and Don take annual canoe trips out of Sawbill, and we enjoy our annual visits with them.

Steven and Joel Hill are another couple who are special friends, greatly enjoyed over the years. They started canoeing out of Sawbill when their three children were small. Steven was teaching in a private school in Ohio and they made the long safari each year for their summer vacation. About 15 years ago, they moved to Maryland. We thought that might end their annual trips but it didn't. The children rarely come now since they are busy with their careers and their own families, but Steven and Jo look forward to their trips as much as ever. Frank especially enjoys visiting with them about Baltimore, his home town.

Another group whose Sawbill adventures ended up in the pages of a book consisted of Wally Neal and Bob Bugenstein from Bloomington; Gerry Rising from Buffalo, New York; and Earl Colburn from Minneapolis. Their annual expeditions started in 1963 and continued through 1998. Since they were already mature professional people when they started this tradition, their longevity is particularly remarkable. In the early days, they heard that long-sleeved white shirts were the best protection against sunburn and insects. They adopted this as their standard uniform, and they stood out in the canoeing population dressed this way. Consequently, their group became known as "The White Shirts." Their book, by Earl Colburn, is titled *A History of the White Shirts*.

Still another group of men, virtually lifelong customers, is led by Tom Glenny from Rockford, Illinois. Tom has a huge farm but he always makes time for at least one — and often several — canoe trips each summer. Tom's friend Dick Brown comes from Colorado to participate in the annual expedition starting at Kawishiwi Lake and ending at Polly Lake and points north. One year, Dick's birthday occurred during their week in the woods. His friends surprised him on the official day by serving cake and ice cream. They accomplished this by taking a cooler with dry ice packed around the ice cream. Tom's sons accompanied the group when they were the appropriate age. Now Stuart Glenny, who farms with his dad, comes with his own family. He has two daughters who love canoeing and are avid and successful anglers.

Larry Mathisen was another customer from Illinois. He was a contractor in Belvidere, Illinois. He started making wilderness canoe trips as a Boy Scout leader, making a trip each year. His own boys learned their outdoor skills from him. Larry was a true Boy Scout, always well prepared, welcoming, and open hearted to all. His trips were customarily along the Kawishiwi-to-Polly route. When he finally "outgrew" scouting, his family — wife, sons, daughter, in-laws, grandchildren — became his canoeing group. One year in the 1990s, the Mathisens were camped at the Kawishiwi campground at the end of their trip when another camper developed an emergency medical condition. Of course, Larry was the one who came to his rescue and drove him to Grand Marais to get help. On his way back up to Kawishiwi late in the night, Larry drove too close to the edge of the one-lane, rough road and went off the road. Then *he* needed help. He had to find another camper to drive him back to Sawbill in order to call a tow truck for his disabled car. In an ideal world, a Good Samaritan should not have had to suffer such bad luck. Several years later, in the summer of 2001, Larry's family once again took a canoe trip out of Kawishiwi. This time, they took Larry's ashes to scatter near his favorite campsite on Polly Lake.

We never had much opportunity to socialize when we were living in the city. Fortunately, we have had the opportunity to meet many wonderful people at Sawbill who have come up to camp or canoe on a regular basis.

The people I've mentioned here are by no means an exhaustive list of "customers remembered." This is only a small sampling of some of the people who have touched our lives and continue to be important to us.

· Chapter 17 ·

—— Operating a Small Business ——

It is interesting to speculate about what makes a business a success. Sawbill Canoe Outfitters could surely be classified as a successful small business now, but it was far from an instant success. There were many years of development and struggle before it became truly viable. Each year was always better than the previous one. That gave us hope and encouraged us to continue. We were very fortunate that we were able to stick with the business through many years of development without depending on it for a living.

We were able to avoid part of the major expense of a business, the cost of employees, because our family members worked 16 hours a day during the season and received no paychecks. We were working for "room and board" and mainly because we were having a good time.

We were very lucky to be in the right place at the right time when interest in wilderness was blossoming and burgeoning. We must also credit the invaluable help of friends. We could never have done it alone.

The entrance sign points the way to our small business.

I believe that the most important factors contributing to the success of the business were the outstanding employees, our focus on customer satisfaction, organizational skills, and our willingness to work hard.

I often feel grateful that we were able to start out with a tiny business while we learned the ropes. Now our business is so big and complex that no one is an expert in all its facets. We try to give our employees every opportunity to know as many aspects of the business as they wish. However, I observe that no employee, however talented, really grasps the entire scope of the business the first season.

A business like ours demands a great variety of skills. Unlike many jobs today, there is very little specialization. We brought to the business camping skills and dreams about managing a business because of our experience in working for Frank's parents at their residential camps in Maryland. Our most valuable contribution was doubtless an understanding of people acquired from our training and experience as psychologists. This enabled us to select and maintain an exceptional crew of helpers. My education also included the study of food and nutrition, which helped in developing the menus for our canoeing adventurers.

Two major things that we didn't know much about were the financial management of a business and how to live remotely without access to public utilities. We were city folk who took electricity and water for granted. We lacked even access to stores and repair technicians when we tried to provide our own utilities.

It was a very good thing to learn these things on a small scale. Bookkeeping for a business is easier to understand when you have 30 transactions than when you have 300. Of course, we did everything with the handicap of no capital and consequently a lack of helpful equipment. People accustomed to current technology cannot imagine bookkeeping without at least a calculator. After a few years of pencil and paper as my only tools, I did get a nonelectric adding machine. Each entry was made by pulling a lever.

Bookkeeping was very simple during the first years. We had a small business and we kept a few simple records. Mostly we accounted for daily receipts, trying to make the cash on hand at the end of the day balance with our record of sales. We also did a simple handwritten inventory at the end of the year.

We had to do these things because of our agreement with Sawbill Lodge. They were to receive 10 percent of our profits in exchange for providing us with the canoes and outfitting equipment they had acquired over the years. So we had to figure out what our profit was. In truth, we didn't have a profit for years. We subsidized the business with our winter earnings from our other jobs. Jean and Dick Raiken needed capital to build their home after they retired in 1960, so they wisely sold us their holdings in the business, and our cooperative arrangement ended.

In 1972, Dick Flint, a former crew member who was by then our attorney, advised that we make our business a closely-held family corporation. This came about primarily because of a concern about liability if one of our customers should be injured in the course of a canoe trip.

Being a corporation requires much more advanced accounting, with complexities such as double-entry bookkeeping and figuring annual depreciation on the assets. I enrolled in a community education course in accounting during the winter, and learned how to handle these new challenges. A few years later, I took a course in computer programming at the University of Minnesota, and in 1980, we moved into the world of computer accounting. While I was purchasing agent and accountant, Frank was in charge of maintenance and repair. He was also our public relations branch.

Operating on a shoestring led to much frustration in the utilities department. We started out with a 10-kilowatt, propane-powered Onan generator to provide electricity and pump water. At critical moments, it would stall. Frank struggled to learn about motors and generators. The nearest Onan dealer was in Minneapolis — not much help in emergencies — so Frank had to puzzle it out on his own with a little help from his friends.

Finally, luck stepped in to rescue us. Two of the leading technicians from Onan's plant in Minneapolis happened to be camping at the Sawbill campground — Larry Riewe and Pete Mickelson. (We came to know very well a lot of people from Onan as we had a lot of repair.) After a long process of troubleshooting the problem, the light dawned on us that the main problem was that we were overloading the little generator. We had been thinking it was just bad luck that the generator always gave out when traffic was heavy. In truth, it had to do with too much demand. We finally recognized that we had to invest in a bigger generator.

Similarly, we dug our first well by hand and hit water at eight feet. After a few seasons, we faced water shortages at crucial times and we had to deal with the need to have professional help. We engaged Rasmussen Well Drilling of Two Harbors. They went down 68 feet. Now we almost never run out of water. Eventually, we put in a big storage tank to provide a backup supply of water. The water in the storage tank saves energy because it is preheated by solar energy before going to the water heaters in the shower house.

It is probably the case that these problems were not immediately obvious because our business was so uneven. Years ago, people did not have the opportunity to take so much vacation time as they do now, causing a big surge of business on Saturdays and Sundays. Gradually, weekends have lengthened with many people arriving on a Thursday morning to start their weekend trips. Saturday is not such a big day for arrivals any more. It is much more common for people to take several vacations during a year so that one of them may be a week in the Boundary Waters.

The major holidays of the summer were the times when a multitude of people descended. Memorial Day weekend has always been for us what Christmas is for the average business. Minnesotans seem frantic to throw off the mantle of winter and get outside to play. Thus they pour into the Boundary Waters.

Similarly, Labor Day seems to inspire a frantic effort to get in one last fix of woods and water and peace and tranquility before school and the winter routine start. The Fourth of July also brought great numbers of people for many years. Now, community celebrations seem to take precedence in the lives of a majority of people and the Fourth is not such a big camping time.

Our business always peaked around the weather conditions and the related matter of how good fishing is. Thus June, often cool and damp, is not our most popular month. Fall trips were virtually unheard of in our early days. Translated, the big demand on our facilities was from mid-July to mid-August. This is especially true for young people and youth groups, which have always been the core of our business. We say that the time they come is after summer school is over and before football practice starts. We are delighted with the quota system that the Forest Service instituted in 1971 because it does a great deal to level out traffic.

When the Forest Service was proposing and discussing the permit system that set quotas for the number of parties that could enter the Boundary Waters Canoe Area Wilderness at each entry point, there was great consternation among affected businesses. Some thought this would reduce the big holiday crowds, and business would be adversely affected.

As it turned out, people simply assessed the situation and redistributed themselves. So the permit system benefited our business and surely all similar businesses as well. Not only did this relieve the environmental stress on the BWCAW, it also reduced the stress on our facilities and crew.

A more even distribution of people needing services is certainly

The main entrance to the store was remodeled in 2001, as part of a major renovation.

beneficial in relieving the strain on our utilities. It is also very helpful for staffing. When we started in business, and probably still today to some extent, it was common practice among resorts to hire most people on an "as needed" basis. This made a lot of sense for the business but was not a good thing for the employee. Employees are, ultimately, the largest expense of doing business. When business is slack, it is very difficult to cover the cost of employees. We did a rare and innovative thing when we hired our first four guides for the whole summer with a guaranteed monthly income. We are very fortunate now to be able to hire top-notch people with very little recruiting effort on our part. One reason for this is that we still guarantee continuous employment and a monthly salary.

Money is just one facet of this situation. The morale and efficiency of crew members suffer when activity ebbs and flows markedly. There was a time in our early years when crew members drifted into the office every morning, sat around visiting, drinking coffee, and twiddling their thumbs until the need arose for them to respond. Job satisfaction is much higher when a person knows what he needs to do and can schedule his time efficiently. This situation led to the development of our work-credit system, which is described in detail in the next chapter. This system allows employees a lot of flexibility in their duties and their schedules. At the same time, it gives the business maximum value during the time they are working. Customers frequently comment on the bustle of activity around Sawbill. Each crew member purposefully pursues his or her assigned duties to provide quality service and customer care.

A dissatisfied customer is unlikely to become a repeat customer. A case in point occurred one summer when I purchased some merchandise from a small company. I mistakenly wrote a check for considerably more than the amount due. (This wasn't the only time I ever made such a mistake but a company would usually tell me about it right away and make an adjustment.) I wrote this company but didn't get an answer. I tried sending a fax and received no answer. Finally, I located a telephone number and called. I talked to a man who said, "I won't send any money back. I won't give you any credit. It's your mistake and I'm keeping your money. Tough toenails to you." So he made a few hundred dollars extra that day but he lost a customer forever. With that kind of attitude, he may not have stayed in business very long.

The point of the story is that putting the customer's best interest first is not only a "Minnesota nice" way to do business but ultimately the road to a successful business. It is so common for remote or specialized businesses to take a bigger than average markup on everything they sell that most people assume we do the same. Many people who camp on the campground regularly go to town to buy their groceries, assuming that a bigger store will be less expensive. In truth, our groceries get a standard markup and are no different in price than bigger stores. We carry everything in our store that a camper might need and we sell at standard prices, always being careful not to take advantage of our customers. The desired goal is to promote repeat business and good word-of-mouth advertising — and we seem to have achieved that goal.

Bill and Cindy Hansen have been totally in charge of the business since 1994. Their roles mirror Frank's and mine. Cindy is the purchasing agent, chief accountant, and the organizer. Bill is the public relations person and an expert in plant maintenance, including radio-telephone equipment, diesel engines, and solar panels.

After years of planning, Bill and Cindy arranged a major renovation of the property in 2001. A large addition to the main building provided new year-round office space, a modernized store, greatly increased storage space, and a far more efficient operation. The outfitting part of the business that had been in the separate dome building was moved back into the main building. Interior decoration and outdoor landscaping make a much more attractive space. Although the appearance of the place is quite different, the basic operation remains essentially unchanged.

· Chapter 18 ·

Work Credit

In the adolescent years of Sawbill, when we were no longer a brand new business but not yet a well-established, middle-aged business, we began to see that there was a lack of organization as to what crew members were supposed to do.

The way the day typically goes at Sawbill involves opening at 7 a.m. A few early birds arrive immediately, eager to buy fishing licenses and rent canoes and get out on the lake. Some even arrive during the night and nap in their cars waiting for the store to open. These eager ones take care of their needs quickly, buy coffee, and set out on their planned journeys. Then things are quiet for several hours. Suddenly, excitement erupts. Customers come in, the telephone starts ringing, vendors call for orders, future customers call with reservations. Maintenance problems become evident and crises are likely to arise. A typical crisis would be that a big group comes in from a trip and they are eager to take showers and we discover that we are out of clean towels.

Back in those adolescent days, Frank and I were always there at

7 a.m. to open up. Frank took care of the customers and I started the book work while things were quiet and peaceful. Gradually, the crew members drifted in and gathered in the office. The previous day's events were reviewed and plans for the coming days were made. Everybody relaxed with a cup of coffee. This continued until customers and events demanded attention either in person or on the telephone. Then the crew, one by one, flew into action. Often, there was more to handle than we could respond to comfortably. Eventually, it dawned on us that we could plan ahead more and make better use of the help we had available. As this realization was occurring, I happened to read a book about a planned community in one of the southern states that was successfully using the work credit system to organize its activities. They had been inspired by B.F. Skinner's book, *Walden Two*, in which he describes a plan for a Utopian community.

B.F. Skinner is a well-known psychologist who was at the University of Minnesota when we were in school there. He later moved on to Harvard, where he stayed for the remainder of his career. Although we never knew him personally, we were very much aware of him and his work. This undoubtedly influenced our attention to his plan.

In *Walden Two*, a group of people gathered to start a new community. At Sawbill, we were a small community living together, not so much by choice as by necessity. However, there were definite similarities. Following suggestions in the book, we started to list all the jobs that needed to be done around Sawbill and to set up a system by which crew members would claim responsibility for the various jobs.

The title "work credit" means that each job has a certain number of credits associated with it. To start the system, the amount of time in hours that each job routinely took was determined and that became the number of credits for that job. One of the main features that Skinner built into the system was that people who accepted less popular jobs would get extra credits for those jobs and conversely, popular jobs would get fewer or only basic credits. Determining which are the popular jobs and which are the unpopular can be a bit tricky. At first, we defined unpopular jobs as those that no one chose in a given week. Those jobs would receive more credits on the following week's schedule. If a job was chosen by three or more people, it was declared to be popular and that job had its credits reduced for the following week.

The popularity of jobs varies from year to year according to the preferences of the people who are working that year. Patterns have emerged over the years, though. Washing cook kits, for example, is often an unpopular job. When our customers come in from a trip, they are expected to turn in their cooking and eating utensils washed and clean. Nevertheless, we rewash and sterilize each item by hand. The hardest part of the job is using steel wool scrubbing pads to remove every speck of black that may be left on cooking utensils as a result of cooking over a wood fire. Propane fires leave some stains on pots, too, and our cook kits are always polished after each use until they look brand new. As an unpopular job, it would get more credits than the time it actually takes. Consequently, there is usually someone who is very willing to take this job.

Transportation is usually a popular job. This means making the daily trip to Tofte, going to the bank and the post office, and picking up the daily deliveries. It also includes driving customers to the different access points. Driving is a job that has considerable appeal to some people. It does take a lot of time since, in our location, nothing is close by. As a popular job, it gets fewer credits than the hours it takes. Still, there is always a willing taker for this job.

In the beginning, all the jobs were listed on a piece of paper. Each crew member received a copy of this document and proceeded to rank the jobs in the order of his or her interest in doing the jobs in the coming week. Once we had each worker's choices, the next step was to coordinate them and determine who was to do what. Implementing the work-credit system was one of the jobs. It was one I always chose because I thought it was great fun. Therefore, every Tuesday afternoon, two other crew members and I sat down and worked out who would be responsible for what jobs during the coming week. We made our work week go from Thursday through Wednesday because weekends tend to be busy and we wanted the weekly transition to take place before the weekend rush began.

A rule we made for ourselves was that each crew member would get at least some part of the job that he or she ranked as first choice. So, if several people ranked a job as number one, we divided the job. Then second choices were assigned and we proceeded down the list. Amazingly, there was considerable diversity of interest and almost every job was chosen by someone. At the end, there would be a few jobs unclaimed, and a few individuals who needed some more hours to fill out their schedule. We would call together all the crew members who had time left on their schedules. All the unclaimed jobs were presented, and the crew members readily volunteered to cover them. The important underlying principle is that everyone gets to choose what he or she will do and agrees in advance to do it. This is the key idea regardless of the details of putting it into practice.

I always advocated this principle when I was counseling with parents about getting their children to participate in chores around the home. There is a strong temptation to be manipulative and to maintain control. Parents often respond to this idea by saying to themselves, "OK, we'll make a list of jobs, but we know what each family member can do and we will just tell them that this is their job and that's the same thing." It's not the same thing at all. The element of free choice is the crucial part of this system. The whole point is that work done willingly goes a lot better than prescribed work.

At Sawbill in the busy season, guests wandering around observing the operation often comment on our efficiency. They see each crew member bustling about performing some task and everything seems to be running smoothly. We owe it all to the work-credit system. The process takes some time and effort but the results make it all worthwhile.

Most businesses assign work by giving each employee a specific set of jobs to do. This becomes part of the hiring procedure. A person is hired to do certain jobs and comes with qualifications that fit those jobs. At Sawbill, most of our jobs are relatively unskilled, easily taught, and also boring. We always hire people who have myriad skills and better-than-average ability to learn new things.

Therefore, we need to make their employment appealing by mixing the less interesting routine tasks with the more demanding and exciting tasks. Any dissatisfaction with jobs is handled by changing jobs every week. The rationale is that if you are not enjoying a job, it is not too onerous to make it through one week, and then you most likely will never have to do that job again.

We have noted over the years that employees have different approaches to their work. Some are most comfortable with learning a job thoroughly and then doing the same thing every week. Others crave variety and novelty and enjoy trying new jobs each week. We have had crew members who are literally in training for starting a business of their own and thus make a strong effort to learn every aspect of our business by participating in every job. Our family members usually make an effort to learn every job. Whatever the individual's preference, the system accommodates it.

An objection often raised by someone hearing of this system for the first time is that some jobs require specialized training and the average person would not be capable of doing all jobs. This is true and we have several responses. We have established guidelines for the more demanding jobs, such as: "You must have worked at Sawbill for six weeks before you can choose this job." That works just like taking a college course that has requirements of earlier courses. This requirement gives new crew members time to get acquainted with the business and the area, for example, before they undertake a job that involves giving out information to customers.

Secondly, we find that people do not bid on jobs unless they feel capable of doing them. However, if someone is willing to try a new and unfamiliar job, then we offer help. For example, bookkeeping calls for some specialized training. Most crew members never bid on this job and it goes each week to someone who is trained and experienced in the work. Everyone has the option of choosing to do this job so it occasionally may go to someone who isn't totally capable of handling it. Then someone else has to take a little extra time to train and supervise during that one week. Then the apprentice makes a decision to continue the learning experience or to leave that job to someone else.

Jobs are broken down into small enough units that no single job takes a lot of time during the week. In fact, if a job is going to take more than 20 hours of the week, it is divided and must be allotted to two different people. This happens primarily with outfitting. During busy times, taking care of all the outfitting groups becomes much too big a job for one person, so the job is divided among several crew members.

The foundation of the work-credit system is job descriptions. A looseleaf notebook contains all the job descriptions. We developed this originally by asking each crew member to write a description of the jobs he or she was doing that week. Then, we spent time in crew meetings reading the job descriptions and revising them according to suggestions that various crew members offered. Over the years, job descriptions have evolved and become established. Now they are essentially revised once a year to reflect changes in the business, such as new equipment or new suppliers.

If job descriptions are the foundation, then the crew meeting is the bedrock. It is so basic that it is easily taken for granted. Our crew gathers once a week after closing time. It is the one time each week when everyone sits down together. The agenda for the meeting comes from an agenda board that hangs in the office. Any crew member can post items for discussion as issues arise. In addition, general plans for the following week are discussed. Each crew member declares his intentions as far as time off. This is the time when problems or glitches in the system can be brought up and discussed, and a remedy proposed, discussed, and agreed upon.

Some effort is required to keep such a meeting from being a gripe session. It is healthy to have a time where gripes can be aired but it can easily be overdone. Invariably, in a group of people living closely together, there are irritations. Just having the opportunity to express one's annoyance often relieves the problem. One rule we encourage is that gripes and dissatisfactions may only be brought up anonymously, without mentioning names. That enables any individual to take the complaint to heart and modify his behavior without feeling personally attacked. Sometimes, the process can lead to problem solving by the group with innovative ideas arising for a solution. More serious problems may need to be handled in individual conferences.

The meeting always includes a time to pass out thanks and kudos for jobs well done or for contributions beyond the required. Crew members are encouraged to drop a note in a box during the week thanking another crew member for a special kindness or assistance or commenting on especially good work or an admirable response to a crisis. These warm fuzzies are passed out at the meeting. A little fun is added by providing munchies, playing a game, or having a special group activity right after the meeting.

No one is required to attend the weekly meeting but anyone staying away must realize that he or she has to abide by the decisions of the group without having input into the decisions. An underlying value of the meeting is that it promotes the idea of a community, with everyone working together rather than the individualistic approach of each person working independently.

Crew meetings take place on Monday evenings. On Tuesday mornings, the crew

Name	Week of: / /
How many days working?	Credits/day:
Cross out the days you will be absent:	Th F S Su M T W

Job	Votes
Store Hours	
Dome Hours	
Total votes (10/working day)	
AM GM S-M-T-WΠ & PBI	8
AM GM Th-F-Sat & PBI	6
Brunch Cook and Clean (3/day)	21
Campground Recycling	0
Canoe Repair and Prep for Sale (2 peopl	20
Clean Main Building (3 folks 1.5/day,9	21
Clean Mobe	10
Clean Showers(2/day) F, S, S, W	0
Computer Accounting (does ORI + DP als	20
Cookkits(2/trip)(extras in the dome)	4
Daily Posting	0
Dinner Cook and Clean (4/day)	28
Food Manager(2/trip,3/breakfast in Do	2
Food Unpack	1
Grocery Manager	0
Handi Person/Woodhaul	0
Mason Bothers (2 folks) order and inv.	6
Merchandise Manager and Grocman (Gre	0
Midday GM Mon-Tues (Work Credit) &	10
Midday GM Sat-Sun & Towels	10
Midday Wed-Fri & Towels	15
Order, Receive, Inventory	0
Outfitting Maint. (10 base + 1/trip) (2	10
Outfitting Manager	2
PM GM Mon-Wed (& Woodhaul)	12
PM GM Sat-Sun (& Woodhaul)	8
PM GM Thur-Fri (& Woodhaul)	8
Pop, Beer and Ice	0
Roll & Put (2 people @ 4 base+1.5/trip	4
Sawbill CG (2x: before/after wkend)	0
Sawbill Newsletter 4-5 times/week	5
Sewing Repair	5
SP Close up store	10
SP Inventory outfitting equip and suppli	20
SP Outside Stuff	10
Temperance Campground (& Crescent)	0
Towels and Rags	0
Transportation	6
Trash & Recycling	4
Trip Unpack(1.5/trip)	2
Vehicle Maint	0

Crew members choose jobs on the weekly work-credit list.

members may be observed poring over a piece of paper. This is the time they indicate their work preferences. On Tuesday afternoons, the office is frequently crowded as crew members gather to see how the job assignments are turning out. There is some of the excitement of a lottery as one never knows just how it will go. Once the results are known, each crew member fills out a personal schedule for the week. This is a time when trades can be negotiated to resolve time conflicts. For the rest of the week, the mark of a Sawbill crew member is the folded paper each one carries in a pocket and studies intently from time to time.

One of the attractive features of this program is that each crew member can decide what hours he or she will work each day. Since our business is open 14 hours a day, from 7 a.m. until 9 p.m., there is the opportunity to choose to work early shifts or late shifts. There are "skylarks" and "night owls" and we always have a mix in our employ. Each person can plan his or her day to include recreational or relaxation time. In good weather, it is popular to arrange time off during the early afternoon for swimming and sunning on the dock or on the deck. Also, each person can arrange his or her work efficiently to take the least possible time. For example, one person is assigned to be present and available for renting canoes and camping equipment during specific hours. Sometimes, no one comes to rent anything for an hour and that hour can also be used for equipment maintenance. By covering two jobs at once, or multitasking, the crew member has the opportunity to cut an hour off his or her working time for that week. By working hard and efficiently, a crew member may be able to do a job more quickly and thus make extra time for personal activities. Some crew members choose to do their work and then go off to other things. Others choose to hang out at the scene of action of the business almost all the time whether they are working or not. The important thing is that people make this decision for themselves.

Sawbill joined the computer age in 1980 with the purchase of an early Apple computer. Bill quickly saw the value of computerizing the work-credit system. It had become quite a chore to do by hand as the number of employees and the complexity of our business

increased. So, he wrote a computer program that is used to this day, with some modifications. The person whose job it is to "do work credit" for the following week polls each crew member to see how many days he or she will be working that week. The other half of the evaluation is to determine what the work needs are for the upcoming week. This information leads to a figure of how many credits each person needs to fulfill his obligation for that week. Then preference sheets are printed out for each crew member. The preference sheet lists the jobs and the number of credits associated with each. Each person's preferences are entered and the computer does all the necessary mathematical calculations such as how many credits each person will have to work in order to cover all the things that need to be done.

Obviously, that varies from week to week, but we make an effort to have enough people

Our first computer was acquired in 1980 to help compile the preference sheets for the work-credit system.

around so that each person has a reasonable schedule. We do this by encouraging our crew members to take their vacation days early in the summer when things are not very busy. Each crew member has one day out of seven off, but we encourage them to save these days off and take them as a block. We also encourage using the time to take canoe trips. Free canoe trips are a perk that goes with the job. It is valuable for us to have employees who have experienced canoe tripping such as the customers will be doing. Crew members often have family obligations as well — a wedding or other celebration for which they must return home — so they can schedule this time as they wish. The only rule is that only a given number of people can be away on any given day so that the business can continue to operate smoothly.

Our work-credit system became considerably more sophisticated in the early 1980s as Bill developed the computer program. While we were living in Bloomington in the late 1960s, we had an American Field Service Intercultural Exchange (AFS) student living with us for the school year and the first part of the summer. Eduardo, who was from Valencia, Spain, graduated from college and went on to earn his PhD in economics from the University of Stockholm. He then worked for the Spanish government in Madrid and now works for the World Tourism Organization. He was visiting us in the early 1980s and was very interested in the work-credit system. He used knowledge he had gained in economics courses to refine the mathematics of our system. Now the different job preferences are weighted according to a mathematical formula that he applied to the system.

We always have plenty of well-qualified people applying for work at Sawbill. New crew members must agree to come for the season. We, in turn, guarantee them full-time employment for the season. Generally, individuals are hired with the understanding that they can come back each summer as long as they see fit. Most crew members return for several seasons.

Since most of our crew members are college students, we do sometimes have a problem covering the spring and fall months when colleges are in session. We have discovered that colleges vary

Camping gear (left) is ready for new trips. Returned gear (right) needs cleanup.

considerably in their schedules. Some colleges begin in early to mid-August and finish up by early to mid-May. Others begin classes in late September and finish well into June. One of our primary considerations in choosing employees is to hire people from schools that are on different schedules. We also like to hire one or two people who are out of school temporarily and can come early and/or stay late. We try to persuade our college graduates to stay on in the fall before starting their new lives. We have some employees who are out of school and thus not bound to college schedules. Frank and I, in retirement, get to fill in sometimes in May, September, or October.

We are thoroughly satisfied with our work-credit system. It has many advantages. It distributes the amount of work evenly so that each crew member feels treated fairly. It gives crew members a say in what they are doing so that they can use their skills to best advantage or learn new skills as they desire. It takes the onerous duty of supervision or discipline off the shoulders of the owners. If a person is not doing his job properly or completely, the situation is almost certainly handled by other crew members who are affected. All jobs are interrelated so that any omission is immediately noted by the person handling the next phase of the work.

For example, cleaning up the returned camping equipment is hardly an appealing or inspiring job. Procrastination in doing it is very understandable. However, the person assigned to packing new trips depends on this cleanup. Should it not be done in a timely or thorough manner, the two crew members would be in immediate consultation and negotiation. Delinquency is not reported to a boss for disciplinary action. Since the crew members all live together, they are highly motivated by social pressure and the desire to get along well together.

We endorse the ideal of equality. Each crew member is equal under the work-credit system. The owners of the business do not have special privileges but take their chances on work assignments just like anyone else. This does not preclude the owners from having control or final authority when the occasion demands it. It just works out that that those occasions are quite rare. Work gets done and everyone lives with some measure of harmony. This is not to suggest that we have found B.F. Skinner's Utopian community, but there is a general satisfaction on the part of both employers and employees. Former crew members often wish they could continue to work under this system in their "real world" careers.

· Chapter 19 ·

—— BWCAW – Federal Role ——

*E*very present-day visitor to the Boundary Waters Canoe Area Wilderness (BWCAW) is aware that "the government" is exercising some control over the area. Almost everyone has a vague recollection of "the government" forcing out a resort or a home owner. The facts are very complex, span a long period of at least a century and a half, and, by many, are not well remembered or understood. A review of the BWCAW's history can lend a better understanding of present-day management.

First of all, what does "the government" mean? The average user in the Sawbill area usually tends to think of "The DNR" as the governmental body in charge. This undoubtedly comes from the experience of purchasing a fishing license issued by the Minnesota Department of Natural Resources (DNR). What are the facts?

The DNR is in charge of the waters, lakes, and streams in the Boundary Waters as well as in all the rest of the state of Minnesota. The land known as the Superior National Forest is under the jurisdiction of the U.S. Forest Service (USFS), an agency of the U.S.

Department of Agriculture (USDA). So, while the waters are under state control, the federal government is the primary manager.

Congress makes the laws that govern the Boundary Waters. They are administered and enforced by the USFS. The top administrator is the Secretary of Agriculture. The whole country is divided into regions. Minnesota is in the Eastern Region, which is headquartered in Milwaukee. Each national forest in the country has a supervisor. The Superior National Forest has its forest headquarters in Duluth. Under that are the smaller district offices in Ely, Aurora, Cook, Grand Marais, and Tofte. A district ranger is in charge of each of these installations. The people who work in the woods are not called rangers, but they are supervised by the ranger. They are officially technicians, specialists, or managers such as wildlife specialists or timber managers. Sometimes the seasonal employees who enforce regulations in the Boundary Waters are affectionately called "wilderness rangers," but the only true rangers are the officials in charge of each Forest Service district.

The USFS and the Minnesota DNR work in close cooperation to manage the BWCAW. Because some of the land within the Boundary Waters is state-owned, the two agencies must work together to maintain campsites and portages. They also cooperate closely in the areas of wildlife habitat, prescribed fire management, and wildfire control.

It should be noted that our national parks are under a totally different jurisdiction — the Department of Interior — and different styles of management and different regulations apply.

Development Versus Conservation

Conflict and differing points of view regarding resources began to develop in the earliest days of settlement in Northeastern Minnesota. Some people observed that uncontrolled exploitation rapidly depleted resources. Clearing a stand of timber that had been growing for hundreds of years eliminated that resource, at least for the ensuing century. In addition, the process of harvesting timber brought in large numbers of people and mechanized equipment, which led to serious problems such as fire. The whole North Shore burned off in successive fires around the turn of the 20th century.

Logging operations in the woods led to fires. For example, railroad train engines threw off sparks, which landed in dry leaves or duff and ignited fires. Wherever there were people, fire became more common and more devastating. Public opinion began to change and to inspire thoughts of conservation. What lay in the future when the lumber and the minerals and the fish were gone? As the population increased, resources were being used up with increasingly greater speed. Some individuals thought controls were needed to preserve life as well as livelihood.

On the other side is the fact that human beings naturally resent control, preferring the freedom to do as they choose. Restrictions on behavior are never well received. Restrictions affecting one's livelihood — hunting and fishing for food, using forest products for shelter — are understandingly unwelcome and vociferously opposed. Two factions developed very early — those who were freely using natural resources and those who wanted to impose controls on the use of resources.

An influential Minnesotan, General Christopher G. Andrews, was among those who thought that resources were being used up too quickly. Andrews was Minnesota's leading advocate of forest conservation in the late 1800s. In 1895, he was appointed the state's chief fire warden and then forestry commissioner, serving until 1911. He persuaded the legislature to establish the first Minnesota state forests in 1899. He championed the creation of what would become the Chippewa National Forest in 1902. He envisioned another national forest in Northeastern Minnesota. He persuaded the federal government to withdraw from sale three large tracts of land along the American-Canadian border in 1902, 1905, and 1908. These were designated as forest reserves. The first of these tracts consisted of 500,000 acres of recently burned-over land that were therefore commercially unattractive. Some of the land was already in the hands of timber companies and being logged.[1]

On February 13, 1909, these three reserves were folded into the Superior National Forest, created by proclamation of President Theodore Roosevelt. At first, the Forest encompassed a little over a million (1,018,636) acres. Gradually, another million acres were purchased so that Superior National Forest now consists of 2,092,997 acres. It extends from the shore of Lake Superior to the Canadian border and from the eastern part of St. Louis County through Cook County. Tofte Ranger Larry Dawson once commented that he was responsible for an area bigger than the state of Rhode Island.

Canadian conservationists were also concerned about logging operations and the rapid decline of moose and caribou that were being heavily harvested to feed the men in the lumber camps. Ontario officials created the Quetico Forest and Game Reserve in April 1909, and this became the Quetico Provincial Park in 1913. The Quetico Park shares a border with Superior National Forest, greatly enlarging the wilderness area. Hunting was declared off limits in the Quetico and that has never changed. Minnesota at first declared part of the Forest a game preserve but later withdrew this provision, so hunting is allowed.

It is important to note that Superior National Forest is not a solid block of land. The 2 million acres of the Forest exist within an area of over 3 million (3,259,719) acres. Many pockets of land are still privately owned or belong to the state of Minnesota, counties, townships, and Grand Portage Reservation. For example, in every township, sections 16 and 36 are set aside as "School Trust Land," the income from which is to benefit the schools. Thus, these are blocks of land now surrounded by the BWCAW. Parenthetically, they are no longer very useful as sources of revenue for the schools. Continuous negotiation is underway to trade blocks of land buried in the middle of the wilderness for blocks of land that could be used to produce revenue, or to sell these blocks to the federal government and invest the money to produce revenue for the schools. These sales or trades are very complicated and normally take years and years to complete. This is not a problem unique to the Boundary Waters or Superior National Forest. Such blocks of land exist in almost every national forest. In 2002, there were still about 250 acres of privately-owned, undeveloped land in the BWCAW. The Forest Service maintains a standing offer to buy the land if any of the owners are willing to sell.

The effort to consolidate the new national forest began almost immediately after it was established. National legislation (the *Weeks Act of 1911*) established a National Forest Reservation Commission whose mission was to consider and approve the purchase of lands for national forest purposes. The federal government moved promptly to buy undeveloped land. The process continued over the years. It became much more difficult when these pockets of land were in private ownership and already developed.

Government control does not occur lightly out of a desire to take charge. As development speeded up, so did the desire to keep some land undeveloped. In the early 1920s, plans were afoot to build major new roads plus spur roads to open up the new forest to summer cottages and resorts. These plans were successfully opposed by the new Isaak Walton League of America. In 1926, Secretary of Agriculture W.M. Jardine announced a policy establishing a new "Roadless Area" wilderness. He spelled out which roads would be built for purposes of fire protection but also decreed that "not less than 1,000 square miles containing the best of the lakes and waterways will be kept as wilderness recreation area." This Roadless Area roughly coincided with today's BWCAW, except for several large parcels on the international boundary that were then already owned by lumber companies. This policy came in response to widespread plans to build roads in the area.

At the same time, Edward W. Backus, owner of a number of business enterprises, including a dam near International Falls, sought to dam the waters all along the international boundary from Rainy Lake to Saganaga Lake to provide his businesses with more power. His ideas were opposed by a group of people who formed the first commission of concerned citizens dedicated to defending the area. This was the Quetico-Superior Council, an international body with headquarters in Minneapolis. Ernest C. Oberholtzer, who lived on Rainy Lake, was elected president. This group succeeded in getting Congress to pass the *Shipstead-Newton-Nolan Act* in 1930. This law withdrew federal land from homesteading, prohibited logging on federal land within 400 feet of recreational waterways in certain areas of the Superior National Forest, and prohibited alteration of the natural water level by dams. Backus's plan to build dams was sidetracked. The Great Depression also thwarted his plans. Two years later his businesses were in receivership.

Metropolitan populations were increasing rapidly in the 1900s and more people were seeking recreational opportunities in the North Woods. While mineral exploration for precious metals never produced any significant riches, word did reach populated areas of the Midwest about the wealth of hunting and fishing opportunities. As early as 1920, an organization in Cook County known as The Ten Thousand Lakes Association was promoting tourism and the establishment of facilities to accommodate tourists who were clamoring to come.

Until 1925, it was not possible to drive all the way along the North Shore, so early outdoor enthusiasts usually came by boat. They found overnight accommodations in the homes of hospitable people such as C.A.A. Nelson in Lutsen and Ben Fenstad in Little Marais, owners of commercial fisheries. The hosts first rented rooms in their homes and then began to build cabins on their property to house their guests. Of course, they provided their guests with meals as there were no restaurants. Often the hosts transported their guests farther into the woods, using horse-drawn wagons. Thus the tourist industry on the North Shore was born. It was inevitable that resorts on inland lakes would soon develop.

Airplanes Become Popular

Before 1930, a number of fledgling resorts were on the Gunflint Trail. Among others, Bill and Justine Kerfoot operated Gunflint Lodge, Russell and Eve Blankenburg were at Seagull, and the Gapens had Gateway Lodge.

The Arbogusts arrived in 1932 to establish Sawbill Lodge. The concept of flying customers to remote places for fishing was gaining popularity. Before long, they were flying their guests to more remote lakes for overnight stays.

On one occasion, all camping equipment and supplies were flown into Cherokee Lake and left at a campsite. The Lodge guests came in by canoe. When they arrived at their campsite, they were a

bit surprised to find it already occupied. A bear was drinking their beer!

Brule Lake was the site of several business enterprises. Mike Fink had a resort near the landing. Harley Dinges rented boats and motors and sold gasoline and bait at his place near the landing. The Pure Oil Company had a resort on the biggest island in the middle of Brule. It was a customer relations fishing retreat, not open to the public. Executives who were likely to sign big contracts to buy gasoline and oil were flown in and entertained. Later the establishment was sold to Ruan, a large truck-rental company that used it for the same purpose. Ken Osman used his private plane to reach the family cabin at the west end of Brule. Nearly 20 resorts in the area used planes for the benefit of their customers.

World War II intervened in the early 1940s. Every able-bodied man was called to serve his country and women took jobs in defense

Emerson Morris was one of many local pilots during the fly-in era.

industries, covering the work left behind by the men in service. Women were also busy offering support services to the armed forces. Gasoline supplies were dedicated to military purposes, so, even if there were any would-be vacationers, there was not much opportunity to travel. Many resorts closed.

However, a long-standing local enterprise reached its peak during the war years — trapping. Fur was in high demand, especially in Europe where it was used in military clothing. Beginning with the first settlers, local residents had always supplemented their incomes with trapping and marketing beaver, otter, fisher, and marten pelts, but the war years were a time when this enterprise yielded big money.

Ray Gervais of Tofte owned and operated Lakeview (a tavern and grocery store) but he had many other enterprises. His father, Joe Gervais, had a tavern in Schroeder and boat rentals on Pine and Beaver lakes (now Crescent and Lichen) and was a famed trapper. Ray, full of energy and drive, bought up tax-forfeited land in the county, built an airport in Tofte, and owned a fleet of five airplanes. An accomplished pilot himself, he employed two other pilots — Morrie Carlson and Ernie Houtala. He had two float planes dedicated to flying anglers to remote lakes. He parked one plane at Nelson's Caribou Resort on Caribou Lake and one at Sawbill Lake.

Ray began to dream of having his own fly-in resort. About 1938, he began building on a point of land he owned in the southwest corner of Cherokee Lake. He built a kitchen and dining building, then three cabins for sleeping.

One of his major businesses was flying into remote lakes to pick up furs. The trapper supplying the furs could then stay out in the woods and continue trapping. Ray's resort became a warehouse or staging area for his fur business. He sold most of his furs to a man named George Kinnunen, who sold them to the Hudson's Bay Company in Canada for shipment to Europe. One summer in the early 1940s, Ray did operate his resort as a fly-in base for fishing.

Ray always felt harassed by Forest Service personnel and state game wardens, feeling that his actions were being stealthily observed and disapproved. Undoubtedly they were disapproved since much of his fur business was illegal. The Forest Service did not encourage his Cherokee resort and let him know that his development was unwelcome. Nevertheless, he persisted and would never have given up voluntarily, had disaster not intervened. His hopes, his body, and his finances were all shattered by a very serious plane crash in the fall of 1945 as he came in for a landing at the Tofte airport. Originally declared dead, he recovered and fought his way back to mobility over the next several years. His body continued to serve him well until March 2002, when he died at the age of 92.

The insurance that he thought was protecting him as a pilot proved useless. The company told him it covered him only if he was flying on a regular commercial schedule. For financial reasons, he was forced to sell the Cherokee resort to the government. In time, high energy and great resourcefulness enabled him to recover financially as well as physically.[2]

Business Development Increases

When the war ended in 1945, attention returned once more to recreational pursuits. Resorts reopened and a new recreational service business — canoe outfitting — was conceived. A number of canoe outfitters sprang up in the Ely area. Wilderness Outfitters and Bill Rom's Canoe Country Outfitters were the largest and most enduring. On the eastern side of the Forest, Gunflint Outfitters began in 1946 as an offshoot of Gunflint Lodge.

As the war drew to a close, demand for timber greatly increased. One Forest Service timber sale of 130 square miles went to the Tomahawk Timber Company of Wisconsin. This parcel was located north of Lake Isabella, which was in the Roadless Area. To accommodate this big lumbering operation, the Forest Service produced a revised management plan in 1948 to exclude the town site with its railroad landing and roads from the Roadless Area. Silver Island Lake, the largest lake in the vicinity, has a Forest Service campground, which now sees heavy use by motorboat anglers, mostly people from northern Minnesota.

Many men moved into the area to work in this huge logging operation, bringing their families with them. By 1948, a new town called Forest Center sprang up and a school was built for the children. Numerous roads were constructed. A new railroad spur was built to transport the timber. The loading area at the end of the railroad was called Sawbill Landing.

Although Sawbill Landing has not existed as a railroad loading dock since the 1950s, it appeared on maps — including the official Forest Service map — for another 50 years. And every year, a number of people referred to the maps and chose Sawbill Landing (thinking it was Sawbill Lake landing) as the place they planned to rent canoes and equipment for their wilderness trip. Arriving at Sawbill Landing, which is now nothing more than an intersection of gravel roads, they were confused and frustrated and faced with a time-consuming drive of 40 miles to Sawbill Canoe Outfitters.

Immediately after the war, interest in airplanes for civilian use skyrocketed. The Forest Service began using airplanes for fire patrol. Remote resorts were built. By 1948, there were 41 such resorts in the interior of what would become the BWCAW, with roughly half serviced by airplanes. Ely had the distinction of being the largest freshwater seaplane base on the continent.

Not surprisingly, the growing volume of air traffic began to change the character of the area and the government stepped in to control development. In December 1949, President Truman signed an executive order stipulating that airplanes must not fly below 4,000 feet above sea level in the area of Superior National Forest known as the Roadless Area. He did this under the auspices of the *Civil Aeronautics Act* passed by Congress in 1938, which established federal control of all air space above the United States. It meant the end of small airplane use in the Roadless Area, which was roughly the northern third of the Forest.

Resorts could no longer fly customers into remote fishing lakes. The order was not intended to interfere with commercial air traffic, which would normally fly above the stipulated air space. Forest Service planes were affected by this order. They now must fly above the air space on fire patrol, for research purposes, or for search and rescue, and can only enter the air space in an emergency. No restrictions were imposed on the other two thirds of the Forest. Private

Forest Service planes gather at Sawbill Lake in 1961.

owners of fly-in resorts were most affected. There was a flurry of legal action brought by the owners. Some deliberately violated the ban to provoke court proceedings. By 1956, the cases had been decided on the side of preserving wilderness values.

Legislation Increases Restrictions

Efforts to consolidate the Forest received a big boost from Minnesota Senator Ed Thye and Representative John Blatnik in 1948. They introduced legislation that authorized the Secretary of Agriculture to acquire land in Superior National Forest by purchase or condemnation; $500,000 was set aside to do it.

By 1955, 90 percent of the land was owned by the federal government, but the remaining land was increasing in value so rapidly that it was becoming very expensive to acquire, and it might soon be totally out of reach. This problem was addressed by Minnesota's Senator Hubert Humphrey and Representative August Andresen, who offered an amendment to the 1948 bill, aimed at speeding up acquisition of the remaining land and making more money available for the purpose. This bill asked for an appropriation of $2.5 million. Emotion began to swirl in Northeastern Minnesota. Private land owners and business operators saw their property being targeted for acquisition. On the other side was the argument that the public interest demanded the preservation of this unique wilderness. Bill Magie, speaking for Friends of the Wilderness, pointed out, "Thirty years ago much of the private land in the Roadless Area could have been purchased for less than what is asked for one property today. Time is running out. The purchase program can no longer wait. We must assure the preservation of the Wilderness Canoe Country for the enjoyment of the boys and girls of tomorrow."

Two resort owners in the Ely area, Joseph Perko and William Zupancich, led the opposition, testing the government's will and the legality of restrictive legislation. They had continued to use airplanes to fly customers to their resorts for three years while lawsuits and appeals were slowly moving through the courts. Immediately after the appeals court finally ruled that the airspace ban of 1949 was legal, on Memorial Day weekend of 1953, at least 50 flights carrying 110 passengers arrived at three resorts. Flights continued until July when U.S. marshals seized the plane. Then the two protesters began transporting their customers by truck over an abandoned railroad grade through the Roadless Area to their Crooked Lake resorts. They brought in a bulldozer and started improving the road. They argued that their business would be ruined if they couldn't build the road. In 1956, a decision was handed down. District Judge Dennis Donovan ruled that Perko and Zupancich had no right of access other than the traditional means of boat, canoe, and portage. This reaffirmed the earlier decision by Judge Gunnar H. Nordbye of the Federal District Court stating that no public roads and no private rights to roads existed within the Roadless Area. The resort owners finally agreed to sell out to the government. It was a major victory for wilderness advocates but court cases challenging the decision continued.[3]

At the same time, the Forest Service was developing additional plans to protect the Forest. The need for rules, regulations, and support services was apparent as more and more people were using the area. For example, many campsites had informally established dumps where campers deposited their cans, glass bottles, and other refuse. In 1956, the Forest Service announced plans to assign three two-person crews to the Forest each season to clean up campsites and portages. By 1972, there were seven crews of five persons each (or 35 people) working the Sawbill area. Forest Service budget cuts led to reducing these numbers until, by 1995, there were again only three two-person crews. They also announced their intentions to work with canoe outfitters to educate the public in good wilderness manners: always drown a campfire with water; bury garbage, cans, and glass; clean up a campsite before leaving.

During the 1950s and early 1960s, use of the area mushroomed. Canoeing increased in popularity and many new canoe outfitting businesses were established. At the same time, advances in technology made motorboats and motors lighter so that boaters could more conveniently take them into more remote lakes — and they did. Snowmobiles entered the picture toward the end of the 1950s, enabling winter travel to the most remote lakes. The logging business was thriving, requiring roads into the sites. Around Sawbill, logging operations existed on each side of us, known as the East Tofte Block and the West Tofte Block. We visited logging sites on Ella Lake (east of us) and between Burnt and Kelly lakes (west of us) while we were out cross-country skiing. In the summer, we felt the strange contradiction as we struggled across portages with our canoes and gear and then suddenly came upon a good gravel road intersecting the portage.

In 1958, the Forest Service renamed the Roadless Area, calling it the Boundary Waters Canoe Area. The final W for Wilderness would be added in 1978.

All this activity and the great increase in usage led to a directive from Secretary of Agriculture Orville Freeman in 1965. His management plan divided the BWCA into a 600,000-acre Interior Zone closed to logging and a 400,000-acre Portal Zone open to logging. It called for the immediate addition of 150,000 acres of the Forest to the no-cut zone with another 100,000 acres to be added by 1975 as existing logging contracts were completed. This would bring the total no-cut area to 612,000 acres by 1975. His directive also addressed motorboat and snowmobile usage by restricting them to designated routes already in use. This plan was widely challenged and led to many legal and administrative battles.

At about the same time, Congress was responding to a national interest in wilderness. The *Wilderness Act of 1964* designated wilderness areas for the whole country and stipulated that permanent structures in these areas were prohibited. This act made the BWCA part of the new Wilderness Preservation System.

As a result, cabins and fire towers scattered throughout the BWCA were removed. The Forest Service had maintained a small cabin on the north end of Cherokee Lake. The DNR had a cabin on Sawbill Lake. Property owners, summer cabin owners, and resort owners located within the new BWCA were forced to make a decision. They were given the option of selling out to the government or taking lifetime occupancy, after which the property would revert to the government with no compensation. Among these property owners were our friends the Osmans, who had a summer cabin on Brule, as did the Frogners. Other well-known residents of the BWCA at the time were Dorothy Molter (on Knife Lake) and Benny Ambrose (on Ottertrack Lake).

The Osmans chose to sell out immediately. They had been feeling that it was time to give up their isolated existence. That did not keep them from being resentful. Even though they were well reimbursed for their property, they were extremely unhappy to relinquish this family-owned retreat.

Dorothy Molter and Benny Ambrose chose to stay. They were given a limited reservation status that they both outlived. In order to allow them to live out their lives in the BWCA, they were made Forest Service volunteers. The Forest Service devoted a lot of effort to taking care of Dorothy in her last years. The popular Dorothy Molter Museum in Ely tells her life story and memorializes the woman fondly known as "the root beer lady."

This restriction affected resorts and canoe outfitters because it banned equipment storage and tent camps in the BWCA. Business owners, as well as individuals, would store one or more canoes near the end of a portage to avoid carrying canoes over the portage. Campsites also would be set up and left in the woods so that customers could camp at remote and secluded sites without portaging equipment. Of course, the best campsites on the lake were always chosen for these "permanent camps."

The official regulation included the following provisions. It was hard to give up these conveniences:

> 1. The erection or use of a permanent or semi-permanent camp within the Boundary Waters Canoe Area is prohibited.
> 2. All camping equipment . . . may be brought into the BWCA only by the person or persons who will use it, and shall be removed by such person or persons upon leaving the area.
> 3. Any camp or item of equipment found . . . will be immediately impounded.

The use of motorboats was undoubtedly the hottest, most controversial issue in the process

Cherokee Lake Cabin (shown here in the 1930s with P.S. Newcomb and Emerson Morris) was removed after Congress passed the Wilderness Act of 1964.

of establishing wilderness. Motorboats were being used in the Boundary Waters area as early as 1922. This did not cause great concern until the 1950s, when traffic increased markedly and the use of motors in interior lakes became much more prevalent. The *1948 Thye-Blatnik Bill* called for motors to be restricted to areas where their use was well established. This idea was also reaffirmed in the *Wilderness Bill of 1964*. As originally written, it included a provision to ban motors on all wilderness lakes. However, Senator Hubert Humphrey, who was a leading sponsor of the legislation, inserted clauses specifically exempting the BWCA. In order to get the bill passed, he responded to the vociferous demands of his northern Minnesota constituents and inserted the following provision: "Nothing in this act shall preclude the continuance within the area of any already established use of motorboats." There are motorboat advocates who still declare that this was a guarantee of motorboat use in perpetuity.

In the Sawbill area, this law led to banning motors on Alton Lake, the most popular fishing lake at that time. The action actually was taken by the state of Minnesota because the access point of Alton Lake is on state land, outside the BWCA. The state passed a rule in 1970 that extended federal rules to any state-owned land. The rules thus endorsed by the state of Minnesota included: the ban on non-burnable cans and bottles; requirements for campers to build fires only in an established fire grate; to leave no fire unattended; to cut no living trees or branches; to leave a clean campsite. Use of motors was prohibited.

The Forest Service promptly removed the narrow-gauge railroad tracks on the Sawbill-to-Alton and Alton-to-Kelso portages. For 30 years, anglers had used the little flatcars on these rails to pull their motorboats over the portages. Some of these users were very upset with the new developments. Some abandoned the area and found other places to vacation and fish. Some remained sufficiently attached to their vacation spots and their fishing holes to make the switch to canoe travel, paddling, and portaging.

Sawbill Outfitters was not upset by this change because the cars were deteriorating to the point of being unsafe. We had tried to obtain replacement parts or to have them restored, but without any success. We were distressed at losing some faithful customers who did not feel able to switch to canoe travel. Opinions differ regarding fishing from canoes. Many people feel that it is totally unrealistic and even unsafe to fish from a canoe. Others fish very successfully from a canoe. The difference may be related to the style of fishing.

A well-kept secret is that fishing success has steadily improved since motors were banned. Noise and the pollution from gasoline fumes and spills may account for this. At the same time, the wilderness controversy and the banning of motors led to major changes in the purposes for visiting the area. Fishing, once the main reason for visiting the Sawbill area, has definitely declined in importance. We have not gathered facts on this issue, but it is safe to estimate that no more than a third of Sawbill's customers come with the intention of doing serious fishing. The rest come seeking wilderness values of solitude, quiet, and experiencing nature. Many do not take fishing gear with them. For others, fishing is incidental.

Various bills were introduced in Congress in the 1970s, culminating with the *BWCAW Act of 1978*. The act designated 1,075,000 acres as wilderness and provided for further purchase of private properties within that area. It added further restrictions on motorboats and other motorized vehicles, and banned logging, mineral exploration, and mining within the wilderness area. The BWCAW was already the most heavily used unit of the national wilderness system. Many businesses served the recreation seekers. Resort owners felt threatened and strongly protested the concept of banning motors. In an effort to find a compromise between business owners and wilderness advocates, sizable lakes on the edges of the BWCAW that were accessible by road were left open to motor use, but the size of the motor was limited to 25 horsepower. Many people had been using larger motors. On other lakes where motor use was already established, motor size was limited to 10 horsepower and provision was made to phase out gradually all use of motors.

The consolation prize for resort owners was the provision that any resort riparian to certain lakes and in commercial operation during 1975, 1976, or 1977 had the option to require the government to buy them out at fair market value. Sawbill Lodge accepted a buyout. Sawbill Canoe Outfitters, not considered riparian to Sawbill Lake, did not have this option. We also had no interest in being bought out. Many of the smaller resorts in the Ely area and some in the Gunflint area exercised this option. Fair market appraisals were very generous. In addition, a business owner could choose to retain one or more buildings and up to three acres of land for personal use. Some casual observers thought that many businesses were being "forced out" but the facts do not support this. It was a choice made by each business. There is no way to know if the businesses that sold out would actually have been negatively impacted by the legislation as was feared. We know that our business was very favorably impacted and that others who chose to stay in business also found this to be the case.

It may seem to casual observers that new regulations come to the Boundary Waters frequently, and it may seem that new rules and regulations are imposed on a whim or without much warning. Nothing could be further from the actual fact. The U.S. Forest Service is quite sensitive to the fact that it represents the public interest and is deliberate to a fault. No change occurs until an issue has been presented in public meetings and debated at length. Anyone affected by a change in rules is specifically invited to attend meetings and everyone is welcome to attend. Notices are posted encouraging public comment. Action takes place slowly because long periods are allowed for public comment. Public opinion is also gathered by doing surveys in the field. A majority of the general public favors preserving some wilderness space, a fact that skews the decisions in that direction.

The Forest Service uses advanced, up-to-date procedures for their decision-making process. First, they gather facts. Their research is very well done. They are concerned with fairness and with treating various factions evenhandedly. They consider carefully how proposed actions may affect businesses and the local economy. When meetings are held, there are periods for presentation of facts and for brainstorming. Decisions are made by consensus. If no consensus can be achieved, they may propose mitigation. An example of mitigation might be stretching the process over a period of time to ease any adverse impact that may result. When legislation called for banning motors in the wilderness, the ban was phased in over several years for some lakes. Possibly the adjustment required of local residents would have been faster if motors had been banned in one fell swoop. Still, that was not possible given the violent opposition, particularly in the Ely area. Protests were literally violent, involving spitting on opponents, throwing rocks, and posting handmade insulting and profane signs on highways.

Brule Lake was an example of how the Forest Service operates. There was strong feeling expressed by many people against banning motors on Brule. Therefore, the *1978 BWCAW Bill* provided specifically that motors could continue to be used on Brule until January 1994, or until businesses already in operation in 1977 were terminated. The last business, Sky Blue Water Resort, closed its doors in 1986 and the motor ban went into effect. Outfitters in the area are unanimous in their observation that use of Brule by canoeists has greatly increased since that time.

The Forest Service has been careful not to impose unnecessary restrictions. For example, while establishing the permit system, it was proposed that all day-users as well as overnight campers should be required to get a permit. That did not happen. Day-users have never been required to apply in advance or pay for a permit. They are asked to fill out a permit at the time of departure just for recordkeeping. Research thus far indicates that day-use is not in conflict with wilderness values. Carrying firearms in the BWCAW is another example of a restriction that has been proposed but ultimately rejected by the Forest Service.

Other interesting proposals made by the public include banning fish locators, temperature probes, or electronic depth finders on the theory that fishing should be done "naturally." Banning boom boxes has been suggested in the interest of preserving the peace and quiet of the wilderness. It has even been suggested that global positioning system (GPS) devices be banned. None of these proposed restrictions has been adopted.

The canoeing public who make their voices heard wanted the

Portage signs showing trail distance to the next lake were removed from the BWCAW.

BWCAW to be even more primitive and requested the removal of picnic tables from campsites. The Forest Service obliged. A vocal majority of canoeists objected to the portage signs, which posted the name of the lake ahead and the length (in rods) of the portage. Those have been removed, as well as the canoe rests on the portages. The vocal minority of motor users has been successful in maintaining motor use on 21 percent of the lakes.

The issues are primarily based on nostalgia. Motor users want to continue beloved recreational pursuits in the same places and in the same manner as they have done in the past. They feel rebellious toward outside controls of their behavior. Paddlers are passionate about solitude and wilderness that contains no trace of human presence. There is a large group of people who can be content with a middle ground. Personally, I love seeing other people out in the Boundary Waters paddling, fishing, or camping — as long as they are considerate of others using the area. Of course, I am disturbed by rowdy, destructive behavior. It is very distressing to see candy wrappers or empty bait cartons scattered on portages, to see vegetation destroyed, or to hear shouting, firecrackers, or gunshots.

Such inconsiderate behavior occurs rarely in the Sawbill area.

On the Forest Service campgrounds that Sawbill Outfitters manages, there have been just a few instances over the years when law enforcement was needed to control behavior. Once, a group of intoxicated young women refused to quiet down and refused to leave — until the sheriff came. Usually the campground host's request is all that is needed to keep noise under control. On one occasion, two young men cut down several trees on their campsite to feed their campfire. The Forest Service cited and fined them. Part of their punishment, imposed by the Tofte district ranger, was a day-long session of planting new trees.

Educating Users of the BWCAW

Sawbill Outfitters has been an ardent supporter of user education for the Boundary Waters. One of our favorite provisions of the *1978 BWCAW Act* states:

> "The Secretary (of Agriculture) is authorized and directed to develop an educational program for the recreational users of the wilderness, which will assist them to understand the purpose, value, and appropriate use of wilderness lands and the functioning of natural ecosystems in wilderness."

Sawbill's Bill Hansen was president of the Boundary Waters Wilderness Education Consortium, which was responsible for developing the educational video that is now required viewing for every member of every group obtaining a permit to enter the BWCAW. It was in place for the 1992 season.

We hear some complaints about repeated watching of the video from visitors who make several trips a year. They are in a hurry to start their trips and resist spending seven minutes watching a video. I can relate to this sense of urgency, but also I love the video and personally watch it many times a year. I sometimes show it to entertain guests who aren't BWCAW users. It combines nostalgic high points of the wilderness experience with suggestions for comfortable and efficient ways to handle chores such as dishwashing

Customers receive an orientation to the Boundary Waters at a 1976 session in Sawbill's dome.

under primitive conditions. Sharpening up camping skills protects the environment. The video illustrates the recommended response to a visit by a bear, and is designed to calm fears about wild animal encounters. It encourages Boundary Waters users to "leave no trace." It is a beautiful and enjoyable production. It has been revised and updated several times since its inception. A longer 21-minute version of the first video was made for distribution to groups contemplating a visit to the BWCAW. An updated version of the video was in place in 2005.

At Sawbill, overnight campers are given a thorough orientation, which includes information on their equipment and food, safety in the woods, and history of the area. I hear Bill reminding people that some of the portages they walk over were used 10,000 years ago by Native Americans. It sets a tone that encourages an attitude of awe and reverence for the wilderness as opposed to rowdy carelessness.

Permit System Comes to the BWCA

The federal government regulation that has had by far the most impact on Sawbill Canoe Outfitters is the permit system. The *Wilderness Act of 1964* gave the Forest Service direction for managing the BWCA. Forest Supervisor Lawrence Neff wrote all concerned parties shortly thereafter: "Those measures legally possible now will be started immediately. Others will follow as rapidly as necessary legal or administrative questions can be resolved." Thus was the permit system born. At the same time, he announced the establishment of a full-time staff position dedicated to BWCA management, and assigned J. Wesley White to fill this position.

The purpose of the permit system is to control the impact of use on the resources — land and water. A wilderness campsite is often beautiful and attractive, with green ground cover, moss, and flowers, or it can be bare ground with mud or swirling dust. The latter condition is the result of heavy use. Many feet mean that vegetation is trampled. A related problem of overuse is that campers going out during a busy time such as holidays might be unable to find an empty campsite and might respond by making a new campsite. This is a serious fire hazard and does not enhance the beauty of the shoreline. Heavy use also contributes to water pollution.

Before proposing the permit system, the Forest Service sponsored research to determine how many people could use the area while still retaining its wilderness quality. They studied actual usage as well as users' perceptions of crowding. They found that 50 percent of all users were starting their trips from three of 70 possible entry points, causing major overcrowding on those three entry lakes. Overcrowding was also occurring at certain times such as holidays. Use in general was much less than the maximum capacity they envisioned as possible without harm to the resource. Forest Supervisor Craig Rupp wrote: "The 1969 pilot study indicates the Canoe Area as a whole, properly managed, can possibly accommodate double the present number of visitors." The effort to relieve crowding was begun with the 1971 canoeing season when it became necessary for visitors to obtain a permit before entering the Boundary Waters. This gave the Forest Service a reliable body of data on the actual use of the area.

Littering by users is another problem the Forest Service takes seriously. As crews cleaned campsites, they were picking up 400,000 pounds (or 200 tons) of litter annually, mostly metal and glass food containers. The Ely Outfitters Association proposed that, beginning in 1971, they would outfit without cans or bottles and use only burnable packaging materials. The Forest Service strongly encouraged all outfitters to follow suit. After a feasibility study, the request was changed to a requirement.

The no-cans-or-bottles goal was eloquently stated in this 1971 notice from the Forest Service:

> "This rule has become necessary to assure that the Canoe Area remains unimpaired for future use and enjoyment and remains a place where the earth and its community of life shall retain an appearance of being untrammeled by man and where the imprint of man is substantially unnoticed."

Immediately after the 1971 season, study began to refine the system. The 1971 experience led to suggestions for reducing party size from 15 to eight. We proposed a party size of nine since our customers often traveled three to a canoe. The rule ultimately evolved into a limitation of 10 people to a party. It was first imposed in the 1973 season. In 1995, it was changed to a limit of nine people with no more than four canoes per party.

By 1976, further study and analysis of the data led to a plan to impose quotas on the number of parties entering the Boundary Waters on a given day at each of the 70 entry points. The purpose was to distribute the use to more lightly-used areas and time periods and thus to avoid destructive overuse of a few areas. Entry limits were established with a target of a maximum of two-thirds or 67 percent occupancy of the campsites available in the area. Computer predictions were invaluable in determining the quota for each entry point. The Sawbill quota was set at 16. However, the Forest Service also set up a phase-in period during which greater occupancy would be allowed, making Sawbill's quota 20 entries per day.

The problem of people who might travel a long distance to start a wilderness trip only to find a certain permit unavailable was addressed by establishing a reservation system. Forest Service research showed that 25 percent of the permits would cover this group. Therefore, 25 percent of the permits could be reserved in advance by contacting the Forest Service. The rest of the permits would continue to be available on a short-term basis.

An important outcome of this new system was that camping could be on designated, established sites only. This had previously been encouraged but could not be enforced.

To assist them in implementing this new user-distribution system, the Forest Service designated certain service-providers such as outfitters or camp directors as "Cooperators." Cooperators could issue permits after first making a telephone call to the Forest Service office to determine availability. Contrary to popular opinion, Cooperators were never

A BWCA travel permit issued in 1973

given any permits that they could issue at their own discretion. The privilege of being a Cooperator could be withdrawn from any business or individual who tried to bend the rules, and this was enforced. Cooperators were enjoined to promote minimum-impact camping as they issued permits and to ask campers to abide by the rules, a copy of which was to be attached to the permit.

Many complexities are involved in a reservation system and these were gradually addressed as the years passed. The matter of "no shows" was addressed in 1977 by a policy of overbooking. Advance reservations could be accepted for 25 percent more than the target number of permits. The major change in 1978 was that 100 percent of permits were included in the reservation system instead of the original 25 percent.

I've observed an unintended consequence to the quota system that actually increases the usage of the area. It has to do with the natural tendency of *Homo sapiens* to rebel. The fact that admission to the BWCAW is not totally free and open but somewhat regulated makes it more appealing to some people. They feel challenged to visit this place, thereby increasing the number of users. I always think of this when I drive the back roads adjacent to the BWCAW and see lake after lake of great beauty totally unregulated and deserted while people are frantically struggling to get on the list to go into the BWCAW. This is sometimes related to their perception that the area is restricted. Often I hear people say that they want to go into the Boundary Waters just to be able to say they have done it.

Minor adjustments have been made over the years in the process for reserving a permit. All permit applications received by January 15 of a given year are pooled and processed at the same time, using random drawing to determine the order of processing. In our experience, no quota is ever filled by January 15. (Quotas for lakes where motors are allowed are the ones that tend to fill up.) However, the private company that takes care of the reservations started calling this a lottery. The word inspires panic in many well-organized, plan-ahead canoeists. Beginning on New Year's Day each year, we start getting frantic telephone calls from these anxious souls who interpret "lottery" to mean that they have to be at the head of the line or they will be totally out of luck. Actually, permits continue to be available throughout the summer. It is almost always possible to get a permit, although it may occasionally be necessary to make minor adjustments to the date of entry or the entry point.

During the 1990s, the concept of public-private partnership was being developed and implemented. In line with this concept, the Forest Service made the reservation system the province of private enterprise in 1994. This means that the toll-free phone number called to make a BWCAW reservation reaches a private business contractor rather than the Forest Service. With some glitches corrected, this is now working well.

The overall conclusion is that the permit system has been very beneficial to the preservation of the wilderness and a good thing for our business as well as others like ours. Sawbill Lake originally had a quota of 20 parties per day. In 1994, it was cut back to 14. Party size was reduced from 10 to nine. This again has only produced the desired result of spreading people out over the appropriate time frame and throughout the area. We are all fortunate that the Forest Service had the wisdom and foresight to curtail development and make this beautiful area a place of peace and quiet. There are thousands of lakes in Minnesota where people can build cabins and use motorized watercraft or airplanes. The Boundary Waters is a unique area where one can experience nature much as it was before humans and technology arrived.

Chapter 20

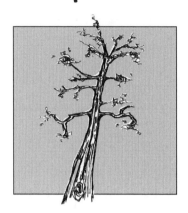

What is Wilderness?

What is wilderness? Do we need it? These questions have been at the heart of 30 years of controversy in Northeastern Minnesota. The debate has come full circle since the first Europeans came to the area in the latter part of the 1800s. They viewed wilderness as something to be conquered and exploited. As metropolitan areas have grown, many people have come to a different conviction. They see wilderness as having value in its own right and advocate minimum human intervention.

Not everyone agrees on the value of wilderness. There are still those who find it threatening and others who find value primarily in development and modern conveniences. Fortunately, not everyone wants to experience wilderness. A profound question that arose as the 1978 BWCAW legislation was being discussed was whether it can still be wilderness if people are present and making use of it. The final compromise was to allow a limited number of people to enter and experience wilderness first-hand. If everyone were eager to visit the BWCAW, it would certainly create a huge management dilemma. It is, in any case, the most heavily used wilderness area in the United States and has been for many years.

A customer sent us the following thoughts about the wilderness experience:

> ". . . when a party leaves Sawbill they will be changed. It may be the rain. Or the tipped canoe. Or the mosquitoes. But it might also be the moon. The smell of the trees. The taste of the water. The chance to let go of the cares and anxieties of every day life. They will return with stories to tell, with muscles that are newly found, with exuberance, and with a tinge of sadness."

"What Is Wilderness?" was the title of an essay written by Sigurd Olson, one of the most beloved leaders in promoting the concept of preserving parts of our country in a natural state — wilderness. He argues that wilderness is essential to everyone, not just those who may visit it in person.[1] This essay appeared in the spring 1968 issue of a publication called *Living Wilderness*. At the time, Olson was president of an organization called The Wilderness Society. Here are the last two paragraphs of his essay:

> "The preservation of wilderness is a humanitarian effort based on the knowledge that man has lived in a natural environment for some two million years and that his physiological and psychic needs come from it. No matter how urbanized or divorced from the natural man he may be, within him is a powerful need for the background from which he evolved. So closely has man been identified with wilderness and so deep are his roots in the ancient rhythms, silences and mysteries of the once unknown, that he cannot forget, and he must return often to recapture his sense of oneness with his environment. Without this opportunity to experience wilderness in his own way and wherever he may be, he will know frustration, boredom and unhappiness.
>
> "Wilderness preservation has to do with man's deepest

inner needs and he can cut his roots to the past at his peril. In the face of our burgeoning population and industrial expansion we can draw courage from the knowledge that in the saving of places of natural beauty and wildness, we are waging a battle for man's spirit. No task is more important, for the wilderness we save today will provide moral and spiritual strength and balance in a world of technology and frenzied speed. Only in a natural environment can man thrive, an environment where there are still places of beauty to go. The effort to protect man's living space from further desecration is one of the greatest challenges of this age. Wilderness is more than camping or hiking, it is a symbol of a way of life that can nourish the spirit."

In 1956, Sigurd Olson published the first of a series of books about the canoe country of Northeastern Minnesota — *The Singing Wilderness*. Olson's life and his mission to preserve some wild places were memorialized in 1972 by Northland College in Ashland, Wisconsin, when they renamed their Institute of Environmental Studies the Sigurd Olson Institute in recognition of his inspiring leadership in the field.

Dr. Grace Lee Nute in her book, *The Voyageur's Highway*, first published in 1941, includes a final chapter in which she argues the case for wilderness.[2] She says that each person has his own definition, but quotes one unidentified man as saying, ". . . there are certain common denominators: simplicity — solitude — nature untouched by man — mental, physical, spiritual rejuvenation. . . . Man has a right to solitude and simplicity. It should be one of the few inalienable rights. They are the essential elements of religion, philosophy, of all exaltation of the spirit. But how to obtain it on a continent rapidly becoming crowded and covered with man's handiwork? Solely, by retaining areas still unspoiled, large enough to give every man his mile, near enough to urban centers to allow every man to get there in an ordinary way. Once despoiled or defiled, these areas are gone — for a geological age."

Wilderness advocate Sigurd Olson sets out on a canoe trip in 1950.

Bruce Babbitt, a former Secretary of the Interior, commented, "Urban growth and development have made it essential for us to look hard at wilderness areas and other green spaces as they dwindle before our very eyes. Each day we lose solitude, along with some of our mental and spiritual refreshment that wilderness areas and green spaces offer to us."

Commemorating the 35th anniversary of the *Wilderness Act* on September 3, 1999, Babbitt's remarks included the following: "The fundamental premise of the *Wilderness Act* is that the process of building roads is a death sentence for an ecosystem. There are all

The wilderness offers spiritual nourishment, solitude, and simplicity.

kinds of scientific studies which show that roads fragment habitat in a way that leads to the disintegration of the ecosystem. . . .

"These fabulous lands are managed for the use and enjoyment of the American people, large enough to be refuges for plants and animals. Moreover, they have become refuges for both wildlife and people. We give these areas a chance to survive by leaving them wild, untamed, and unimpaired for future use and enjoyment as wilderness."

Dr. Miron "Bud" Heinselman, Forest Service researcher and lifelong visitor to and advocate for the BWCAW, expressed his convictions in these statements: "Will we forsake those who have gone before us and allow the flood-tides of civilization to overwhelm this beautiful country? I plead for the wilderness . . . I speak for the unborn generations that will follow us — who have as much right as we to know the mournful howl of a timber wolf on a far-off ridge, or the haunting laughter of the loons echoing among the moonlit islands. . . . The Superior-Quetico Wilderness Canoe Country breeds a loyalty and reverence that surpasses all reason and spans the generations."[3]

Wilderness is difficult to define. Sigurd Olson captures the essence most poignantly in the opening of his first book, *The Singing Wilderness*.[4]

> "The singing wilderness has to do with the calling of the loons, northern lights, and the great silences of a land lying north of Lake Superior. It is concerned with the simple joys, the timelessness and perspective found in a way of life that is close to the past . . . I hear it best in the wilderness lake country of the Quetico-Superior, where travel is still by pack and canoe over the ancient trails of the Indians and Voyageurs. . . .
>
> "There is magic in the feel of a paddle and the movement of a canoe, a magic compounded of distance, adventure, solitude, and peace. The way of a canoe is the way of the wilderness and of a freedom almost forgotten. It is an antidote to insecurity, the open door to waterways of ages past and a way of life with profound and abiding satisfactions. . . .
>
> "The movement of a canoe is like a reed in the wind. Silence is part of it, and the sounds of lapping water, bird songs, and wind in the trees. It is part of the medium through which it floats, the sky, the water, the shores.
>
> "A man is part of his canoe and therefore part of all it knows. The instant he dips a paddle, he flows as it flows,

the canoe yielding to his slightest touch, responsive to his every whim and thought. The paddle is an extension of his arm as his arm is part of his body.

" . . . no part of any country is inaccessible where there are waterways with portages between them. The canoe gives a sense of unbounded range and freedom, unlimited movement and exploration."

Notes

Chapter 1: Our Story Begins
1. Tofte, John Jr. "Casey." Interview, 1990.

Chapter 3: Forest Service – Then and Now
1. Sundling, Hugo. "Quetico-Superior: 1909-1984." Handout, 75th Anniversary Celebration at Atikokan, Ontario, 1984.
2. Tofte, John Jr. "Casey." Interview, 1990.
3. Mulligan, John Edward. Interviews, compiled by J. Wesley White, 1977.
4. White, Wesley. "Historical Sketches of the Quetico-Superior" *Superior National Forest*, vol. 9, April 1970.

Chapter 5: Sawbill Lodge
1. Arbogust, Wilson. "The History of Sawbill Lodge." Written for Cook County Historical Society records.
2. Whitesell, Corinne Brown. Interview, 2001.

Chapter 8: Corps Values – The CCC
1. "CCC." *Minnesota Conservation Volunteer*. Minnesota Department of Natural Resources, July-August 1983.
2. Arbogust, Harold. Letter, October 21, 2002.
3. Erickson, Olga. Interview, March 9, 2001.

Chapter 9: The Sawbill Trail
1. Tofte, Ted. "Building the Sawbill Trail." *Tofte General Store Gazette*, vol. 2, issue 1, Summer 1979.
2. Morris, R. Emerson. Letter, June 13, 1994.
3. Hansen, Earl. Interview, 2000.
4. "Paving the Way to Compromise on Sawbill Trail," *Duluth Star Tribune*, September 14, 1992.

Chapter 15: Fire in the Woods

1. Heinselman, Miron. *The Boundary Waters Wilderness Ecosystem.* University of Minnesota Press, Minneapolis and London, 1996.
2. Mulligan, John Edward. Interview, by Grand Marais Ranger Earl Niewald, 1975.
3. Wolff, Julius F. Jr. "Some Major Forest Fires in the Sawbill Country." Reprint from *Minnesota History*, vol. 36, no. 4, December 1958.
4. McKeever, Roger. Interview, 1998.
5. Perich, Shawn. "Plouff Creek Fire Memories" *Cook County News-Herald*, June 22, 1998.

Chapter 19: BWCAW Management

1. Searle, R. Newell. *Saving Quetico-Superior: A Land Set Apart.* Minnesota Historical Society Press, 1977.
2. Gervais, Gerald and Ronald. Interview, March 6, 2002.
3. White, Wesley. "Historical Sketches of the Quetico-Superior." *Superior National Forest*, vol. 5, February 1968.

Chapter 20: What is Wilderness?

1. Olson, Sigurd F. "What is Wilderness?" *Horizons*. Sigurd Olson Environmental Institute, Northland College, Fall 1999.
2. Nute, Grace Lee. *The Voyageur's Highway.* Minnesota Historical Society, St. Paul, MN, 1941.
3. Heinselman, Miron. *The Boundary Waters Wilderness Ecosystem.* University of Minnesota Press, Minneapolis and London, 1996.
4. Olson, Sigurd F. *The Singing Wilderness.* Alfred A. Knopf, Inc., New York, NY, 1956.

Bibliography

Publications

Arbogust, Wilson. *Sawbill Lodge*. Cook County Historical Society, 1998.

Boundary Waters Wilderness News, 1992 Annual Report. Friends of the Boundary Waters Wilderness, Minneapolis, MN.

"CCC," *Minnesota Conservation Volunteer*, Minnesota Department of Natural Resources, July-August 1983.

Heinselman, Miron. *The Boundary Waters Wilderness Ecosystem*. University of Minnesota Press, Minneapolis and London, 1996.

Nute, Grace Lee. *The Voyageur's Highway*. Minnesota Historical Society, St. Paul, MN, 1941.

Olson, Sigurd F. *The Singing Wilderness*. Alfred A. Knopf, Inc., New York, NY, 1956.

———. "What Is Wilderness?" *Horizons*. Sigurd Olson Environmental Institute, Northland College, Fall 1999.

Paddock, Joe. "Keeper of the Wild." Minnesota Historical Society Press, 2001.

"Paving the Way to Compromise on Sawbill Trail," *Duluth Star Tribune*, September 14, 1992.

Perich, Shawn. "Plouff Creek Fire Memories." *Cook County News-Herald*, June 22, 1998.

Raff, Willis. *Pioneers in the Wilderness*. Cook County Historical Society, Grand Marais, MN, 1981.

"Recent Events That Have Shaped the Boundary Waters Canoe Area Wilderness." *Wilderness News*. The Quetico-Superior Foundation, Minneapolis, MN, Winter 1994.

Searle, R. Newell. *Saving Quetico-Superior: A Land Set Apart*. Minnesota Historical Society Press, 1977.

Sundling, Hugo. "Quetico-Superior: 1909-1984." Handout for 75th Anniversary Celebration at Atikokan, Ontario, 1984.

Tofte, Ted. "Building The Sawbill Trail." *Tofte General Store Gazette*, vol. 2, issue 1, Summer 1979.

White, Wesley. "Historical Sketches of the Quetico-Superior." *Superior National Forest*, vol. 5, February 1968.

Wolff, Julius F., Jr. "Some Major Forest Fires in the Sawbill Country." Reprint from *Minnesota History*, vol. 36, no. 4, December 1958.

Interviews

Erickson, Olga. March 9, 2001.
Gervais, Gerald. March 6, 2002.
Gervais, Ronald. March 6, 2002.
Hanson, Bud. 2002.
Hansen, Earl. 2000.
Hunt, Robley. 2001.
McKeever, Roger. 1998.
Mulligan, John Edward. Interviews compiled by J. Wesley White, 1977.
Mulligan, John Edward. Interview by Gunflint District Ranger Earl Niewald, 1975.
Tofte, John Jr. "Casey." 1990.
Whitesell, Corinne Brown. 2001.

Letters

Andersen, Harold E. June 19, 1972.
Arbogust, Harold. October 21, 2002.
Arbogust, Wilson. 1999.
Howell, Jane Arbogust. 1999.
Morris, R. Emerson. June 13, 1994.
Neff, Lawrence P. January 12, 1965.
Reid, James E. December 4, 1970.
Rupp, Craig W. January 30, 1970; July 2, 1970; October 22, 1970; February 17, 1971.
Torrence, James F. October 10, 1975; November 20, 1975.